WOMEN
and
JEWISH LAW

WOMEN
and
JEWISH LAW

An Exploration of Women's Issues
in Halakhic Sources

RACHEL BIALE

SCHOCKEN BOOKS · NEW YORK

First published by Schocken Books 1984
10 9 8 7 6 5 4 3 2   86 87
Copyright © 1984 by Schocken Books Inc.

Library of Congress Cataloging in Publication Data
Biale, Rachel.
Women and Jewish law.
Includes bibliographical references and index.
1. Women—Legal status, laws, etc. (Jewish law)
2. Women, Jewish—Religious life. I. Title.
LAW   296.1'8   83–40457

Designed by Nancy Dale Muldoon
Manufactured in the United States of America
ISBN 0–8052–3887–5 (hardcover)
ISBN 0–8052–0810–0 (paperback)

The author acknowledges with gratitude permission to re-
print excerpts from the following books: *The Soncino Talmud*, translated into English with Notes, Glossary, and In-
dices under the editorship of I. Epstein (London: Soncino
Press, 1961), 18 vols. All rights reserved by The Soncino
Press Ltd., London. *The Torah: The Five Books of Moses*,
editor-in-chief, Harry Orlinsky (Philadelphia: The Jewish
Publication Society of America, 1962). Copyright by the
Jewish Publication Society of America.

For my parents
ANINA and CHAIM KORATI

✦✦✦✦

CONTENTS

	Preface	ix
	Introduction	3
1.	WOMEN AND THE *MITZVOT*	10
2.	MARRIAGE	44
3.	DIVORCE	70
4.	THE *AGUNAH* AND THE *YEVAMAH*	102
5.	SEXUALITY AND MARITAL RELATIONS	121
6.	*NIDDAH*: LAWS OF THE MENSTRUANT	147
7.	SEXUALITY OUTSIDE OF MARRIAGE: INCEST, ADULTERY, PROMISCUITY, AND LESBIANISM	175
8.	PROCREATION AND CONTRACEPTION	198
9.	ABORTION	219
10.	RAPE	239
	Epilogue	256
	Notes	267
	Halakhic Sources	285
	Glossary	287
	Index	289

PREFACE

IN THE spring of 1977 I taught a course at the Hillel Foundation at the University of California at Berkeley on the subject of women in Jewish law. Instead of reading a secondary, interpretive work, the class immersed itself in study of the original sources: Bible, Talmud, medieval codes, and commentaries. In subsequent years I taught the course twice more, to students in the Judaic Studies Program of the State University of New York at Binghamton. Again the focus was exposure to original texts in an effort to learn firsthand how the traditional scholars of the Halakhah (Jewish law) reasoned and argued.

The original impetus behind this book was therefore pedagogical. Instead of using the Jewish legal sources to defend a particular position, which is generally the purpose of virtually every other book on women in Jewish law, I thought it important to provide readers with a selection of the sources themselves reflecting a wide spectrum of traditional opinion. But since many of the sources are difficult to understand and often ambiguous in meaning, I have added extensive explanations and commentaries to make them more accessible to the general reader. The result is something of a hybrid between an anthology of sources and an interpretive history of Jewish law pertaining to women. It is my hope that by including extensive texts rather than brief excerpts, and by commenting only on the texts themselves, I have been able to preserve the original pedagogical purpose of the book.

I am grateful to my students at the Lehrhaus Judaica in Berkeley and at the State University of New York at Binghamton for their enthusiasm, questions, and insights.

I am grateful to Prof. Temma Kaplan, Rabbi Chaim Seidler-

Feller, Noam Zion, and Prof. Amos Funkenstein for reading portions of the manuscript at different stages in its development. As
my teacher, Amos Funkenstein gave me the analytical method,
and encouraged me in the hutzpah, to undertake this book. Rabbi
David Feldman kindly read the galleys for this book and construc-
tively challenged some of my interpretations. I am also grateful for
the persistent efforts, encouragement, and criticisms of Bonny
Fetterman, my editor at Schocken Books.

Above all, I thank my husband, David. If it were not for his help
this book would still be a large pile of papers covered with
splotches of black ink. Last to be acknowledged is my son Noam,
who has been the most wonderful interference I could possibly
hope for.

WOMEN
and
JEWISH LAW

INTRODUCTION

INTEREST in the history of women has accompanied the growth of self-awareness and political consciousness generated by the women's movement. Similarly, Jewish women have focused much attention on the status and life of women in Jewish society. In order to understand the contemporary reality of Jewish women's lives we must learn of their past, of the place of women in traditional Jewish society. This book offers some of the sources which are critical for the study of women in traditional Jewish life. These are sources of Halakhah, Jewish law, which formed the backbone of Jewish life before secularization.

The centrality of the Halakhah to Jewish life and its inaccessibility to contemporary readers not reared in traditional Jewish learning, or "study of Torah," inform the purpose of this book. The Halakhah is inaccessible to the untrained reader because its methods of argumentation are so complex that they often seem impenetrable, and because of the sheer volume of the literature. Moreover, in the case of women, not only contemporary secular readers lack access to halakhic sources; women within Orthodox Jewish society, today and in the past, have rarely had the necessary training for the study of the law, and never the requisite status and recognition for formulating Halakhah.

Women have participated in the evolution of the Halakhah only in the "prenatal" and "postpartum" stages of the process. They encountered problems and conflicts in daily life and raised questions that required halakhic decisions: from the minutia of the laws of *kashrut* (dietary laws) in their kitchens, to the momentous problems of marriage, divorce, procreation, abortion, and rape. At the end of the process women, like men, implemented the rulings

3

of the halakhic authorities who were exclusively male. At times women have argued halakhic issues with the recognized authorities of their day. The Talmud (Nedarim 50b) tells of a woman who came before Rav Judah to ask a halakhic question, and provocatively disputed his ruling. But such a case was probably rare, and she was deemed brazen: punished by heaven, "she burst and died." As a rule, women in the past as well as women in the present have been halakhically silent.

The collection of halakhic sources in this book is intended as a first step toward drawing women into the circle of the Halakhah. Such an attempt is necessarily fraught with considerable problems and limitations. The Talmud is traditionally called an "ocean," which symbolizes its vastness and depth, and immersion in the Talmud is just the first step toward learning of the Halakhah. Only the greatest scholars can master its full range. Moreover, any comprehensive treatment of an aspect of the Halakhah would be so detailed and technical as to exclude most readers. Therefore, far from pretending to present a definitive and complete study of women in Jewish law, I have chosen to select some of the most central issues and central texts from biblical to contemporary times. I have also sought texts that demonstrate the flexibility and originality of rabbinic thinking as well as those that represent the major positions on each issue. No doubt there will be those who would select other texts, but I have tried to follow the rabbinic principle that "he who tries to grasp too much, grasps nothing at all."

I have also tried to limit this study to the law itself. A social history of Jewish women remains to be written, and given the increasing impact of women's history on Jewish historians, probably will be written in the coming years. The status of women in Jewish law is only one aspect, one source, for that story. I have tried not to draw conclusions about the actual life of women from the law, except where it seemed warranted. Law sometimes lags behind social reality and sometimes anticipates it. At times attitudes change in popular mores and behavior, and only later enter codified law, while at others the law may permit much more than popular attitudes will tolerate.

The sources in this book reflect the trends of development and change in the Halakhah and demonstrate the continuing controversies over fundamental issues. The material in each chapter is organized in historical progression, usually starting with biblical legislation, moving to the Mishnah and Gemara (the two historically successive parts of the Talmud) and then to medieval and modern codes, commentaries, and responsa. Together with this historical structure I have also tried to organize each chapter to present a wide variety of opinions, from those of the majority to the dissenting voices.

My selection of halakhic sources, like any selection from a vast literature, is informed by a certain view of the Halakhah. I believe that historically the Halakhah has been characterized more by disagreement (*mahloket*) than by consensus, more by mechanisms of change than by forces of rigid conservatism. I do not dispute the fact that there is consensus in the Halakhah on many issues, and that its fundamental impetus is to preserve the customs of the past. However, historical study of halakhic sources shows that the mechanisms for change and the openness of the tradition in preserving minority opinions have been primary factors in assuring the perpetuation of the legal system. A historical perspective further shows that the attempt to present a monolithic and extremely conservative portrait of the Halakhah is more a characteristic of the response of modern Jewish Orthodoxy to secularism than a central feature of the Halakhah in earlier periods.

Thus the sources in this book reflect development, change, and controversy in the Halakhah. They also demonstrate that despite the difficulties in drawing general conclusions about the treatment of "women's issues" in the Halakhah, we can see a gradual and persistent effort to redress the fundamental imbalance in power between men and women which characterizes biblical law. The evolution of the laws of divorce illustrates this trend. In the Bible, divorce is a unilateral action of a husband; it permits no right of appeal to the wife and precludes the possibility of a woman's initiating divorce proceedings against her husband.

Rabbinic law, in the course of about ten centuries, makes four major changes in the laws of divorce to improve women's lot.

First, the Halakhah requires a complex legal procedure for writting a bill of divorce (get) which, while it cannot prevent a determined husband from divorcing his wife "unjustly," at least reduces the possibility of rash, thoughtless divorces effected in the heat of anger. Second, the Talmud introduces a number of circumstances which may serve as grounds for a woman to seek a divorce from her husband (she still cannot divorce him, but rather may appeal to a Jewish court to compel him to divorce her). Furthermore, postbiblical Halakhah introduces the ketubah, a marriage document which in actuality is a sort of "divorce insurance." In the ketubah, which the groom gives to the bride at the wedding, he promises substantial payments in the event of a divorce (or his death), thus securing the divorcée some measure of economic protection. Finally, in the Middle Ages the ban of Rabbenu Gershom (tenth century) forbids divorcing a woman against her consent. The unilateral power of men to effect divorce remains a major factor in the Halakhah, but it is considerably tempered by postbiblical rulings.

Other areas of Halakhah reveal a similar trend. The laws of onah, the sexual relations between husband and wife, for example, seem intended to redress the imbalance in sexual power and initiative between men and women in a traditional family and society. The rabbis, apparently perceiving that men are more likely to control sexual relations in a marriage, and to demand sexual satisfaction when they desire it, require a man to satisfy his wife's sexual needs, and at the same time forbid him to rape his wife. The times of "conjugal duties" are prescribed in the Mishnah "according to the rabbis' estimate of the woman's notion of what would satisfy her," and furthermore, "if he sees that she is asking him for that act, by attracting his attention and adorning herself in front of him, then he is commanded to please her in this matter of mitzvah" (Avraham ben David, Ba'alei Ha-Nefesh, Sha'ar Ha-Kedushah).

Despite the trend toward increasing woman's rights and protection in many areas of Halakhah, two major notes of caution are necessary. First, in some areas of women's lives, perhaps most important in those related to sexuality, the Halakhah was probably more permissive and more generous to women than life itself. In the case of sexual relations between husband and wife the Halakhah grants all the rights for sexual satisfaction to the woman and places all the restraints on the man. I suspect that in reality, despite the laws of *onah*, sex more often was initiated and conducted to satisfy the husband's sexual needs, and women often responded to men's sexual demands against their own wishes and pleasures. Another example of the gap between Halakhah and actual practice is the laws regarding the menstruant woman (*niddah*). The Halakhah requires severe restrictions of the normal intimacies between husband and wife during the *niddah* period, but does not prescribe social and religious ostracism. However, popular attitudes toward the *niddah* included the notion that her very breath and footsteps contaminate, so that one should avoid any contact with her, even greeting her with social pleasantries. It was common practice for the *niddah* to abstain from the synagogue during the period of her impurity.

A gap between common practice, folk beliefs, and popular attitudes on the one hand, and formal legal principles on the other, is a feature of all organized societies governed by law. Common wisdom has it that laws normally lag behind social reality. Permissive, liberalizing attitudes begin with changes in popular mores and behavior, and only later enter codified law. If this is true, it is clearly true only part of the time. In the case of some of the halakhic material presented in this book the law may have preceded common practice in what to the contemporary eye are liberal, compassionate attitudes toward women.

The second note of caution about the "liberal," or even "liberating," trend in the Halakhah pertaining to women concerns its limitations. Much as the rabbis and later legal authorities at times impress and even surprise us with their comprehension of the condition of women in their society, and their efforts to better it, whatever could be done to increase women's legal rights and protect them remained within a legal system which women could never penetrate. The authority to make halakhic decisions has always been the province of men. Every ordained rabbi (ordination today is usually granted by a formal institution—a *yeshiva* or rabbinical school—but legally is valid when conferred by an individual rabbi of recognized stature) is qualified to determine Halakhah. But halakhic decisions of historical significance are made in each generation by those rabbis who can display both extraordinary learning in their published works (responsa, halakhic codes, and commentaries) and can count on a substantial following in the community. The two factors of course usually emerge hand in hand. The fact that both factors reflect subjective judgment means that while our view of the prominent halakhic authorities of the past is fairly well established, at any given historical moment there are many competing claims for the "authoritative halakhic voice" of the times. Until very recently women played no role in the struggle for recognition among halakhists and in the evolution of the Halakhah. While women could and did gain more halakhic rights in the course of generations, they never gained halakhic power. They have been silent recipients, outsiders to the process.

I believe that it is time for women to try to penetrate the world of the Halakhah. They need to acquire the tools to comprehend halakhic reasoning, study past halakhic rulings, and finally, formulate their own views of the Halakhah. Women must take upon themselves the study of Torah from which they are legally exempt. Indeed, all Jews who are preoccupied with fashioning a Jewish life have a stake in understanding the Halakhah. Regardless of their definition, secular or religious, all forms of contemporary Jewish life must arise out of a confrontation with the past. Whether one lives in harmony with tradition or in tension with it, one must contend with that tradition. Comprehending the Halakhah is necessary for a Jewish life, whether one seeks to follow Jewish law or depart from it.

For those who choose to study the Halakhah without following its prescriptions there is tension and perplexity in store. Why study these laws when one has no intention of heeding them? Can one study and understand the Halakhah while rejecting its fundamentally imperative nature? It seems to me that between the alternatives of studying the Halakhah in order to live by it and studying it as a rarefied academic pursuit there is a third course. It is a way of learning which engages the sources in intellectual and personal spheres, allowing them to become part of one's vocabulary and world of associations, without necessarily becoming prescriptions for daily life.

In order to engage in meaningful Jewish discourse today, and to formulate personal and communal ways of "being Jewish" in the modern period, it is necessary to acquire a shared "Jewish language," which is the language of the traditional Jewish sources. If we master the language of these sources and use them as an anchor, we can talk about contemporary problems in a way that connects them to what is already known and crystallized. Otherwise we sever the connection with the past on which our world rests. In order to understand what puzzles and concerns us in the present we must turn to the past, even though it may at first be more confusing, obscure, and alien than our present. In the case of Halakhah, for many Jews today, and for Jewish women in particular, learning the language of the past is learning a foreign language. Yet this language is crucial, not only in order to understand the history of the Halakhah and what Jewish life has been, but also to formulate Jewish life and aspirations today.

✳ 1 ✳
WOMEN AND THE MITZVOT

Principles of Obligation and Exemption

The life of any traditional Jew, whether a man or a woman, is guided, even dictated, by the *mitzvot* (the commandments). The *mitzvot* encompass almost all conceivable spheres of human activity, and through prohibitions and prescriptions fashion private and public Jewish life, often down to the most minute details. The great majority of the *mitzvot* apply equally to men and women, from the universal prohibition "Thou shalt not murder," to the exacting details of the laws of *kashrut* and the observance of the Sabbath. Yet there are exceptions to the general rule, and these fall into two categories: those *mitzvot* which are linked to gender and apply only to men (circumcision) or only to women (laws regarding menstruation), and *mitzvot* which are not directly related to biological differences yet are "gender biased." The latter group of course requires more study and analysis since the reasons for the differentiation between men and women are not self-evident. It is those *mitzvot* which apply only to men or only to women but which are not necessitated by gender differences that will occupy our attention in this chapter.

In the Bible we find commandments of both types. There are exclusive male commandments which are related to man's biological characteristics: circumcision, the impurity caused by ejaculation, the prohibition on trimming the sidelocks, etc. For women there are other commandments, such as the laws regarding the impurity of the menstruant and the sacrifice a woman must bring after giving birth. Other commandments that apply only to one of the sexes are less clearly related to biological differences. For example, the *mitzvah* of *pidyon ha-ben*, redeem-

10

ing the firstborn if it is a male, applies to males only because prior to the selection of Aaron and his lineage to the priesthood, firstborn males were apparently given up for this service. The redemption frees the firstborn son from this duty. However, the fact that the priesthood was exclusively male reflects, in itself, a gender bias, not a biological difference. In fact, other ancient religions included women as priestesses. The prohibition on multiple sexual relations for women but not for men should probably be understood as a reflection of the biological reality that maternity is self-evident while paternity is presumed (this is probably the underlying reason why personal status such as "who is a Jew" is determined by the mother). Finally, such *mitzvot* as the requirement of three yearly pilgrimages for men but not for women, the laws of inheritance, etc., are examples of "gender-biased legislation"; they reflect not biological differences but differences in male and female roles in the social order of biblical times. This social order maintained rigid boundaries between male and female roles (despite rare exceptions such as Deborah, who functioned as a judge) and the *mitzvot* which pertain only to men or only to women reflect and perpetuate the differentiation. The division between males and females in their role and place in society is best summarized in a law which pertains to both sexes: a man may not wear women's clothes nor a woman men's clothes (Deut. 22 : 5).

Though these biblical laws reflect a clear social order they do not seem to flow from systematic legislative thinking. There is no explicit formulation in the Bible of principles of exemption or exclusion of women (or men) in one set of obligations over another. In the Mishnah, however, we do find an explicit statement about the differences in legal obligations between men and women and an attempt to systematize them:

All positive commandments which are time-bound [*mitzvot aseh she-ha-zeman graman*]: men are obligated and women are exempt. But all positive commandments which are not time-bound are binding upon both men and women. All negative commandments [*mitzvot lo ta'aseh*], whether time-bound or not time-bound, are binding upon both men and women, excepting: "You shall not round [the sidelocks], neither shall you mar [the corner of your beard]," and "He shall not defile himself to the dead." [Kiddushin 33b]

The Mishnah states a general principle of exemption for women based on the division of the mitzvot according to two criteria. The first division is that of mitzvot aseh, prescriptions, vs. mitzvot lo ta'aseh, prohibitions. The second criterion is time: some mitzvot are time-bound and some are not. For example, the prohibition on lighting a fire on the Sabbath is obviously time-bound since on any other day of the week one is free to light a fire. The prohibition on eating unkosher food is not time-bound while the requirement of eating a particular food, the matzah, is time-bound since it only applies on Passover. In other words, all of the mitzvot within the body of Jewish law fall into four groups:

1. Positive mitzvot which are time-bound
2. Positive mitzvot which are not time-bound
3. Negative mitzvot which are time-bound
4. Negative mitzvot which are not time-bound

According to the principle cited in Kiddushin 33b the mitzvot in groups 2, 3, and 4 apply equally to men and women, while those in group 1, time-bound positive mitzvot (mitzvot aseh she-ha-ze-man graman), are incumbent upon men only. We must note, without entering into a detailed discussion, that the Mishnah uses the term "exemption" in regard to these mitzvot, leaving open the possibility that while women need not fulfill these mitzvot, they may observe them if they so choose. Several scholars have shown that halakhic opinions on the issue of assuming obligations from which one is exempt are varied. The halakhists range from those who permit and look favorably upon assuming obligations voluntarily, to those who permit the performance of the mitzvah but disallow saying the blessing which usually accompanies the act, and finally to those who rule against assuming obligations (especially for women) altogether.[1]

The Mishnah in Kiddushin 33b seems to offer a neat and clear-cut rule for the exemption of women from certain mitzvot (despite the three exceptions that it enumerates: trimming the locks and the beard, from which women are exempt for obvious reasons; and avoiding contact with a corpse, which applies only to male priests since women pass on the priestly lineage but do not have any priestly functions). But the Mishnah does not give an explanation for this principle of exemption. What lies behind this principle? Is it based on differences between men and women in legal status, in spiritual-religious status, or in social and cultural roles?

A number of modern writers have justified the principle of the Mishnah in terms of practical considerations of the woman's domestic role in society. Women in traditional Jewish society were encumbered by the duties of a housewife and mother. The demands of children and home chores dictate a woman's "timetable." Time-bound *mitzvot* would interfere with this domestic timetable and place an unreasonable burden on women.[2] This point is particularly relevant in explaining the fact that while women are bound by the obligation to pray, they are exempt from praying at set times. Other writers, those who defend the role of women in Jewish Orthodoxy today, have elevated the principle beyond mere practical considerations, arguing for fundamental spiritual reasons which bind women to a domestic role and set them apart from the clock that dictates the lives of men.[3]

A medieval commentator, David ben Joseph Abudarham, explains the reason for the exemption of women from time-bound positive *mitzvot* in different terms—as due to a basic conflict between the commands of God and the demands of a husband:

The reason women are exempt from time-bound positive *mitzvot* is that a woman is bound to her husband to fulfill his needs. Were she obligated in time-bound positive *mitzvot*, it could happen that while she is performing a *mitzvah*, her husband would order her to do his commandment. If she would perform the commandment of the Creator and leave aside his commandment, woe to her from her husband! If she does her husband's commandment and leaves aside the Creator's, woe to her from her Maker! Therefore, the Creator has exempted her from his commandments, so that she may have peace with her husband. [David ben Joseph Abudarham (fourteenth century, Spain), Sefer Abudarham, Part III, "The Blessing over (Fulfilling) the Commandments"]

According to *Sefer Abudarham,* the reason for women's exemption is that a woman is a servant of two masters, and may be caught in the crossfire of jealousies between them. Interestingly, it is God who "bows out" of the competition, allowing the husband's commands to prevail. Presumably God is less given to small jealousies and power struggles, and can afford to lay some of his requirements aside in order to preserve peace.

The rivalry between God and husband over female obedience is not merely a picturesque way of explaining the exemption of women from certain *mitzvot*. Indeed it seems to underscore a profound point, though I am not sure it was one intended by the author of *Sefer Abudarham*. The halakhic and religious position of women is strained by a tension between two views of women. God, in the "rivalry" of our text, holds a fundamental theological and ethical position which recognizes no stratification of human beings, no inferiority of women to men. All persons are of equal value, spiritually and morally, and all human life is equally sanctified. On the other hand, the husband represents an attitude grounded in daily life and social reality, where there are distinctions of religion, class, learning, and of course gender. Women are inferior to men in economic power, social standing, legal rights, and religious role and importance. While in ultimate moral and spiritual terms a woman's life is equal to a man's, her concrete, day-to-day life is marked by subservience to men. This tension appears in Genesis in the two creation myths. In one account woman is created equally with man "in God's image," and in the other account is created to meet man's needs.

Turning to a detailed analysis of the rule that women are exempt from time-bound positive *mitzvot*, we discover that there are more exceptions to the rule than cited in the original *mishnah*. These exceptions are of two types: there are time-bound positive *mitzvot* from which women are not exempt, and there are also *mitzvot* which are not time-bound and yet women are exempt from the duty to perform them. The exceptions are of such significance that the Gemara itself begins the discussion of this *mishnah* with a question about the validity of the general principle:

All positive commandments which are time-bound, etc.: Our rabbis taught: which are the time-bound positive commandments? *Sukkah, lulav, shofar*, fringes [*tzitzit*], and phylacteries [*tefillin*].

Now, is this a general principle? But unleavened bread [*matzah*], rejoicing [on holidays], and assembling are positive *mitzvot* which are time-bound and yet incumbent upon women. Furthermore, study of Torah, procreation, and redemption of the [firstborn] son [*pidyon haben*], are positive *mitzvot* which are not time-bound and yet women are exempt [from them]. Rabbi Yohanan answered: We cannot learn from general principles even where exceptions are stated. [Kiddushin 33b–34a]

The Gemara begins its commentary on the mishnaic rule "all positive *mitzvot* which are time-bound: men are obligated and women are exempt" by citing the major *mitzvot* which fall into this category. Thus women are exempt from the obligation to dwell in a *sukkah* on the Feast of Tabernacles (Sukkot) and from the duty to take up a palm branch (*lulav*) on that holiday. They are also exempt from the *mitzvah* of hearing the *shofar* blown on the New Year (Rosh Ha-Shanah) and Yom Kippur. Aside from the above *mitzvot* which are particular to certain holidays, women are also exempted from two *mitzvot* which are time-bound and are usually carried on every day: the obligation to wear fringes (*tzitzit*) whenever one wears a four-cornered garment (which is fulfilled by Orthodox Jews by going "beyond the call of duty" and wearing a fringed four-cornered garment, a *talit katan*, as a regular part of daily dress), and the obligation to wear phylacteries (*tefillin*) in the course of the morning prayer.[4]

The five *mitzvot* cited by the Gemara are major examples of time-bound positive *mitzvot* from which women are exempt. Since they are only examples the Gemara later wonders why they were chosen by the rabbis: Perhaps there was some doubt as to whether they were indeed covered by the general rule. The subsequent discussion in the Gemara (omitted here) reconstructs possible reasons why one might have had some questions about the five *mitzvot*. The Gemara does not doubt that women are exempt from these *mitzvot* but shows alternative ways of justifying their exemption. The Gemara concludes that these mitzvot were in fact cited as proofs of the general rule exempting women from time-bound positive mitzvot.

This discussion however indicates that there was some question as to the universality of the exemption principle. Otherwise, why would it be necessary to go through convoluted arguments to show that the principle is a principle? Indeed the doubts about this general principle are brought out boldly when the exceptions to the rule are enumerated. There are, first of all, time-bound positive mitzvot which are incumbent upon women. The Gemara cites three: eating matzah on Passover, the obligation to rejoice on the holidays, and the duty of the whole community to assemble in order to hear the reading of the Torah (hak'hel). Second, there are several positive mitzvot from which women are exempt despite the fact that they are not time-bound and therefore, according to the general principle, should apply to women. These exceptions include study of Torah, procreation, and redemption of the first-born (if it is male): three very important mitzvot.

Some of the exceptions cited in the Gemara have a scriptural basis, such as the mitzvah of assembling (hak'hel), which the Bible explicitly applies to "men, women and children" (Deut. 31 : 12), and some have a rabbinical origin, like the ruling "A man is obligated to procreate but a woman is not" (Yevamot 65b). The Gemara goes into the details of justifying each of the exemptions that it cites. We shall leave that discussion aside to return to the central question of the passage: Is the principle of Kiddushin 33b a general principle? It seems that it is certainly not a general principle since the exceptions are so significant. Why then is it stated as a principle? The response of Rabbi Yohanan to this question essentially skirts the problem. He says: "We cannot learn from general principles, even where exceptions are stated." Rabbi Yohanan argues that even though we have a general principle stated and exceptions enumerated in the mishnah in Kiddushin 33b, we cannot deduce that all other cases follow the general principle. Other exceptions may crop up, and yet they do not threaten the validity of the general principle. In effect, Rabbi Yohanan "saves" the general principle of the exemption of women from time-bound positive mitzvot by undermining the meaning of "general principle."

Enumerating the exceptions to the rule that women are exempt from all time-bound positive mitzvot raises serious doubts that historically this principle governed which mitzvot women fulfilled and which they did not. Rather than an a priori rule about exemptions of women from certain mitzvot, what probably occurred historically was a gradual evolution of daily practice and communal customs which allowed women not to perform certain mitzvot. Eventually the customs acquired the force of law and the halakhic justification probably emerged initially on a case-by-case basis. The principle that women are exempt from all time-bound positive mitzvot and obligated in all others was probably an after-the-fact attempt to explain and systematize the reality that women did not perform all the mitzvot equally with men. Therefore it is not surprising at all that there are a good many exceptions to the rule and that the exceptions encompass some very central mitzvot. It also seems that another common denominator does exist among all the mitzvot from which women are exempt; it is not a legal-logical principle but a social-cultural one. As we shall see by analyzing the major mitzvot from which women are exempt— prayer, Torah reading, and the study of Torah—the common thread uniting them is that they are all obligations outside the realm of women's domestic role. They are the central duties of public religious life, a life which is focused on men.

Prayer

Prayer is a central activity in the life of a religious Jew. As the avenue of communication with God it is required of both men and women.

Mishnah: Women, slaves, and minors are exempt from reciting the Shema and from putting on phylacteries, but they are subject to the obligations of prayer, and mezuzah, and grace after meals.

Gemara: That they are exempt from the shema is self-evident—it is a positive mitzvah which is time-bound. You might say that because it

mentions the kingship of heaven it is different. We are therefore told that
it is not so.

. . . They are subject to the obligation of prayer: because it is [supplica-
tion for] mercy. You might think that because it is written in connection
with it: "Evening and morning and at noonday" (Psalms 55 : 18) it is like
a time-bound positive *mitzvah*. Therefore we are told.

. . . And grace after meals: This is self-evident? You might think [other-
wise] because it is written "When the Lord gives you in the evening meat
to eat and in the morning bread" (Ex. 16 : 8). Therefore we are told.
[Berakhot 20a–20b]

Although women do not have the same legal status as minors and
slaves, they are grouped together in this passage because they
share a secondary role in ritual life. The *mishnah* in Berakhot
cites three types of prayer: reciting the Shema (verses from Deuteronomy [6 : 4–9; 11 : 13–21] and Numbers [15 : 37–41] which begin with "Hear O Israel the Lord our God is One" and contain
admonitions to remember God and follow the law) in the morning
and evening, prayer for divine mercy, and reciting grace after
meals. Women are exempt from the first form of prayer, the
Shema, since it is clearly a time-bound *mitzvah*. This must be
clarified according to the Gemara since the Shema contains a declaration of the "kingdom of heaven," i.e., the reign of God, and
one might think that the importance of such a declaration of the
central creed of Judaism overrules the exemption of women. Indeed, despite the definitive ruling exempting women from the
duty of reciting the Shema, the *Shulhan Arukh* states "The proper
thing is to teach them [women and slaves] [to recite it] so that they
accept upon themselves the reign of Heaven" (Orah Hayyim
70 : 1), and Moses Isserles adds "so that they should at least recite
the first line."

The third prayer mentioned in Berakhot is the grace after meals.
The obligation to recite a blessing after a meal is scriptural. Deuteronomy 8 : 10 states: "You shall eat and shall be satisfied, and
you shall bless the Lord your God for the good land which He has
given you." It seems self-evident that women are required to recite
the grace since it is a thanksgiving over the food which they too
eat and is not dependent on time. However, since food is else-

where associated with set times ("in the evening meat to eat," etc.) one might have thought that women are exempt from saying grace. Therefore, the Gemara explains, the text tells us explicitly that women are obligated to say the grace.

The Shema and grace after meals are specific, defined prayers. The second form of prayer addressed in the mishnah is nonspecific; it is prayer in general. Women are subject to the obligation of prayer because prayer is fundamentally a way of asking for divine forgiveness, and everyone, men and women (as well as slaves and minors), "needs God's mercy" (Rashi, commentary on Berakhot 20b). In fact, it is a woman, Hannah the mother of Samuel, whose praying (1 Samuel chapter 2) serves as the model for supplicative prayer (Berakhot 31a). Yet as with grace after meals, one might think that general prayer is time-bound as well, because of the verse which calls for prayer "evening, morning, and noonday." Therefore the ruling of the mishnah is necessary lest we think that prayer is a time-bound mitzvah and conclude that women are exempt from it.

While the passage in Berakhot and subsequently Rashi, Tosafot, Maimonides, and other later commentators all hold that women are obligated in prayer as are men, we find evidence that in practice women did not perform the duty of prayer in the same way as men:

"Women and slaves even though they are exempt from reciting the shema are obligated in prayer because it is a positive mitzvah which is not time-bound" (Shulhan Arukh, Orah Hayyim 106 : 2).

Commentary: "A positive mitzvah"—so wrote Maimonides who held that prayer is a scriptural commandment for it is written "And worship Him with all your heart" etc., and according to the scriptural mitzvah it is sufficient to pray once a day and according to whatever content he chooses. And therefore women have been accustomed not to pray in a set manner since immediately in the morning, around the time of washing, they say some kind of request [as a prayer] and according to scriptural law that is sufficient. And it is possible that the rabbis also did not obligate them for more than that. [Abraham Gumbiner (1635–1683): Magen Avraham—Commentary on the Shulhan Arukh, Orah Hayyim 106 : 2]

The author of the *Magen Avraham* cites Maimonides in order to try to explain the prevailing custom of women not to pray in a set consistent manner. He feels compelled to explain this practice because all previous halakhists rule that women are obligated to pray. He himself holds that opinion, and explains in another place that "Even though prayer does have a set time, since they have said 'Would that a man spent all his day praying!' it is a *mitzvah* that is not dependent on time" (*Magen Avraham*, Orah Hayyim 70 : 1).

The *Magen Avraham* explains the practice of women in prayer through the distinction between the scriptural obligation of prayer and the rabbinical obligation. The scriptural obligation does not require a set time or a set text for the prayer (see Maimonides, *Mishneh Torah*, Hilkhot Tefillah 1 : 1), only some sort of request for divine mercy made once a day. The rabbinical definition of the *mitzvah* of prayer introduces a set text and set times. Thus the rabbinical aspect of the duty of prayer is a time-bound *mitzvah* and women are exempt from it. Women fulfill their scriptural duty of prayer by making a personal address to God as they start their day and thereby, according to *Magen Avraham*, they legitimately discharge their obligation. He goes further, suggesting that the practice has been sanctioned by the rabbis who "possibly did not obligate them for more," though he remains vague on this and does not cite a specific proof.

In fact what we see in the commentary of *Magen Avraham* is that women acted *as if* they were exempt from the set daily prayers which men were required to perform. A division developed between "women's prayer," which was private and individual in content and time, and "men's prayer," which was in codified formulas and scheduled at certain times of the day (*Shaharit*, *Minhah*, and *Ma'ariv*, the latter being a lesser obligation). Certainly, women at times participated in the set prayers, but this was a matter of personal choice and was not a requirement. The private prayer of women did not remain totally individual either. Special prayers for women, or *tehinot*, were composed for special occasions such as births and weddings. Yet women's prayers remained essentially private, personal, and spontaneous supplication.[5]

There is another important aspect of prayer where we find a division between men and women, and that is the forum for prayer. As we have said, women mostly pray at their own times and in private. Men, on the other hand, pray at set times and preferably in public. Prayer in public requires the presence of a quorum, a *minyan*, and usually takes place in a synagogue, although that is not legally necessary. The definition of a quorum does not only exempt women, it totally excludes them. A *minyan* is defined as a group of ten adult males and it is derived from the biblical concept of *edah*. *Edah* means a congregation, and it is used to describe a group numbering ten men in Numbers 14 (ten of the twelve spies who went to tour the Promised Land while the Israelites were in the desert).

The requirement of a *minyan* for certain prayers on certain occasions is clearly stated in the Talmud (Megillah 23b). The occasions included are, among others, reading the Torah and the *haftarah* (the prophetic text accompanying the Pentateuch portion), recitation of Kaddish and sanctification prayers (*Kedushah* and *Barekhu*), consolation of mourners, and the seven blessings of marriage. The requirement of a *minyan* for daily prayer is a somewhat more complex and questionable matter. Prayer in a *minyan* is clearly preferable to private prayer, but the Talmud does not explicitly state that prayer in a *minyan* is a duty. The later authorities are split on this question. Rashi holds that prayer in a *minyan* is a *mitzvah* and a man should actively seek out a *minyan* to pray with (Rashi on Pesahim 46a). Nachmanides represents the alternative view: prayer in a *minyan* is not an individual *mitzvah* so that one is not required to seek out a *minyan*. Yet if a *minyan* is already available, the ten men who comprise it should pray together as a congregation rather than separately as ten individuals (*Milhamot Ha-Shem*, Megillah 5a). The halakhic argument behind these views is complex and we need not enter it. What concerns us is the relevance of these views to the role of women in public prayer.

Nowhere in the halakhic literature is the possibility of including women in a *minyan* discussed as a "real life" issue except of course in current literature written to address contemporary demands that women have equal rights in public worship. Contemporary writers cannot hope to find explicit rulings on this issue in earlier halakhic sources, but rather must seek indirect evidence to show whether women can or cannot be legally counted in a *minyan*. David Feldman, a Conservative rabbi, argues, for example, that women could not be counted in a *minyan* because they do not have the same obligation to pray as do men. Feldman follows the opinion of Rashi that the obligation to pray in a *minyan* is a *mitzvah*, and is bound up with the *mitzvah* of praying set prayers three times a day. Since women are exempt from the time-bound *mitzvah* of prayer (being obligated only for unfixed prayer) they do not have the same obligation as men. "A *minyan*," argues Feldman, "is made up of ten people who share the same obligation," and therefore women cannot be included among men.[6]

Moshe Meiselman rejects the inclusion of women in a *minyan* on other grounds. In his book *Jewish Woman in Jewish Law*, Meiselman implicitly follows the view of Nachmanides that prayer in a *minyan* is only a communal obligation. Ten men together automatically comprise a congregation (*edah*) and as such have the obligation to pray together as a *minyan*. Women, according to Meiselman, do not form a congregation, even when ten of them come together, because in Judaism women are viewed as private persons:

It would seem that the reason ten women do not form a minyan is reflective of the private emphasis of their directive. Men are public figures and hence bind together to form a public unit. Women are more private and hence remain ten individuals. [p. 140]

Meiselman's reasoning applies not only to women's exclusion from a regular *minyan*, but also the extreme case he discusses of ten women forming their own *minyan*. According to Meiselman, since women's nature is essentially private, they can neither mix with men to form a congregation nor do it by themselves. In comparison Feldman, who bars women from a *minyan* because they do not share the same duty of prayer with men, would probably allow the formation of an all-women's *minyan*, since that *minyan* would be made up of "ten people who share the same degree of obligation."

Feldman bases his logic on the kind of *minyan* for which women would be counted according to earlier authorities such as Rabbenu Nissim (Ran, fourteenth century). The special case is that of a *minyan* gathered for the reading of the Megillah (the Book of Esther) on Purim. The reading of the Megillah must be a public reading because it is a *mitzvah* to publicize the miraculous victory of the Jews over their enemies in the days of Ahasuerus (probably the Persian king Xerxes, fifth century B.C.E.). Therefore a *minyan* is a necessity. Furthermore it is the duty of every person to read the Megillah (i.e., actively take part in publicizing the miracle), although this duty may be discharged through another person's reading on one's behalf. Those who actually read the Megillah out loud discharge the obligation of everyone in the audience to read, while the audience in turn comprises the necessary "public" for the reading. Women are not only qualified to read the Megillah, they are actually obligated to participate in the reading.

Rabbi Joshua ben Levi also said: Women are under the obligation to read the Megillah since they also profited by the miracle then wrought. [Megillah 4a]

Women are then obligated to read the Megillah since the reading is the reminder of the miraculous delivery of the Jews, both men and women alike. Possibly the central role of a woman, Esther, in the victory of the Jews underlies Joshua ben Levi's sentiment.

Following the statement of the Mishnah, all commentators agree that women are obligated to hear the reading of the Megillah, and most accept the logical extension that women may discharge each other's obligation by reading for each other (though of course most halakhists would not have advocated the new phenomenon of an exclusively female *minyan* unless there were no men available). However, Rabbenu Nissim goes much further than this. He argues that in the case of a *minyan* for the purpose of reading the Megillah women should be counted along with men since they are equally obligated to hear and publicize its story:

How can it be that women may help fulfill the men's obligation and cannot be counted as part of the *minyan* for this purpose? Rather, they are definitely to be counted [in the *minyan*]. [Rabbenu Nissim (Ran), Commentary on Megillah 23a][7]

However, the opinion of the Ran, although it has some following, is a minority opinion. Most authorities disqualify women from a *minyan* for the Megillah reading just as they exclude them from a regular *minyan* for daily prayer or recitation of Kaddish.

Torah Reading

The reading of the Megillah touches on another important aspect of the participation of women in public worship: their role in the weekly reading of the Torah. Since the reading of the Torah is clearly a time-bound *mitzvah* it would seem that women should not be obligated to participate. Yet the biblical commandment to assemble the whole people to hear the Torah read explicitly includes women (as well as children and foreign residents):

[9]Moses wrote down this Teaching and gave it to the priests, sons of Levi, who carried the Ark of the LORD's Covenant, and to the elders of Israel. [10]And Moses instructed them as follows: Every seventh year, the year set for remission, at the Feast of Booths,[11] when all Israel comes to appear before the LORD your God in the place which He will choose, you shall read this Teaching aloud in the presence of all Israel.[12] Gather the people—men, women, children, and the strangers in your communities—that they may hear and so learn to revere the LORD your God and to observe faithfully every word of this Teaching. [Deut. 31 : 9–12]

The purpose of the reading of the Torah to the assembly of all of Israel is to teach the law. In biblical times the public reading of the Torah was to take place only once in seven years, and included a summary of the law and the history of the people of Israel (namely, the book of Deuteronomy up to Chapter 31). If the reading of the whole Torah by weekly portions is derived from this biblical duty of public reading, then the duty of hearing the Torah read on the Sabbath should fall equally on men and women. Indeed some authorities follow this logic and argue that women are obligated to hear the weekly reading of the Torah.[8]

Other authorities do not oblige women to hear the reading of the
Torah every Sabbath as they do not derive this *mitzvah* from the
obligation of assembly (*hak'hel*) but from other legislation attributed to Ezra. In his religious and social reforms during the establishment of the second Temple (sixth century B.C.E.), Ezra instituted public readings of the Torah every Monday, Thursday, and
Sabbath. But Ezra's legislation does not explicitly include women,
as does the *mitzvah* of assembly in Deuteronomy 31. Furthermore,
many rabbis argue that reading the Torah is analogous to study of
Torah, since both are ways of fulfilling the commandment "And
you shall teach them [the laws] repeatedly to your sons and speak
of them when you sit in your home and when you walk in the
road, and when you lie down and when you rise" (Deut. 6 : 7).
The *mitzvah* of studying the Torah, as we shall soon see, applies
only to men. Thus if the reading of the Torah is essentially part of
the *mitzvah* of study of the law rather than an extension of the
mitzvah of *hak'hel* (assembly), women are exempt from it. Most
halakhic authorities after the Talmud tend to rule in this manner,
regarding the reading of the Torah as a time-bound *mitzvah* originating with Ezra and related to study of Torah. Therefore they
exempt women from the obligation to hear the reading of the
Torah.

It is obvious that if women are not obligated to hear the reading of
the Torah they are not obligated to read the Torah out loud, and
would certainly be excluded from reading the Torah on behalf of
the congregation. Hence those who follow the majority and rule
that women are not obligated to hear the Torah also bar them from
aliyah la-Torah: the ceremonial act whereby members of the congregation "go up to the Torah" to read, or more often, to recite the
blessings over the Torah and then have a reader read out loud for
them.[10] The *aliyah la-Torah* has been a central issue in the current
controversy over women's participation in synagogue ritual. *Aliyot*
for women are generally accepted in the Reform movement in
North America but are totally unacceptable in Orthodox synagogues. Within the Conservative movement the debate continues.[11]

Against the dominant post-talmudic tendency to exclude women
from both hearing and reading the Torah, there is a talmudic pas-

sage that suggests that in principle, if not in practice, women are legally qualified to read the Torah:

> Our rabbis taught: All are qualified to be among the seven [who read the Torah], even a minor and a woman, but the Sages said that a woman should not read because of the congregation's esteem [kvod ha-tzibbur]. [Megillah 23a][12]

The Talmud apparently assumes that women are included in the obligation of hearing the public reading of the Torah, and therefore in principle are qualified to be among the seven readers of the weekly portion. Only the consideration of kvod ha-tzibbur, which is not related to the legal issue of obligation, in the end bars women from actually reading.

What is kvod ha-tzibbur? The Talmud does not furnish a precise definition of the term, nor do medieval commentators ask what it means. One possibility suggested by some more recent writers is that it refers to proper etiquette between the sexes in public. A woman reading the Torah may be fulfilling a duty equal to that of men, but she is also causing sexual distraction during the most important service of the week. Sexual distraction is considered a grave problem in the Halakhah. Traditional practice makes provisions so that women should not be seen or heard by men during services. Women are separated from men by a mehitzah, which in practice in most Orthodox synagogues is not only a partition (as the term literally means), but a seating section behind and/or above the main part of the synagogue where the men sit. A woman's voice is considered a sexual provocation (kol be-ishah ervah), so that a woman may not read or recite before men. The view that kvod ha-tzibbur refers to the proper atmosphere free of sexual overtones is supported by the fact that only women, and not minors or slaves, are barred from reading the Torah because of this consideration.[13]

Nevertheless there is room for doubt that the term kvod ha-tzibbur is intended here as a reference to sexual distraction. In the Talmud and other writings the rabbis use precise terms to refer to sexual distraction such as mahshavot zarot (foreign thoughts), yetzer ha-ra (evil impulse), pritzut (licentiousness) or ervah (sexual transgression). Why would the Talmud use a vague term when it had plenty of ways of saying explicitly that women should not read the Torah because men would be sexually distracted?

Kvod ha-tzibbur may mean something else. Literally, the term means "the honor of the congregation." How would a woman's reading the Torah threaten the honor of the congregation? The solution may be found in a similar situation cited in Berakhot 20b: a woman may recite the grace after meals on behalf of her husband under certain circumstances, yet the rabbis say: "A curse light on the man whose wife or children have to say the grace for him." The wife or children would have to say the grace on a man's behalf if he were not observant enough or, more likely, not educated enough to say it himself. Thus a woman can legally say grace for her husband, but the very act casts doubt on the husband's education and piety. It puts him to shame, and that is evidently what would happen if women were to read the Torah.

David Feldman, who suggests this view of *kvod ha-tzibbur*, cites a responsum of Maharam of Rothenburg which indirectly supports his interpretation:

And in a town made up entirely of *kohanim* [priests] with not a single Israelite, we say that a *kohen* will read twice and then women will read, for "All are qualified to be among the seven, even a slave and a woman and a minor.". . . But the rabbis said that a "woman should not read because of *kvod ha-tzibbur*," so how is it that *kvod ha-tzibbur* is suspended? Because of the blemish cast upon the *kohanim:* lest they say that they are sons of divorcées. [Maharam of Rothenburg (thirteenth century), Responsa, No. 47]

The weekly Torah portion is divided among seven readers: the first one a Kohen; the second a Levite; and the last five Israelites. In the town in question there were no Levites or Israelites. Who should read the portions usually read by Levites and Israelites? The answer of Maharam of Rothenburg is that women should read all the portions which are normally not read by priests, despite the violation of *kvod ha-tzibbur*. The reason is that although there are other men in the congregation who could read, they are all *kohanim*. If they were to read the portions of non-*kohanim*, people might suspect that they are not "true *kohanim*" but *hala-lim* ("sons of divorcées," i.e., sons of *kohanim* who married divorcées and were therefore demoted from the status of priests). In other words women are to read the Torah in order to protect the reputation and the honor of the men in the congregation.

What we can conclude from Maharam of Rothenburg's responsum is that reading the Torah reflects on the status of the reader and of the congregation. In the unusual case of the town of *kohanim* the possible doubt about their priestly status takes precedence. In normal cases a congregation that allowed women to read the Torah would cast doubt on the piety of its male members. As in the case of a man whose wife recites the grace after meals for him, one would think that in a congregation where women are given *aliyot* the men are too ignorant to read the Torah. Ben Zion Uziel, who was a chief rabbi in Israel, adopted this interpretation of *kvod ha-tzibbur* in passing, in a passage discussing the problem of men and women mixing in business, social, and religious interactions. In his Responsa, *Mishpetei Uziel* (Hoshen Mishpat No. 6), he says: "The meaning of *kvod ha-tzibbur* is that they should not say that there is no one among the men who knows how to read the Torah, not that it is a matter of sexual distraction [*pritzut*]."

Underlying the logic behind the concept of *kvod ha-tzibbur* is a simple assumption: women are second best in public prayer. Wherever possible men should read the Torah. If women read it, despite the fact that in principle they are qualified to do so, it means that there is something wrong with the male congregants. The simple meaning of *kvod ha-tzibbur* is that women reading the Torah put men, and the congregation as a whole, to shame. It is no wonder that allowing women to participate in *aliyot* and in reading the Torah have become major issues among Jewish feminists today. Barring women from *aliyot* is really a reflection, and perpetuation, of that aspect in Jewish law which makes women second-class members of the community.

The secondary place of women in society seems to be particularly pronounced in the sphere of public ritual life in that the exemption/exclusion of women from certain *mitzvot* forms a pattern. Women are exempt from the duty of set daily prayers, so they rarely participate in synagogue services during the week. They are also exempt from the *mitzvah* of wearing *tefillin* (phylacteries), which is the focal point of the morning prayers. The reading of the Torah is the climax of the weekly cycle of worship. Women are exempted by many halakhic authorities even from hearing the reading of the Torah, and are barred from active participation in Torah reading through *aliyot*. Therefore it seems that women are exempt from most *mitzvot* which comprise public prayer. In actual practice exemption is hardly distinguished from exclusion; public ritual life is the province of men. Women are second-class participants in public ritual and, conversely, public ritual is secondary in the lives of traditional Jewish women.

Study of Torah

The study of Torah is as central to the religious life of a Jew as prayer, and is in fact understood traditionally as a form of worship, *avodat ha-shem*, perhaps its highest form. Women are exempt from the duty of studying the Torah despite the fact that it is a positive *mitzvah* which is not bound by time. This exemption does not imply that women are not required to know the law; since they are bound by most laws they are obligated to know them. Rather, women are not required to engage in the study of Torah as an end in its own right, whether as a form of worship or as a professional pursuit.

The grounds for exempting women from the *mitzvah* of studying Torah are not related to the rule of *Kiddushin* 33b about time-bound positive *mitzvot*. They are separately defined in another passage in Kiddushin:

Mishnah: All obligations of the son upon the father, men are bound and women are exempt. But obligations of the father upon the son, both men and women are bound.

Rav Judah [said]: This is the meaning of "All obligations of the son upon the father" those [*mitzvot*] one must perform for a son, "men are bound by but women are exempt." We thus learn what our rabbis had taught: The father is obligated with respect to his son to circumcise him, teach him Torah, take a wife for him, and teach him a craft. Some say: to teach him to swim too. [Kiddushin 29a]

In Kiddushin 29a we find a second principle which results in exemption of women from certain *mitzvot*. Women are exempted from the "obligations of the son upon the father" (*mitzvot ha-ben al ha-av*), that is, acts which a father must do for his son. These *mitzvot* are circumcision, redeeming the son if he is a firstborn (*pidyon ha-ben*), teaching him Torah as well as a craft, and arranging for his marriage. These *mitzvot* are the cornerstones of making a child a worthy Jew and preparing him for adult life. For that reason some rabbis add the obligation "to teach him to swim": a basic "survival skill."

It is interesting to contrast the text of Kiddushin 29a which places the responsibility of preparing a child for a proper Jewish life as an adult on the *father*, with the popular image of the traditional Jewish woman. The image one encounters time and again in literature, memoirs, and sentimental and polemical writings glorifying the role of women in traditional Judaism points to the woman as the bearer of tradition in the home, and as the one who passes the heritage to her children. The relation between the image and the historical reality is an elusive problem beyond our scope here, but it is important to note that the image is grounded in popular ethos, perhaps magnified by sentimentalism, and is not based on the requirements of the Halakhah.

Complementing the prescribed parental obligations is a parallel set of *mitzvot*: the "obligations of the father upon the son" (*mitzvot ha-av al ha-ben*). These are the child's duties toward the parents: primarily the fifth commandment, "Honor thy father and thy mother," and they are incumbent on both men and women. This ruling is somewhat mitigated, however, by the obligations of a woman toward her husband:

A man and a woman are equally obligated in showing honor and awe to father and mother, but the woman is not able to perform all the duties since she is bound to her husband. Therefore she is exempt from honoring her father and mother while she is married, but obligated if she is divorced or widowed. [*Shulhan Arukh*, Yoreh De'ah 240 : 17]

The exemption of women from honoring their parents does not mean that they are allowed to be disrespectful; rather, they are exempt from the active performance of this duty, namely, supporting the parents, doing whatever they bid, attending to their daily needs, etc. Even so, the commentary *Siftei Kohen* on the *Shulhan Arukh* states here: "Yet it seems that if her husband does not restrict her, she is obligated like a man in anything she can do."[14]

In the case of obligations of the father toward the son, as we have seen, women are exempted. Not only are they exempted, they are excluded. Women do not perform these *mitzvot* for their children, nor are they recipients of these acts as daughters. They do not teach and are not taught, do not redeem the firstborn and are not redeemed if they are born first, etc. The reason behind this exclusion of women must have to do with the differential definition of the parental function of father and mother and the different adult roles that boys and girls were expected to grow into. The Gemara does not address the cultural-social reasons for this law. Typically it focuses on presenting a logical mechanism internal to the text, rather than justifying the law with a general statement about social reality, such as "women do not study or teach the Torah." As might be expected of "men of the law," the rabbis generally try to frame social reality in the structure of legal logic.

We can observe the legal mechanisms behind the exemption/exclusion of women from the obligations of the father toward the son in the case of study of Torah:

"To teach him Torah": How do we know it? Because it is written "And you shall teach them to your sons" (Deut. 11 : 19). And if his father did not teach him, he must teach himself, for it is written "And you shall study." How do we know that she is not obligated [to teach her children]? Because it is written *ve-limadetem* [And you shall teach], [which can also be read] *u-lemadetem* [and you shall study]. Whoever is commanded to study is commanded to teach. Whoever is not commanded to study is not commanded to teach.

And how do we know that she is not commanded to teach herself? Because it is written *ve-limadetem—u-lemadetem*: the one whom others are commanded to teach is commanded to teach himself, and the one whom others are not commanded to teach, is not commanded to teach himself. How then do we know that others are not commanded to teach her? Because it is written: "And you shall teach them to your sons"—not to your daughters. [Kiddushin 29b]

The logical principle in this passage is based on the fact that the key word in Deuteronomy 11 : 19 can be read to mean either *learn* (study) or *teach*, depending on the vowels one supplies. The traditional Torah text was written without vowels and this type of exegesis is very common. The word *ve-limadetem* means "to teach" (literally, "to cause others to learn") while *u-lemadetem* means "you shall learn." In English the two related actions, learning and teaching, are expressed by two totally different words. In Hebrew this is done by using the same root in two different verb forms. This linguistic shift from one verb to the other accommodates the logical progression in the passage:

1. The one whom others are commanded to teach must teach himself (i.e., study).
2. The one who must teach himself must teach others.

If we place father and son into this logical structure we see a cycle created whereby one generation teaches the next. A son must be taught Torah by his father; he therefore must also teach himself Torah (if his father did not teach him or once he becomes an adult), and in turn, according to the second principle, he must teach others, namely, his sons.

Men in every generation are within the cycle of learning and teaching. Women are always outside it. Why? Because the negation of the logical principle is also consistent:

1. The one whom others are not commanded to teach is not commanded to teach oneself.
2. The one who is not commanded to teach oneself is not commanded to teach others.

Only in regard to men do we have a biblical verse which commands others to teach them: "And you shall teach them to your *sons*."

There is no commandment to teach the law to the daughters. Women do not have to be taught, and therefore do not have to teach themselves and do not have to teach others. They remain outside the bond of teaching which connects father and son in every generation. By the same logic women are exempt from redemption of the firstborn and from either learning or teaching a craft; others are not commanded to do those things for them.

Does being exempt from the study of Torah mean being excluded from it as well? On this the sources are divided. Some hold that women need not, but may, study Torah, and even encourage them to do so. Others attempt to bar women from the study of Torah altogether.

She had scarcely finished drinking when her face turns green, her eyes protrude and her veins swell, and it is proclaimed: "Remove her that the Temple court not be defiled!" If she possesses a merit it suspends the effect [of the water]: some merit suspends it for one year, some merit for two, and some for three. Hence declared Ben Azzai: A man must teach his daughter Torah so that if she has to drink she may know that the merit suspends the effect. Rabbi Eliezer said: Whoever teaches his daughter Torah teaches her nonsense [*tiflut*]! [Sotah 20a]

Can it enter your mind [that it is actually] nonsense? Read, rather: as though he teaches her nonsense. Rav Abbahu said: What is Rabbi Eliezer's reason? Because it is written: "I, wisdom, am present in subtlety [*ormah*]" (Prov. 8:12), i.e., when wisdom enters a man subtlety enters with it. [Sotah 21b]

The context of the competing statements of Ben Azzai and Rabbi Eliezer is the ordeal of the *sotah*. The *sotah* is a woman suspected of adultery against whom there is no actual evidence. Neither husband nor anyone else can testify to any facts to prove the suspicions. Such a woman is brought to the Temple where her guilt or innocence is determined through the ordeal of drinking the bitter water (Numbers 5; see the detailed discussion below in Chapter 7 on Sexuality Outside of Marriage). Presumably if she is innocent the water has no effect on her; if she is guilty the water causes an immediate physiological reaction. The Mishnah elaborates what the bodily reactions are, but adds a provision: if the woman is meritorious the reaction may be delayed up to three years so her guilt would not be evident. In this context Ben Azzai declares that a man should teach his daughter Torah. The reason is that if she is brought to the ordeal of the bitter water and is guilty, she should not think that she has been vindicated if the water causes no reaction. She should know that the effect has been suspended due to her past merit and that her guilt remains.

The statement of Ben Azzai is treated by Rabbi Eliezer as a general pronouncement. Indeed that is how it should be understood, because the discussion of the ordeal of the *sotah* in the Mishnah is totally theoretical. The ordeal was certainly abandoned by the second Temple period, and possibly even during the first, so Ben Azzai is not thinking of an actual need to know the rules regarding the *sotah*. Rather the principle is the important thing: a man should teach his daughter Torah not only so that she can follow the laws, but also so that she has an understanding of law and can deduce what lies beneath the surface.

Rabbi Eliezer objects strenuously to this general principle. He states: "Whoever teaches his daughter Torah teaches her nonsense." The word *tiflut* is often translated more strongly as "obscenity." The Gemara hastens to defend the holiness of the Torah: lest one think that the Torah itself becomes *tiflut* when taught to a woman, the Gemara states: "it is *as though* he teaches her *tiflut*."

Despite his strong language, even Rabbi Eliezer would not totally reject teaching women Torah. He would favor teaching them the laws they need to know in order to conduct a proper Jewish life. But he opposes teaching them anything beyond that, such as the underlying meanings and reasons which Ben Azzai would teach. Those things would be like nonsense if taught to women. The distinction between teaching specific laws and teaching the meaning of the Torah is clarified in the commentary of the Gemara. The wisdom of the Torah is subtle and with its study subtlety enters a man's mind. The rest is left unsaid in the Gemara, but the assumption is that men can acquire subtlety but it is beyond the capacity of women.

A case cited in the Jerusalem Talmud demonstrates that Rabbi Eliezer opposed teaching women anything beyond the laws they must follow:

A certain lady asked Rabbi Eliezer why the one sin in the case of the golden calf was punished by three deaths. He said to her: A woman's wisdom is only in her spinning wheel, for it is written "And any woman of wise heart, with her hands she wove" (Ex. 35 : 25). His son Hyrcanus said to him: why did you not give her some proper answer from the Torah? Now you have lost me three hundred *kur* [a measure] a year in tithe!" He said to him: "Let the words of Torah be burnt and not be given to women!" When she went out the students said to him: "This one you got rid of, but what do you answer to us?" [Jersualem Talmud, Sotah 3 : 16a]

The wealthy lady (who apparently bankrolled Eliezer's son with her yearly tithe) asked Rabbi Eliezer a scholarly question. It was not a question about executing the law, but a question about the interpretation of the Torah, and indeed a legitimate question since Eliezer's students demanded a serious answer after she left. Rabbi Eliezer refused to answer the woman's question and insultingly told her that her wisdom is in her hands, in spinning and weaving wool, not in her head.

As against the position of Rabbi Eliezer we find the view of Ben Azzai, not just in his pronouncement "A man should teach his daughter Torah," but also in evidence about the actual practice in the talmudic period. Though these were exceptions, there were women who went far beyond the practical learning of *halakhot* and studied Torah in some depth. The most celebrated case is that of Beruriah, the wife of Rabbi Meir, who studied Torah, and as we can gather from the talmudic anecdotes about her, could claim to be a scholar in her own right.[15] We also find cases of women who were sufficiently versed in the law to challenge the practice or ruling of rabbis they came in contact with (see Eruvin 53b and Nedarim 50b). These were unusual cases; most women were taught only what they needed for their daily life. Yet the controversy as to whether or not women may engage in study of Torah for its own sake continued in the post-talmudic sources. Most authorities lean toward restricting, if not ruling out, any in-depth Torah study for women. An interesting non-halakhic example is *Sefer Hasidim* (twelfth or thirteenth century, Germany):

A man must teach his daughters the *mitzvot*, that is, the halakhic rulings. And as to what they have said, that "he who teaches his daughter Torah teaches her *tiflut*," that is in regard to the depths of learning: the reasons for the *mitzvot* and the secrets of the Torah, which you do not teach to a woman or a minor. But the *halakhah* concerning the *mitzvot* he must teach her, for if she does not know the *halakhot* of Shabbat [the Sabbath] how can she properly keep it? And the same goes for all the commandments, in order that she be careful in their performance.

However, it is impossible for a bachelor to teach girls even if the father were to stand right there and watch over them, so that they are not together in privacy. For [even then] his desires or hers might surge and overcome them. Furthermore the voice of a woman is an *ervah*. Rather, the father should teach his daughter and his wife. [*Sefer Hasidim*, Paragraph 313, edited by R. Margolis (Bologna: Rescension)]

The *Sefer Hasidim* calls for teaching women the legal aspects of Torah so that they gain comprehensive and detailed command of the Halakhah. What is useless, according to the *Sefer Hasidim*, is teaching women the philosophical ("the reasons for the commandments") and the mystical interpretations of the Torah ("the secrets of the Torah").

The *Sefer Hasidim* advocates a fairly broad Torah education for women. One might even consider hiring a teacher-tutor for his daughter. The text hastens to add a provision against hiring a bachelor as a tutor for a girl, not because of the question of study of Torah for women, but because of the danger of sexual temptation on either side. The question of whether a married man may be hired to educate a daughter is left moot since the text simply recommends that a man should teach his daughter and his wife himself. The likelihood of a bachelor's applying for the position of a tutor for women (undoubtedly not a high-status job) is probably much greater than that of a married man's seeking it. At any rate, the important point here is that teaching a daughter Torah is acceptable, provided that one takes effective measures to safeguard against sexual temptation.

As against the *Sefer Hasidim*, the authoritative *Shulhan Arukh* views women's study of Torah with disfavor. The *Shulhan Arukh* acknowledges that women may study Torah and even gain reward from heaven, but nevertheless recommends against it:

A woman who has studied Torah gains a reward, but not like the reward of a man, because she is not commanded to study but does it [of her own will]. Yet even though she does gain a reward, the Sages have com-manded that a man should not teach his daughter Torah, because most women do not have the intention of truly learning and they turn the teachings of the Torah into nonsense, in accordance with their limited understanding.

The Sages have said: "Whoever teaches his daughter Torah teaches her *tiflut*": this they said about the Oral Law. As to the Written Torah [the Pentateuch], to begin with, one should not teach it to her, but if he already has, it is not as if he teaches her *tiflut*. [*Shulhan Arukh*, Yoreh De'ah, Hilkhot Talmud Torah 246 : 6]

The *Shulhan Arukh* begins by acknowledging that a woman who studies Torah gains some reward from heaven, so there can be no question of a transgression. A woman's reward is lesser than a man's because when she studies Torah she does it of her own choice, presumably for some personal gain or satisfaction, while a man does it because he is commanded. In the Halakhah the re-ward or value of fulfilling an obligation, a *mitzvah*, is considered greater than that of doing a "good deed" out of one's own volition.

Despite the reward women do gain in studying Torah, Joseph Karo, author of the *Shulhan Arukh*, sides rather closely with the position of Rabbi Eliezer. He cites Eliezer's view in the name of all the rabbis and explains the danger in teaching women or allowing them the opportunity to study. First, women do not really have the proper intention in studying and do not really wish to become learned. Second, women have limited understanding and if they study Torah they would misinterpret and misconstrue its teach-ing, turning it into "nonsense." For the *Shulhan Arukh* the mean-ing of *tiflut* is not just that teaching women Torah is a useless waste of time, and worth no more than teaching nonsense; there is actually a danger that they will pervert the meaning of the Torah and end up with a mistaken notion of its teachings.

Finally, the *Shulhan Arukh* makes a distinction between the Oral Law (the Mishnah, the Talmud, and subsequent exegetical and legal literature) and the Pentateuch itself. Teaching the Oral Law is definitely ruled out because of its complexity; it is certain to be like teaching nonsense. The Pentateuch, on the other hand, is simpler. One should not really teach it either, but if one already has, it is not a total waste. Moses Isserles, in his commentary on the *Shulhan Arukh,* does not quite agree. He states: "But nevertheless, a woman must learn those laws which pertain to women." Those laws are numerous and often complex, especially in the case of the laws of *niddah* (see Chapter 6 on *niddah*), the menstruant woman. Nevertheless, while following the laws governing women's lives requires a fairly detailed knowledge of Halakhah, it does not require much in the way of understanding halakhic reasoning as such.

In twentieth-century eastern Europe the education of girls became a controversial issue with the emergence of an institutionalized framework in the Bais Yaakov schools for girls.[16] While formal education for girls did eventually gain acceptance in the Orthodox world, it generally remained, as the *Shulhan Arukh* recommends, limited to teaching *mitzvot* for practical needs and inculcating the ideals of being "a worthy daughter of Israel," namely, fulfilling a maternal and domestic role, offering *tzedakah* (philanthropy) to the poor, and upholding modesty (*tzni'ut*). As against the mainstream view of female education, which may be termed "separate and unequal," Yeshayahu Leibowitz, an Orthodox writer in Israel noted for his provocative views on Judaism and the Halakhah, has recently argued for an equal Jewish education for men and women:

The matter of the study of Torah is totally different from all [the *mitzvot* from which women are exempt].[17]

True, this too is a positive *mitzvah* [*mitzvat aseh*], and one of the most important of positive *mitzvot*, but after repeated discussions of this question in the history of Halakhah it was determined in the accepted Halakhah that women are exempt from it. And this is a grave error and a great misfortune in historical Judaism. . . . Barring women from the study of Torah is not freeing them from an obligation (as in the case of some other *mitzvot*) but rather a denial of a basic Jewish right. Women's "Jewishness" thus becomes inferior to that of men.[18]

Leibowitz advocates equal Torah education for boys and girls, and holds that such equality can only be achieved if boys and girls are taught together in the same schools and the same classes.

Leibowitz's view is regarded as radical and anomalous within the Orthodox community in Israel. In this community girls con-

tinue to receive only a limited Jewish education which emphasizes practical knowledge of the *mitzvot* with little theoretical
understanding of the Halakhah, and developing upright pious
"Jewish daughters" with little importance given to intellectual
development. In the United States today the Reform and Reconstructionist movements advocate full equality of education for all
ages and levels, including rabbinical training and ordination.[19]
The Conservative movement has very recently reversed a long
debated policy by voting for the inclusion of women in rabbinical
training and for their ordination as rabbis.[20] The Orthodox community includes a wide spectrum of attitudes, but even the most
liberal "modern Orthodox" still hold to the principle of separate
education for males and females, and separate is not equal.

The traditional role of women in the study of Torah is in encouraging and enabling their husbands and sons to pursue it. The
glorification of this female role is common currency in contemporary polemics about the role of women in Judaism, but it appears
in the Talmud:

Greater is the promise made by the Holy One, blessed be He, to women
than to men, for it says: "Rise up, ye women that are at ease, ye confident
daughters, listen to my speech." Rav said to Rabbi Hiyyah: Whereby do
women gain this merit? By making their sons go to the synagogue to learn
and their husbands go to the *Bet Midrash* [school] to study the teachings
of the rabbis, and by waiting for their husbands until they return from the
Bet Midrash. [Berakhot 17a]

Women gain their merit by enabling and encouraging their husbands and sons to study the Torah. The Talmud brings many
stories demonstrating the piety and merit of women who sacrificed their own needs and marital happiness in order to enable
their husbands to study Torah. The classic case is Rachel, the wife
of Rabbi Akiva. She married him when he was a poor, ignorant
shepherd because of his promise to go study. She then lost all her
wealth when she was ousted by her father and spent twenty-four
years in "living widowhood" while Rabbi Akiva was studying.
Only at the end of this long period did she finally return to her
husband and regain her former status (Ketubot 62b). Not all stories

of such devotion ended happily, and there is even one story of a wife who waited so long that "she lost the powers of procreation" (Ketubot 62b).

In his commentary on the *Shulhan Arukh* passage cited above, Moses Isserles states the same principle: "A woman is not required to teach her son Torah, yet, when she aids her son and husband in studying Torah she partakes in their reward." Women's role as enablers to their husbands in study of Torah symbolizes the general position of women in Jewish religious life. The total number of *mitzvot* from which women are exempted is rather small, but their weight is significant. The exemptions substantially exclude women from the realm of public religious life. At best, women remain passive participants in public prayer and reading of the Torah. In the final analysis the status of women in relation to the *mitzvot* is a result of the position of women in traditional Jewish society: they have no public role and their proper sphere is the home. The private nature of women's prayer is a result of the same exclusion of women from public life.

There are three *mitzvot* which are expressly the special province of women and they illustrate the same point. These three *mitzvot* are *niddah* (the laws of the menstruant woman), *hallah* (burning a tenth part of the dough of the bread as a symbol of the tithe paid to the priests), and lighting the Sabbath candles. All three of these *mitzvot* pertain to the specific sphere of marital and domestic life. *Niddah* regulates the rhythm of sexual relations and is, of course, exclusively female for biological reasons. *Hallah* symbolizes the woman's role as baker of the bread, and by extension, in charge of the household. The Sabbath candles accent the woman's place in the home where she lights the candles just before the Sabbath begins, while her husband is in the synagogue praying with the men.

Women's religious duties as well as their special rights (*onah*, sexual rights, for example) center in the sphere of marriage and family life. Indeed most of this book concerns legal issues which pertain to marriage, divorce, and marital life. Although women and the legal issues surrounding them contribute many cases to the halakhic literature, women had no direct influence on the evolution of the Halakhah that governed their lives.

On Assuming Mitzvot

Much of the contemporary debate on women and the *mitzvot* has focused on the issue of assuming obligations: can women, who are as a group exempt from certain *mitzvot*, assume the obligation to perform these *mitzvot* and will this constitute halakhic equality with men? The call for women to assume the "yoke of the law" has centered on the *mitzvot* we have discussed: prayer, *aliyah la-Torah*, and the study of Torah. These obligations in particular are seen as the keys to areas of Jewish life from which women have been excluded: public worship—through Torah reading and participation in a *minyan*, and halakhic learning which, through formal sanction (rabbinic ordination) or informal recognition of erudition, would ultimately enable women to enter the process of formulating Halakhah. The implications of this debate are far-reaching and many feel that the assumption of *mitzvot* may prove to be the route for integrating women across the board into male-dominated areas of religious and spiritual life.

The discussion begins with a general question: can women, and others such as minors or men in mourning who are exempt from certain daily prayers, take upon themselves the duty of performing *mitzvot* from which they are halakhically exempt? The answer given by most authorities is "yes." In other words, exemption does not mean exclusion. However, some opposition to this remains. For example, the Talmud says that Mikhal, the daughter of King Saul, used to put on *tefillin* and "the sages did not protest" (Rosh Ha-Shanah 33a) but Moses Isserles, despite his halakhic ruling that women may assume obligations, states in his commentary on the *Shulhan Arukh*: "we do protest" (Moses Isserles, Commentary on the *Shulhan Arukh*: Orah Hayyim: 38 : 3). Perhaps Isserles' objection to donning *tefillin* is the demonstrative nature of the act and the implication, in public, of women's equal role in ritual. However, as we have said, the majority view is that

"women may obligate themselves." The major split in the Halakhah concerns the status of such obligations performed by
women. Maimonides holds that while women may assume obligations from which they are exempt, they may not recite the blessings that accompany them. The blessings all begin with the same
formula: "Blessed art Thou O Lord our God, King of the universe,
Who has sanctified us with His commandments and commanded
us to . . ." perform a given *mitzvah*. Since women are not commanded to perform certain *mitzvot*, they cannot recite the blessings. Maimonides further rules that while they may perform the
act, it is not equal to the *mitzvah* performed by a man. This view is
based on the concept that performing a *mitzvah* one has been
commanded to perform has greater merit than assuming obligations one has not been commanded to perform.

The opposing view is represented by Rabbenu Tam: he holds
that a woman who assumes an obligation may recite the blessing
accompanying it. Furthermore, a woman performing a *mitzvah*
she has taken upon herself is allowed, like men, to violate laws
superseded by this *mitzvah*. For example, a woman who assumes
the obligation of blowing a *shofar* on Rosh Ha-Shanah is allowed
to handle the *shofar* in order to perform the duty (handling the
shofar for any other reason is a violation of the holiday observance). Rabbi Isaac Ha-Levi, Rashi's teacher, not only permitted
women to recite the blessing accompanying the *mitzvah* but required it. This position holds that once a woman takes on a *mitzvah* by assuming the obligation, she is accountable for all aspects
and implications of the new duty.

Other questions arise for those halakhists like Rabbenu Tam and
Isaac Ha-Levi who rule that women may recite the blessing along
with the *mitzvah* they have taken on. Do women gain the same
reward for performing an assumed *mitzvah* that men gain for it?
Do women who assume an obligation share an equal status with
men who are already commanded? And most significantly, can
women who assume a given *mitzvah* as their duty now perform
this *mitzvah* on men's behalf (as in the case of reading the Torah
or the Megillah)? The halakhic opinions prior to some recent ones
all hold that women do not gain full equality with men even

though they may perform the *mitzvah* and recite the blessing in an identical manner. Joseph Karo rules "A woman who has studied Torah has a reward but not as much as the reward of a man, because she is not commanded and performs it [of her own will]." (*Shulhan Arukh*: Yoreh De'ah: 246 : 6). The Tosafot rules in the same manner, explaining that a man who fulfills an obligation does it anxiously since he is commanded, while the woman who is exempt and chooses to assume the obligation can "take it or leave it" (Tosafot to Kiddushin 31a). The general consensus is that women may not discharge men's obligations for *mitzvot* they have taken upon themselves. Although assuming an obligation is a serious commitment (analogous to a vow), the fact remains that performing the *mitzvah* is based on a voluntary choice for a woman while it is a divinely mandated responsibility for a man. Moreover, while an individual woman may assume an obligation and perform it devotedly, women in general have no responsibility for this *mitzvah*. As a group or sub-congregation, women are still exempt from this *mitzvah* while all men, whether they perform it or not, are equally subject to the duty in the eyes of the law.

As we have seen, the issue of assuming obligations points to a possibly radical change in the religious status of women. If women were to choose in great numbers to assume the obligations of daily prayer, Torah reading, wearing *tefillin*, or the study of Torah, they would create a very different profile of Jewish worship and learning. Then, they might press for a bolder ruling on the final barrier to full participation and equality of women in Jewish religious life: that their performance of *mitzvot* be deemed equal to men's. If the community of women as a whole assumes the obligation for a *mitzvah* from which women are exempt, the obligation could then be expressed as a modern day *takanah* which, like the *takanot* of previous generations, has the force of law and becomes an integral part of the Halakhah.

MARRIAGE

FINDING a spouse, marriage, and the creation of a new family are the hallmarks of maturity and self-fulfillment in almost all cultures. The Pentateuch and the historical books of the Bible generally supply us with accounts of the marriages of their more prominent figures. The most detailed of those accounts are the stories of the marriages of the two patriarchs, Isaac and Jacob. We learn of the importance of lineage in the story of how Abraham's slave traveled to Mesopotamia to find a bride for his son Isaac (Genesis 24). We learn about love and devotion in the story of Jacob, who worked on his father-in-law's estate for seven years to gain his first bride, Leah, and another seven years to marry his second, beloved bride, Rachel (Genesis 29). But when we look for specific legislation about marriage we find a void. There are no explicit prescriptions concerning requirements for marriage (such as minimum age, marriage within one's class, etc.) nor regarding the exact procedure necessary for effecting marriage.

Rather than direct legislation about marriage we find reference to the act of marriage as if in passing, in the context of legislation about some other matter. For example, Deuteronomy 24 : 5 states that "When a man takes a new wife he shall not go out with the army for one year, nor shall he be taxed to supply the army." The purpose of this text is to legislate the exemption of a newly married man from military duty. It concerns a special consequence of "taking a new wife," but tells us nothing about how a man goes about doing that. Similarly, Deuteronomy 22 : 13 deals with a man who "takes a wife and comes to her" (i.e., has intercourse with her), and then accuses her of not having been a virgin before their cohabitation, but does not explicate how "taking a wife" is carried out in the first place. All the biblical references to marriage are characterized by a lack of explicit legislation on how to effect marriage.

Most of the references to marriage in the Bible have two more features in common:

1. The use of the term "to take" (*la-kahat*) to designate marriage
2. The automatic association of marriage ("taking") and sexual relations

If the nature of the legal act of "taking" is unclear, what comes after it is as clear as could be: the groom and bride have sexual intercourse. Now there are two possible views of biblical marriage: either the "taking" is the same thing as having intercourse and marriage was simply effected through sexual relations and cohabitation, or taking in marriage did involve procedure and ceremony but these were determined by family customs and communal practice. In the latter case it may have been unnecessary to add legislation to well-established custom, or possibly even problematic if there were considerable variances in local practices and family traditions. Most likely the reality lay somewhere in between. Probably sexual relations were the act which made a marriage take effect, yet they were surely preceded and followed by certain ceremonies and celebrations. Especially among the affluent classes in society we can expect that marriage was accompanied by a set procedure. At least we have explicit evidence in the case of Isaac and Rebecca that engagement was formulated and celebrated according to family custom.[1]

The Bible then supplies us with plenty of evidence about marriage but with no explicit prescriptions. Postbiblical Halakhah relies therefore on *interpretation* of the biblical text in legislating marriage. The cornerstone of this legislation is the legalistic interpretation of the term "taking" which characterizes biblical references to marriage. A second element in the Halakhah is the clear connection between the act of marriage and the act of sexual intercourse. This element, as we shall see, becomes a problematic one when we enter the talmudic discussion.

The central text for the Halakhah on marriage is the very first paragraph of Tractate Kiddushin (Betrothals). The first *mishnah* in the tractate contains in brief the fundamental laws of marriage as well as the complications and problems which ensue from them. These are the primary issues in our discussion, and we shall therefore follow the text of Kiddushin 2a throughout this chapter.

Mishnah: A woman is acquired in three ways and acquires herself in two. She is acquired by money, by deed, or by intercourse. "By money": Bet Shammai maintain: a *dinar* or the worth of a *dinar*. Bet Hillel rule: a *perutah* or the worth of a *perutah*. And how much is a *perutah*? An eighth of an Italian *issar*.

And she acquires herself by divorce or by the death of her husband. A *yevamah* is acquired by intercourse and acquires herself by *halitzah* or by the *yabam*'s death.

Gemara: "A woman is acquired." Why does he state here: "A woman is acquired," while elsewhere he teaches "A man betrothes" (Kiddushin 41a)? Because he wishes to state "money." And how do we know that money effects betrothal [*kiddushin*]? By deriving the meaning of "taking" from the field of Ephron. Here it is written "When a man takes a wife" (Deut. 24 : 1) and there it is written "I will give you money for the field, take it from me" (Gen. 23 : 12). Moreover "taking" is designated acquisition (*kinyan*), for it is written: "The field which Abraham acquired" (Gen. 49 : 30), and also "men shall acquire fields for money" (Jer. 32 : 15). Therefore, he teaches "A woman is acquired." Then let him state there (Kiddushin 41a) "A man acquires." He first employs biblical phraseology but subsequently the rabbinical idiom. Now, what does the rabbinical idiom [*mekadesh*] connote? That he interdicts her to all men as *hekdesh*. But why not teach here "a man acquires"? Because he wants to teach the second clause "and acquires herself," which refers to the woman. He therefore teaches the first clause likewise, with reference to her. Then let him state: "A man acquires . . . and makes her acquire"? [No] Because there is the husband's death where it is not he who acquires [herself] for her, but Heaven who confers [herself] upon her. Alternatively, were it taught "he acquires" I might have thought even against her will, hence it is stated: "A woman is acquired"; only with her consent, and not without it. [Kiddushin 2a–b]

The *mishnah* opens with a general statement: "A woman is acquired in three ways and acquires herself in two." The central term in this phrase requires explanation: what is the meaning of "acquire" and what does it have to do with marriage? Indeed the

Gemara which follows immediately addresses this very question. The term "acquisition," *kinyan*, normally refers to purchase of property. The term commonly used by the rabbis to refer to marriage is *kiddushin* (betrothal), just like the name of the tractate. The Gemara begins with the question of why this mishnaic text uses the term "acquire" instead of "betroth" (*mekadesh*) which is used in other passages about marriage. The answer is: "Because he [the rabbi who cited this *halakhah*] wishes to state 'money.' " In other words, money is clearly connected to the term "acquire," since acquisition of property is done through payment of money. The *mishnah* wants to teach us that marriage, like acquisition, can also be effected through payment of money. How do we know that? asks the Gemara. "By deriving the meaning of 'taking' from the field of Ephron." The field of Ephron was purchased by Abraham for a burial plot. We know that Abraham "acquired" it because we are told that he paid for it a certain sum of money and because another text (Gen. 49 : 30) refers to the field with that specific term "acquired" (*kanah*). The field which Abraham acquired is also referred to in the biblical text as a field which was "taken." Therefore the purchase of the field of Ephron teaches us that "taking" and "acquiring" mean the same thing. They both mean acquisition by payment of money. Now we know that marriage is referred to in the biblical texts as "taking" ("when a man takes a wife," etc.). Thus we may place marriage in a chain of identities: purchase by money = "acquisition" = "taking" = marriage. And thus we learn that a woman may be acquired "by money" from the very formulation "A woman is acquired [*niknet*]."

However, this acquisition of a woman by money is not purchase of property. For one thing, a man may not sell the woman he "acquires" for a wife. For another, the amount of money required for acquiring a woman is so small that we could not possibly think that we are dealing with a regular financial transaction here. Even though there is a dispute between Bet Hillel and Bet Shammai as to the sum of money required for *kinyan* ("Bet Shammai maintain: a *dinar* or the worth of a *dinar*. Bet Hillel rule: a *perutah* or the worth of a *perutah*"), both schools cite minimal sums. Bet Hillel cites the smallest coin, a perutah, and their ruling is accepted as halakhah. All of this goes to show that the amount of money is immaterial because the acquisition is symbolic. If the exchange of money is not an actual purchase, what then is the "real" meaning of acquiring a woman in marriage? What are the actual legal implications of this act?

The Gemara illuminates the meaning of marriage by contrasting the terminology used here, "acquiring," and the terminology used elsewhere in the Mishnah, kiddushin. About the use of "acquire" here and "betroth" (mekadesh) later in this tractate the Gemara says: "He uses biblical phraseology here but subsequently the rabbinical idiom." To the question of what the rabbinical term kiddushin means and connotes the Gemara answers: "That he interdicts her to all other men as hekdesh." Hekdesh is a term which describes an object that has been set aside for some purpose, usually a ritual one, and may not be touched by anyone nor used to any other end. This is the original meaning of the word kadosh, "holy" or "sanctified," an object or place that is set aside from all other (profane) things and remains separated from them. In the act of kiddushin (betrothal) a man sets his wife aside and forbids her to all other men. According to the Halakhah a married woman has an exclusive sexual relationship with her husband. She is "out of bounds" to all other men and is "forbidden to the rest of the world" (asurah le-kulei alma).

The act of acquisition is an act in which the man sets the woman aside for himself only. The term kiddushin is crucial for making this point since it includes the notion of exclusivity. The notion of acquisition does not prevent sharing. One might have thought if only the term kinyan was used that, just as a man may share property he had purchased with others, so he may share the wife he had "acquired" with fellowmen. Therefore the concept of "taking" in marriage is a fusion of kinyan and hekdesh.

The notion of kiddushin, that the husband "interdicts her to all other men," applies to women only. A woman who is married is only allowed to have sexual relations with her husband. Her husband, however, is not forbidden to have relations with other women, provided that those other women are not married themselves. This passage is a reflection of the system of polygyny which prevailed in the Halakhah. A man may have several wives while a woman may only have one husband. Undoubtedly, one of the reasons for this restriction was to protect children from doubts concerning paternity.

The Talmud illustrates the notion of polygyny (inaccurately also called polygamy; polygyny refers to multiple wives, polygamy to multiple partners of either sex) with a concrete example:

Raba said: [If he says] "Become betrothed to a half of me," she is betrothed. [If he says] "Half of you is betrothed to me," she is not betrothed.[2] [Kiddushin 7a]

Raba states that a man who asks a woman to marry half of him is contracting a valid marriage. Another half of him may marry another woman. In fact, according to the Halakhah which Raba relies on, a man may "split himself" into many more parts, that is, he may marry as many women as he wishes. The Talmud states only one limitation on the number of wives a man may marry and this law only applies to the king. The king is not allowed to marry more than eighteen women, for a larger number would interfere with the fulfillment of his political duties, as we learn from the case of Solomon who had a thousand wives (Sanhedrin 21a). A woman, on the other hand, may only marry one man so that a man who asks to betroth only half of his bride ("Half of you is betrothed to me") is attempting the impossible. Such a betrothal is not valid and "she is not betrothed."

Raba's ruling as well as other passages in the Talmud make it clear that polygyny is permitted. A man may marry as many wives as he wishes as long as he continues to fulfill his marital and sexual obligations (see Chapter 5 on Sexuality and Marital Relations) toward all of them. The rabbis speculated that four wives are the realistic maximum so that the husband can devote one week out of the month to each to fulfill the duty of onah (Yevamot 44a). However, a reading of the Talmud as a historical document shows that these were theoretical speculations. We do not hear of a single rabbi who had more than one wife and we have no specific case cited in which a rabbi had a plaintiff who had several wives. Even in the Bible the practice of polygyny seems to be limited to the Patriarchs and the kings, and as a rule we do not hear of it in the life of the common man.

Though it seems that polygyny was not practiced in the postbiblical period it remains very significant that it was halakhically acceptable. This changed in the Middle Ages for those Jews living in Christian countries. Christianity forbade polygyny altogether, so for Jews living under Christian rule and influence it gradually became less and less tenable and more and more embarrassing to permit it in their laws. By the ninth and tenth centuries the aversion to polygyny (which was most probably never actually practiced by the Jews in Europe) began to take the form of prohibitions set in community practice and rules (takanot). Traditionally the definitive order against polygyny is attributed to Rabbenu Gershom Me'or Ha-Golah (960–1028) even though we have evidence that it had already been accepted in many communities before his time.[3]

The herem [writ of excommunication] according to the ruling of our communities declared by Rabbenu Gershom Me'or Ha-Golah that it is forbidden to marry two wives, may only be revoked by one hundred rabbis from three regions and three different communities. [Responsa of Rabbi Meir (Maharam) of Rothenburg (ca. 1220–1293), No. 1022 (Prague edition)]

The prohibition of Rabbenu Gershom on polygyny is stated in the form of a herem, a threat of excommunication. The rabbis derived much of their power and legal authority from the fact that they could order a person who breaks the rules of the community to be excommunicated and ban any contact with him. When new legislation such as the prohibition on polygyny is introduced there is a problem: one cannot go back and change the Talmud and the statements there which permit this practice. The prohibition is therefore introduced as a new layer, a new ruling called a takanah. Since the Bible and Talmud do not forbid it, the prohibition on polygyny must be backed up with a different source of authority, namely, the authority of the community and its leading rabbis. Anyone who violates the *takanah* cannot be threatened with appropriate retribution since neither the Bible nor the Mishnah and Talmud prescribe punishment for polygyny. Therefore the violator must be threatened by being banned from the community whose *takanah* he has violated.

The ban of Rabbenu Gershom on polygyny was only accepted by a portion of the worldwide Jewish community of the Middle Ages, by Ashkenazic Jewry which was within the domain of Christianity. The Jews who resided in Islamic countries did not accept this ban and among them polygyny was practiced, even though it was rather rare.[5] This was possible in Islamic countries since polygyny is permitted in Islam (a man may marry up to four wives). In the State of Israel, where Ashkenazic and Sephardic Jews have come together, the differing practices posed a problem. A prohibition on polygyny was enacted by the State of Israel as part of the definition and consolidation of the rabbinical laws applying to personal status (*dinei ishut*), and was imposed on Jews from all countries alike. However, those Jews who arrived in Israel with more than one wife (and this was particularly true among the Jews of Yemen) were allowed to maintain their polygynous marriages.

Finally, it must be understood that the ban of Rabbenu Gershom does not have the status of an immutable law and in very special circumstances may be revoked. Such revocation requires, as stated in the responsum of the Maharam, the consent of one hundred rabbis from three different regions. The circumstances warranting revocation of the ban of Rabbenu Gershom are extraordinary, such as when the wife cannot accept a writ of divorce (get) because she has disappeared, when she has apparently died but there is no proof of her death, when she has become insane, or when she stubbornly refuses without reasonable cause to consent to a get (regarding the requirement that the woman accept the writ of divorce, see Chapter 3). In other words, in extreme cases where a man is bound to a woman he can neither live with nor divorce, the ban of Rabbenu Gershom may be lifted so the man may marry a second wife.[4] We can appreciate the importance of this "loophole" when we realize that it is not available for women. A woman can never be allowed to marry another man unless her husband divorces her or dies, even if her husband is insane or has been gone and not heard of for thirty years. A woman in such circumstances is called an *agunah* (one who is bound), and we shall return to the grave problems of such a situation in Chapter 4.

The Mishnah cites a second way of effecting marriage: "by deed." How is the validity of the deed for effecting *kiddushin* proven? The use of a deed (*shtar*) for effecting marriage is drawn from its use to dissolve marriage:

How do we know that with a deed [one can effect marriage] as well? It is logical. Since money which cannot release [from marriage] enters [one into marriage], then a deed which does release should not enter one [into marriage] as well?

And should you say: "A deed should release and enter"? The "attacker" [*kategor*] should become the "defender" [*sanegor*]? The words of one are different from the words of the other. Could you say the same about money, perhaps? Namely, that this money is different from that money? The nature of money is the same here and there. [Kiddushin 5a]

The use of a deed is derived from the procedure of divorce. One uses money in order to effect marriage but cannot use money to dissolve marriage through divorce. Since divorce is the graver act of the two, a deed which *can* release from marriage (i.e., a *get*) should certainly have the power to enter one into marriage. This logical argument may be assailed by a question: If a deed which dissolves a marriage is the "attacker" of the marriage, is it reasonable to say that the very same thing, a deed, can be the "defender" of marriage, i.e., that it can effect marriage to begin with? The answer is that it is sensible because there is a difference between the words of one deed and the other: these words enter one into marriage while those release the bonds of marriage. Perhaps, then, by the same logic we could argue that money may be used to effect divorce. Since money effects marriage we could argue that it ought to dissolve marriage as well, and say that the money used for *kiddushin* is different from the money used for a divorce. No, answers the Gemara, you could not make that argument since money is the same whenever you use it; a coin is always a coin.

The third and simplest way to effect marriage is by intercourse, and no exegesis is needed to prove that. The biblical text is plain and clear on this score: when a man takes a wife he has sexual intercourse with her. The term for intercourse, *bi'ah*, is derived from the common biblical euphemisms *"ba aleha"* ("he came upon her") or *"ba eleha"* ("he came unto her").

The *mishnah* in Kiddushin 2a states the three ways of effecting *kiddushin* directly and makes no distinction between them. Any of the three ways is valid, as stated in the Jerusalem Talmud: "Either with money, or with a deed, or with intercourse" (JT, Kiddushin 1 : 1). However, in the talmudic discussion we see the emergence of some changes:

1. Disapproval of betrothal by intercourse
2. Disapproval of betrothal with disregard for proper decorum: with money or an object the literal worth of a *perutah*, or betrothal in the marketplace.
3. Introduction of a requirement of prior arrangement of the marriage (*shiddukhin*).

These changes are summarized in the following passage about a man who betrothed a woman with an object worth no less but no more than a *perutah:*

A certain man betrothed with a myrtle branch in the marketplace. Thereupon Rabbi Aha ben Huna sent to Rabbi Joseph: "How is it [the law] in such a case?" He sent back: "Have him flogged in accordance with Rav, and demand a divorce in accordance with Samuel." For Rav punished anyone who betrothed in the marketplace, or by intercourse, or without prior engagement, or who annuled a divorce, or lodged a protest against a divorce. . . .

The Nehardeans maintain: For all those Rav inflicted no punishment, excepting for betrothal by intercourse without prior arrangement. Others state: Even with prior arrangement—on account of licentiousness. [Kiddushin 12b]

The case of the man who betrothed in the marketplace with a myrtle branch raised questions in Rabbi Aha's mind. True, the marriage seemed to be valid because a myrtle branch can be said to be "the worth of a *perutah*." But the *kiddushin* lacked the proper spirit and decorum. Indeed that was also the view of the rabbi he consulted, Rabbi Joseph. Rabbi Joseph responded by citing the divergent opinions of Rav and Samuel, each requiring a different punishment, and advised Rabbi Aha to apply both measures. The man should be flogged in accordance with the opinion of Rav. Flogging was the punishment for *mardut*, rebelliousness and disregard for rabbinical authority and for the customs of the community. Despite the flogging Rav apparently let the marriage stand. This we conclude from the fact that Samuel, who is in disagreement with Rav, required that the man be compelled to divorce his new wife. Rabbi Joseph in his answer to Aha recommends that the man both be flogged and forced to divorce his wife, in other words, a more stringent view than the view of either Rav or Samuel.

Rav is attributed with a whole list of cases in which he punished the offender with flogging: "Anyone who betrothed in the marketplace, or by intercourse, or without prior arrangement, etc." All these cases involve actions which are not *illegal* (on the contrary, betrothal by intercourse is mandated in the Mishnah) but which violate accepted custom and undermine the authority of the rabbis. There is another tradition cited here which minimizes the number of cases in which Rav called for punishment by flogging. It is the tradition cited in the name of the Nehardeans who claimed that Rav only punished one offense by flogging: betrothal by intercourse without prior arrangement. According to the Nehardeans, Rav permitted betrothal by intercourse as long as the marriage had been prearranged and agreed upon by the family of the bride (that is the full meaning of *shiddukhin*). He only forbade, and thus punished, betrothal which was effected by intercourse "on the spot," without consultation and approval. This tradition is disputed by "others" who claim that Rav flogged anyone who betrothed by intercourse, even if there were *shiddukhin* beforehand. This last opinion furnishes a reason as well: "on account of licentiousness." That is, betrothal by intercourse could all too easily smack of sexual motivation. If one betrothes by intercourse there is room to wonder whether the full solemnity of *kiddushin* was intended in the act, or whether sexual pleasure was foremost in the man's mind.

The last two opinions in the passage from the Gemara indicate

clearly that betrothal by intercourse was considered the least desirable, the least proper, and the most suspect form of effecting
marriage. Though the Bible and the Mishnah not only permit but
prescribe intercourse as a way of effecting *kiddushin*, the Talmud
attempts to suppress its use. The difficulty rabbis like Rav and
Samuel have with betrothal by a *perutah* or an object literally
worth a *perutah* is similar, as is the problem with betrothal in the
marketplace and betrothal, through any means, without *shiddukhin*. All these instances have the same feature in common: betrothal is effected without parental approval or involvement, without
communal sanction, and without rabbinic control. This is the
crux of the problem with the three ways of effecting marriage.
They require very simple procedures and prescribe no form of
outside control. With betrothal by intercourse there is additionally the "taint" of free sexual relations.

Marriage is a very serious matter. In a traditional society it determines not only the nature of family life and personal happiness
of the couple, but also cements the social and economic standing
of the families. Social expectations and economic needs seem to
mandate that marriage be controlled by the parents of the bride
and groom and that society's representatives sanction the marriage and participate in its celebration. Yet according to the Halakhah in Kiddushin, a man may marry at his will as long as he
finds a woman who consents to intercourse or accepts a *perutah*
from him. There is a clear conflict between the letter of the law
and the requirements of family and society. It should therefore not
be surprising that despite the explicit ruling in the Mishnah that a
man may betroth with a *perutah* or by intercourse, these practices
are suppressed by later Halakhah. Since these ways of effecting
marriage cannot be expressly forbidden (one cannot change the
biblical or mishnaic text) they are severely discouraged by flogging or by forcing the dissolution of such marriages. Maimonides
summarizes the rulings on the three ways of effecting *kiddushin*
clearly and succinctly:

Even though the essence of the act is thus ["A woman is acquired in three
ways etc."], nevertheless, the children of Israel have accustomed them-

selves to betroth with money or its equivalent. Also, if a man wants to betroth with a deed he may do so. But we do not acquire with intercourse as the first means. If a man does betroth with intercourse he is flogged for rebelliousness so that Israel should not become promiscuous in this matter, despite the fact that his betrothal stands as valid betrothal. And the same holds for one who betrothes without engagement or one who betrothes in the marketplace: he is flogged for rebelliousness so that this does not accustom people to licentiousness. [Maimonides, *Mishneh Torah*, Seder Nashim, Hilkhot Ishut 3 : 21–22]

The Halakhah after the Mishnaic period took pains to eliminate the practice of betrothing by intercourse, with an insignificant object worth no more than a perutah, and without proper preparation and decorum. Betrothal was preceded by engagement (*shiddukhin*) and effected with a marriage contract (*ketubah*) and an object of significant value. Intercourse was postponed until after the ceremony of *kiddushin* and acquired new significance as the necessary consummation of betrothal.

The legal validity of intercourse, an exchange of a *perutah*, etc., for effecting marriage could not be erased or undone. Problems resulting from this fact remain a constant feature in the Halakhah. The most common problems were various forms of elopement (*nisu'ei seter*). These were marriages against the wish of the parents, or marriages in which a particularly young or naïve bride was conned into accepting betrothal.

For generations after Maimonides the problem of inappropriate marriages persisted. The community had to legislate severe punishments in order to assure that marriages take place in front of two witnesses and a *minyan* of non-witnesses in the proper ceremonial manner of *huppah ve-kiddushin* to assure the sanction of family and the religious establishment. Thus, for example, the minutes of the council of the community of Lithuania recorded in the seventeenth century include a *takanah* (ruling) which punishes anyone who marries without proper ceremony and community sanction with flogging and excommunication:

Anyone who deliberately and brazenly violates the customs of Israel by marrying a woman or a virgin without [a *minyan*] and a *huppah* shall, together with the witnesses who assisted him in this foul deed, be excommunicated and ostracized in this world and in the world to come. Their sin shall not be forgiven and the court shall punish them severely by hanging them from a post and administering forty lashes without any possibility of ransom [bail]. They shall be punished and tortured with all manner of suffering and excommunications as a means of preventing the promiscuity of the generation. [*Minute Book of the Council of Lithuania,* Item No. 43 (S. Dubnow edition)][7]

The extremely severe punishments mandated in this ruling (forty lashes without the possibility of substituting a fine for some of them could in some cases amount to a death sentence!) suggest the extent of the opposition to marriages against the wishes of the parents and the sanction of the community.

The problem of elopement was particularly severe in the mishnaic and talmudic periods and the early Middle Ages, because in addition to betrothing at an early age (even before the girl reached twelve) it was common to wait a year between betrothal (*kiddushin*) and full-fledged married life (*nisu'in*). This meant that for a year the bride and groom were legally fully married but were not living as husband and wife. The waiting period was susceptible to a change of heart by either party, or to the entry of another man interested in the bride. The Talmud reports a case of a man who "snatched" a woman who had been betrothed as a minor, had become an adult, and was about to enter her marriage:

> . . . it once happened in Naresh that a man betrothed a girl when she was a minor. When she became an adult and he placed her on the bridal chair another man came and snatched her away from him. Even though Rav's disciples, Rabbi Bruna and Rabbi Hananel, were present, they did not require her to obtain a bill of divorce from the second man . . . Rav Ashi said: He acted improperly so they treated him improperly also and annulled his betrothal. Said Rabina to Rav Ashi: [Your explanation is] satisfactory where the man betrothed with money; what if he betrothed by intercourse? The rabbis declared his intercourse to be an act of mere fornication. [Yevamot 110a]

As the girl in Naresh was preparing to enter her marriage with the man who had betrothed her earlier, another man came and "snatched" her, that is, took her and betrothed her. There was some disagreement between the rabbis about the response to this situation. The disciples of Rav who were present felt that the woman was fully married to her groom so that the betrothal of the "snatcher" (presumably by intercourse) did not hold (since she was legally forbidden to him) and she could return to her groom without needing a divorce from the second man. Rav Ashi felt that the initial betrothal did not have effect since it was done before the girl reached maturity and had not yet been followed by intercourse and *nisu'in*. Thus Rav Ashi believes that the betrothal of the "snatcher" did hold, and in order to do justice and return the woman to her groom the rabbis annulled this betrothal.

Rav Ashi explains that the rabbis retaliated against the "snatcher" for his improper betrothal by doing him a nasty turn and annulling his act of *kiddushin*. Rabina wonders about this annulment. If the betrothal was done by money the rabbis have the authority to expropriate the man's money retroactively so that legally speaking the money was not his at the time of the betrothal and he could not validly betroth with it. But, asks Rabina, the rabbis cannot very well retroactively eliminate his ability to have intercourse. Therefore, if betrothed by intercourse, how can the betrothal be annulled? The answer of Rav Ashi is that the rabbis have the power to declare retroactively that the act of intercourse was an act of mere sexual promiscuity (*be'ilat zenut*) and not an act of betrothal.

The possibility of annulling a marriage could furnish a solution for the problem of elopement and inappropriate marriage. However, it is a rather difficult procedure to defend since both retroactive expropriation and declaration of intercourse as *be'ilat zenut* require a considerable stretch of logic and legal reasoning. It was reserved for very extreme cases, and cancelling an inappropriate marriage by divorce was a preferable avenue.

The problem of the waiting period was handled in different ways in the major centers of Jewish life. In Alexandria, for example, it was common to add a clause to the *ketubah* (the marriage contract), which was written during the *kiddushin*, whereby the *kiddushin* would be voided if the groom did not actually take the bride into his home to begin their married life within a year of the writing of the *ketubah*. In ancient Israel it was common to

write an agreement (simphon) which made the kiddushin dependent on nisu'in's taking place within a specified time (usually a
year).[8] In Babylonia arrangements based on conditional clauses
were rejected because the prevailing halakhic view was that marriage cannot be conditional (ein tnai be-nisu'in).[9] Generally, the
family of the bride took great care to protect her during the vulnerable period between kiddushin and nisu'in, while gradually a
new custom emerged: kiddushin and nisu'in were joined into one
two-part ceremony.[10]

We would imagine that most cases of elopement involved a
couple who wanted to marry against the wishes of the parents.
However, if we return to the case of the girl at Naresh (Yevamot
110a), it seems that there the bride herself was opposed to the
(second) marriage which was later annulled. Otherwise it would
be difficult to understand the story which implies that she returned to her first husband. Yet this is puzzling. If the girl happily
returned to her first husband after the annulment of the second
betrothal, why did she allow herself to be "snatched" and betrothed by the second man to begin with? Had she no say in the
matter of her own betrothal?

The Gemara in Kiddushin 2a makes it very clear that the bride
must consent to her own marriage. The phrasing in the mishnah,
"a woman is acquired," is brought as proof that the woman's
consent is necessary: "were it taught 'he acquires,' I might have
thought even against her will, hence it is stated: 'A woman is
acquired'; only with her consent, and not without it." The mishnah is purposefully phrased to indicate that the woman has her
say in kiddushin; so states the Gemara. However, in the subsequent discussion of the Gemara on how exactly a woman has to
give her consent we find an opening for problems. The woman's
consent, according to the Gemara, does not require definite articu-
lation. Silence on the woman's part may be construed as consent
(shtikah ke-hodayah). In other words, if a woman is given a sum
of money or an article as a token of betrothal and does not protest
the act, she is betrothed. This allows for certain circumstances
when a woman may be betrothed without full-fledged consent.
The problems pertain especially to the situation of a very young

girl, perhaps like the girl of Naresh, either conned by deception and false promises, or ignorant of the details of the Halakhah.

Despite these problems most marriages went along smoothly with parental approval and proper consent of the bride. Yet even in the proper marriages there were often questions about the completeness of the woman's consent. This was not because of deception or trickery on the groom's part, but because most marriages in Jewish society were arranged by the parents. Social conventions dictated that a daughter submit to the marital choice of her parents, so the bride's consent was closer to acquiescence than to choice and decision. Additionally, as we shall soon see, women were often married at a very young age, twelve or even earlier, so that their "consent" was hardly well considered and mature.

There is a tension between the laws which require the woman's consent (and by prescribing simple ways of effecting *kiddushin*, place marriage in the control of the couple) and social convention which puts marriage in the hands of the parents. We have seen this tension at work in the gradual suppression of betrothal by intercourse and of the minimum sum of one *perutah*. Both were suppressed, we have argued, because they allowed valid betrothals which involved no parental or communal supervision. Similarly, when parents arranged the marriages of their children, they in fact often ignored the requirement of true consent.

An interesting example of the problem of marriage without parental consent appears in an eighteenth-century responsum from Germany reporting what must have been a rather scandalous case:

[There was a case of] a rich man's son who betrothed a maiden, one of the servants of the household ... and later he regretted his action and changed his mind, and his father and other family members opposed this also. . . . For generally, the maids in any household set their eyes on the sons of the wealthy and give themselves to them easily in order to get them accustomed to having them and then to be betrothed by them. And since this one acted improperly . . . we too shall act with her improperly. [Jacob Reischer, *Responsa Shevut Yaakov* Part 2, No. 112]

The case is a classic one: the son of a rich man is apparently seduced by the maid. Young and naïve, he falls in love with her and betrothes her. Later on, probably faced by the outrage of the family, and undoubtedly by various threats of shaming and disinheritance from the father, he changes his mind and wants to revoke his betrothal. Indeed Reischer asserts that maids in wealthy households "generally . . . set their eyes on the sons" and offer themselves in order to be wed by them. If not actually a common occurrence, this was certainly a common fear. Reischer rules that since the betrothal was achieved through improper means (the maid's seducing a naïve boy) it should be annulled. Reischer presumes that the maid managed to con the boy into betrothing her by seduction and manipulation, and thus rules on the matter as if she had been the active agent in the betrothal.

The case described above is unusual in the sense that it is the woman who presumably maneuvers the man into an improper marriage. More often it was the other way: a man cons a woman into marriage. This is so for two reasons: first, the man is the active legal agent in effecting betrothal, and social conventions generally viewed the man as the one who seeks a bride.[11] Second, though a woman needs to consent to the betrothal, mere passive acceptance of the token of marriage constitutes consent according to the Halakhah.

It seems that despite the letter of the law which in Kiddushin 2a prescribes a simple transaction between groom and bride as two free agents, marriage in fact was placed under tight controls, mostly parental controls. This is not surprising when we realize and appreciate the centrality of marriage in Jewish society. Everything, it seems, hangs on marriage: social status, economic gains and stability, personal fulfillment, sexual satisfaction and control, and of course biological continuity. It is quite logical that marriage should not be left to the whims and desires of the young.

The functions marriage fulfills—legally, socially, and personally—are summarized in the Tur's opening paragraph in Even Ha-Ezer, the section covering the laws regarding personal status:

Blessed be the name of God who desires the good of his creations, for He knew that it is not good for man to be alone and therefore made a helpmate [ezer ke-negdo] for him, and furthermore, that the purpose of the creation of man is procreation and multiplication and that it is not possible without a mate and therefore He commanded him to cleave to the mate He had made for him. Therefore, a man is required to marry a wife in order to procreate and multiply. And he who does not engage in procreation is like one who spills blood, for it is written [whoever spills] "man's blood" (Gen. 9 : 6) and right next to it "And you shall be fruitful and multiply" (Gen. 9 : 1). And he is like the one who lessens the Divine image since it is written "In the image of God He had made man, and you, be fruitful and multiply" (Gen. 1 : 27–28). And he causes the Divine spirit [shekhinah] to depart from Israel.

And whoever lives without a wife lives without well-being, without blessing, without a home, without Torah, without a protective wall, without peace. And Rabbi Eliezer said: whoever has no wife is not a man, and once he marries a woman his transgressions vanish into thin air, as it is written: "He who has found a wife has found well-being and shall please God." [Jacob ben Asher, Arba'ah Turim, Even Ha-Ezer, Chap. 1, Laws of Procreation, I]

Even Ha-Ezer is the volume in Jacob ben Asher's code of law Arba'ah Turim (or Tur for short), which encompasses the laws of family life. It is named for the phrase in Genesis 2 : 18 which describes the creation of a companion for the first man as the creation of a helpmate for him (ezer ke-negdo). The introduction to the laws of marriage here is by no means accidental or haphazard. It is a carefully phrased summary of the essentials of the institution and purpose of marriage.

The first purpose of marriage according to the formulation in the Tur is to furnish companionship since "He knew that it is not good for man to be alone and therefore made a helpmate for him" (Gen. 2 : 18). It is rather remarkable that the author of the Tur places the psychological need for intimacy and protection against loneliness as the first goal of marriage, taking precedence over the biological need of procreation.

Procreation is the second purpose of marriage. Self-propagation is the "intention" of creation for all living species. Not to engage in procreation is likened to three things: murder, lessening the divine image, and causing the divine presence to depart from the community of Israel. The three violations illustrate the three levels of meaning and purpose in procreation. The first level is the biological one common to all living creatures: procreation means creating life; not procreating means destroying potential life. "He who does not engage in procreation is like one who spills blood" because by not replacing himself with his progeny he is like the one who commits suicide. The second level is particular to the human race. Procreation is man's way of creating something in his own image and the image of God. It is man's way of reenacting the original creation of a man "in our own image" (Gen. 1 : 26). This meaning of procreation is most fully developed in the Kabbalah, which postulates a process of union of male and female principles within God. The third purpose of procreation is anchored in the national framework, since it maintains the special tie between God and the people of Israel. The link between procreation and God's special relationship with Israel can clearly be seen in the ceremony of circumcision (brit milah). Circumcision, as described in Genesis 17 when first performed by Abraham on himself and his sons Ishmael and Isaac, is a pact of alliance between God and Abraham in which fertility is the central promise. Therefore a Jew who does not engage in procreation in effect refrains from perpetuating the special pact (brit) between God and Israel. He thus diminishes the divine presence (the Shekhinah) within the Jewish community.

The transgressions which one commits if he refrains from procreation are followed by a list of bounties that the bachelor does not experience. A man without a wife lives without well-being, without blessing, without a home. Rabbi Eliezer goes even further: "whoever has no wife is not a man." The gloomy lot of the bachelor is compared with the good fortune of the man who marries. He not only gains all the blessings that the bachelor misses, but even his past transgressions are forgiven: "they vanish into thin air."

The Tur does not mention the blessings that a woman finds in marriage nor her obligation in the act of procreation. The reason is twofold. First, the Tur is, of course, addressed to men and thus admonishes and encourages men to marry. Second, in line with the prevailing assumption in the rabbinic tradition, Jacob ben Asher presumes that "A woman wants to marry more than a man wants to marry" (Yevamot 113a). No special encouragement and promise of benefit is needed for a woman, for she would marry as soon as an appropriate opportunity arises. The Talmud expresses this presumed desire to marry in a succinct statement: "A woman prefers to be impoverished and be married than be wealthy and unmarried" (Sotah 20a). Similarly, the rabbis assumed that a woman has a natural desire to bear children. As we shall see in greater detail in Chapter 8 on procreation and contraception, the rabbis purposefully refrained from making procreation a duty for women.

In addition to companionship, happiness, and procreation, marriage serves another central purpose: the control of the sexual impulse (yetzer ha-ra):

A man who has reached the age of twenty years and has not yet married a wife spends all his days in sin. In sin? Do not actually think so, but rather say: [he spends all his days] in thoughts of sin. [Kiddushin 29b]

The sexual impulse is omnipresent and must find expression. An unmarried man does not have a wife with whom he can satisfy his sexual desires. He must therefore turn to other women, at least in fantasy. The bachelor is not suspected of actually committing sexual transgressions, but he is assumed to be committing them in thought. Without a wife, he is sure to turn his fantasies to women who are not permitted to him.

Marriage, of course, is no insurance against temptation. The rabbis in all generations saw temptation as an ever-present force in the lives of men. As for women, some rabbis saw them as equally given to sexual temptation while some regarded them as immune from it.[12] Marriage provides a channeling of erotic desire which is sufficient for most men to at least prevent excessive dwelling on it and any overt acts of adultery. Therefore while "one is forbidden to even look into the face of a single woman" when it is done for erotic pleasure, one may look "in order to see if she is attractive in his eyes so that he might marry her" (Maimonides, Mishneh Torah, Book of Holiness, 21 : 3).

There is another threat of sexual transgression to the bachelor, and that is the sin of hashhatat zera: improper emission of seed. Ejaculation outside of heterosexual intercourse is undesirable at

best. If it occurs without intention, such as in one's sleep (ba'al
keri), one immerses in water to remove the impurity it causes. The
pious might take on some form of penance as well. Any other
"improper emission" is analogous to the act of Onan (Genesis 38),
who purposefully "cast his seed upon the ground" to avoid fulfilling his duty as a levir (he was practicing coitus interruptus)
and was killed by God as a punishment. Certainly any form of
masturbation would be a grave offense. Such was the fear of male
masturbation that the Talmud states that whereas in the case of a
woman examination of the genitals is worthy (in order to determine the onset of menstruation), in the case of a man "the hand
that goes below the belly-button should be cut off" (Niddah 2 : 1).

Sex within marriage is the safeguard against improper sexual
fantasies and activities. The unmarried man has no protection
against them. The unmarried woman is less vulnerable to temptation since women are generally expected to be less likely to act on
their sexual impulses, even if they are subject to temptation. The
greater sexual danger to unmarried women is from men, in the
form of seduction, elopement, or rape. A woman is expected to
pass from one protected status, that of a daughter, to another, that
of a wife. This transition is expected to take place in early puberty.

The traditional way to control sexuality is to channel it into the
marital relationship even before it emerges. Early marriage, just at
the beginning of puberty (age twelve for girls and thirteen for
boys), which was the practice in many Jewish communities,
served to curtail the sexual impulse and prevent transgressions.
Early marriage served yet another very important function: it allowed the parents to control the choice of spouse and the terms of
marriage.

The Talmud states, "An eighteen-year-old to the wedding canopy" (Pirkei Avot 5 : 21) about males, and "A man is forbidden to
betroth his daughter while she is a minor, [he should wait] until
she grows up and says: I want so-and-so" (Kiddushin 41a) about
females. Nevertheless the common practice was to marry sons and
daughters earlier. In Middle Eastern and North African countries
the practice in Jewish communities was to marry girls around the
age of twelve or even earlier, while the grooms were usually con-

siderably older. In eastern Europe couples were usually closer in age, both having just reached puberty. The justification for early marriage was the statement in Yevamot 62b: "He who marries off his sons and daughters close to their coming of age [samukh le-fir-kan] is the one of whom it is said: 'And you shall know that your tent is at peace.' " "Close to their coming of age" was understood to refer to the reaching of puberty and sexual maturity. Therefore the Tur states: "He who marries early, at age thirteen, is fulfilling the mitzvah in an exemplary manner" (Tur, Even Ha-Ezer 1 : 9). The Tur adds a precaution: "But prior to age thirteen he should not marry them because it is like promiscuity [zenut]." One should not marry off his children before they reach thirteen because they will not have reached sexual maturity and cannot carry on a fruitful sexual relationship. Sex with no potential for conception whatsoever is analogous to masturbation and "wasting seed" (hashhatat zerah).

Yet despite the Tur's ruling that thirteen for a boy and twelve for a girl is the earliest age for marriage, earlier marriages were not unheard of. Such early marriages posed a halakhic problem since they violated talmudic prescriptions as well as rulings such as the Tur's.[13] They were practiced primarily for economic and social reasons: in order to secure optimal matches at the time they were available. Another reason was the dowry, the neduniyah. Since one was not sure that today's assets will be here tomorrow, when money for a neduniyah was available a match was made and the terms agreed upon. This explanation appears in Tosafot's commentary on Kiddushin:

"A man is forbidden to marry off his daughter when she is a minor": . . . Nevertheless, it is our custom to betroth our daughters even if they are minors because day after day the [oppression of] Exile [galut] increases and if a man has the possibility of giving his daughter a dowry now [he betrothes her], lest he not have it later on and she will remain an agunah forever. [Tosafot, Kiddushin 41a]

Tosafot explain that the economic situation is such that people do not trust what tomorrow will bring and thus marry their daughters off as soon as they can afford to. It is interesting that the text refers to a girl who is not married as soon as the chance arises as an *agunah* (a "grass widow," a woman unable to marry because she is bound to a husband who is no longer there). Surely her status would not legally be that of an *agunah* for she will be free to marry. But in practice she might never have the chance and thus would remain unmarried all her life, as if she were barred from marriage like an *agunah*.

Early marriages, prior to age thirteen for boys and twelve for girls, posed definite halakhic problems. But perhaps even graver were the psychological problems which resulted from such premature marriages. The Haskalah (Enlightenment) literature is rich in descriptions of personal tragedy and marital strife resulting from immature betrothals, certainly a biased view since the Haskalah made an ideological point of condemning traditional marriage. The *maskilim* criticized the early age of marriage, the complete control over spouse selection by the parents, and the subjugation of the choice to economics and social standing. They offered instead the ideal of romantic love.[14] But even halakhic writings, reflecting the traditional Orthodox position, often transmit the tragic consequences of premature marriages. Such marriages could easily lead to sexual dysfunction, marital disharmony, and unhappiness. We have no way of making statistical estimates about the fate of couples married at extremely young ages. We probably should assume that most such marriages prevailed even if the initial period of married life was traumatic and unhappy. In some extreme cases premature marriages ended tragically. Such a case became a cause célèbre in rabbinic circles in the second half of the eighteenth century. As reported by Yehezkel Landau in his responsa *Noda bi-Yehudah* (second edition), Responsum 52, a boy and a girl were married when he was twelve and she eleven. They lived together in her parents' home, more as brother and sister than as husband and wife. There were no sexual relations between them. With time they were mocked by their peers and acquaintances because their marriage was a nonmarriage. They felt increasing pressure to consummate the marriage, and finally one night the boy came to his bride. In the middle of the sexual act someone knocked on the door and the boy, in his fear, had a premature ejaculation. Penetration was never achieved and when the rabbi examined the sheet the next morning he found on it only traces of semen and no "blood of virginity" (see Deut. 22 : 15–18). There was great commotion and shame, and soon afterward the boy disappeared. He was never heard from again and the girl became an *agunah*: bound to a husband she did not have and unable to marry anyone else. The girl's parents sought the opinion of many rabbis in an attempt to release her from the marriage and allow her to remarry.

The halakhic discussion in the case of this girl who became an *agunah* was a complicated one since there were two questions involved: the validity of premature marriage in general and the validity of this particular marriage which was not consummated. The legal problems involved in premature marriages were difficult because there are halakhic grounds for forbidding such marriages, yet after the fact, most of them were allowed to stand. The problem is similar to that of betrothal by intercourse or "with a myrtle branch." In principle such *kiddushin* are forbidden, as we have already seen, but once effected they are valid (Kiddushin 12b). Furthermore many cases of premature marriages occurred during times of upheaval: either periods of imminent threat of war and dispersal, or times when there were decrees or rumors of impending decrees forbidding or restricting Jewish marriages. Thus factors of instability and fear played perhaps a greater role than strict legal considerations in determining the age of marriage in different periods and different places.

Marriage occupies the central place in personal and communal life in traditional Jewish society. It serves as the instrument of control over economic fortunes, social status, sexual activity, and self-perpetuation.[15] It also offers intimacy, emotional fulfillment, and a sphere for eroticism. Inevitably, societal constraints and control come into conflict with personal aspirations. Though the Halakhah starts with laws of marriage which allow it as an independent act of a couple, easily performed and with few legal and economic constraints, it gradually imposes more and more restrictions, wresting control of marriage from the hands of the young couple and putting it in the hands of parents and the communal establishment. Women, much more than men, are controlled by others in traditional Jewish society when it comes to effecting marriage. Usually the choice of a husband is made by the parents, as are the negotiations over dowry and future financial terms. The woman's role in the actual legal act of marriage is passive: she accepts the betrothal by silent acquiescence; only if she wants to protest need she say any words during the ceremony.

Just as she is a passive participant in effecting marriage, so the woman is a passive agent in the dissolution of marriage by divorce. In the case of marriage, as we have shown, the woman's passive role can lead to the problems of elopement, being conned into an undesirable marriage, and being married by her father to a man she did not herself choose for her husband. In the case of divorce, as we shall see in the next chapter, the consequences of the woman's passivity can be much more tragic. She can remain married to a hated husband against her will or, alternatively, be abandoned by her husband and never able to remarry (an *agunah*). Her fate is not in her hands because she can only be a passive recipient of a divorce, never its initiator.

✳ 3 ✳
DIVORCE

AS IN the case of the laws of marriage, when we search the Bible for material on divorce we do not find systematic or detailed legislation. However, we do find one passage on divorce which elaborates enough to give us some notion of the nature of divorce in biblical law. Deuteronomy 24 deals with a special case of divorce: forbidding a divorcée who remarried and then divorced yet again to return to her first husband. In passing, within a circumstantial clause describing the initial divorce, the passage reveals quite a lot about the practice and procedure of divorce in general.

[1]A man takes a wife and possesses her. She fails to please him because he finds some [matter of] indecency (*ervat davar*) about her, and he writes her a bill of divorcement, hands it to her, and sends her away from his house;[2] she leaves his household and becomes the wife of another man,[3] then the second man rejects her, writes her a bill of divorcement, hands it to her, and sends her away from his house; or the man who married her last dies,[4] then the husband who divorced her first shall not take her to wife again, since she has been defiled—for that would be abhorrent to the LORD. You must not bring sin upon the land which the LORD your God is giving you as a heritage. [Deut. 24 : 1–4]

Let us begin with the end of the passage where we finally reach the legislative statement. The point of this passage is that a woman's first husband who had sent her away may not take her again to be his wife after she "had been defiled" by marriage to another man. The woman is "defiled," but only with regard to her first husband. She is free to go and marry yet a third man. Nachmanides explains this legislation in an ingenious manner:

The reason for this prohibition is so that they should not exchange wives with one another. One would write her a bill of divorce [a *get*] in the evening and in the morning she would return to him. [Nachmanides (Ramban) on Deut. 24 : 4]

If it were not for this prohibition a man could divorce his wife one day, she could marry another man "for the night," and then be divorced by him and return to marry her first husband: a simple system of "wife swapping"!

This law may have a preventive aim as Nachmanides proposes, but more likely it is primarily a reflection of a tension within biblical law between acceptance of divorce and elements of a position opposed to divorce altogether. The clearest example of this antidivorce sentiment is in the prophecy of Malachi: "God stood in testament between you and your first wife and now you have turned treacherously against her. . . . Do not turn against the wife of your youth for the one who sends away [his wife] is hateful. . . ."[1] We also deduce that antidivorce sentiments remained alive in postbiblical Judaism from the teachings of Jesus and the prohibition on divorce in the Church.[2]

Within actual legislation, opposition to divorce remained confined to the special laws for priests. The priests were forbidden to marry divorcées (Leviticus 21), though they were not forbidden to divorce their wives. This strange asymmetry can only be understood if we understand the prohibition on marrying a divorcée as part of the strict laws of purity by which the priests were bound. The same term is applied to a divorcée as to various agents (corpses, reptiles, etc.) which cause ritual impurity. For the priests, who had to observe more stringent laws of purity than the rest of the nation because of their service in the Temple, a woman who had had sexual relations with another man (i.e., a divorcée or a zonah, one who had sexual relations outside marriage) was "defiled" and forbidden. Perhaps there was actually some theory of priestly "purity of blood" which extended the meaning of ritual purity to encompass sexual relations and familial lineage.

The prohibition in Deuteronomy 24 : 1–5, which considers a woman who married a second time "defiled" in respect to her first husband and forbidden to remarry him, is a vestige of the antidivorce sentiment expressed in the priestly code and in Malachi's

prophecy. But it is a minor vestige: the overall thrust of Deuteronomy 24 is to portray divorce as an accepted part of human life. As
a legal transaction divorce is simple and quick: the husband simply "writes her a bill of divorcement, hands it to her, and sends
her away from his house" (verse 1).

The legitimacy of divorce is accentuated in postbiblical Halakhah. The Mishnah focuses on the power of the get to release the
woman from her husband and allow her to marry anew, rather
than presenting it as a negative indictment of the divorcée:

Mishnah: The essence of the get is the words: Behold you are hereby
permitted to any man. Rabbi Judah says: [He must add]: And this shall be
to you from me a writ of divorce and a letter of release and a bill of
dismissal, wherewith you may go and marry any man that you please.
[Gittin 85 a–b]

Two formulations of the get appear here, the second requiring
more detailed phrasing. Both are in agreement, however, that the
essence of the get is that it frees the woman to go and marry
whomever she pleases.

To say that the essence of a divorce bill is to free the woman to
marry another man is not to suggest that divorce was encouraged,
taken lightly, or carried no consequences of societal judgment,
stigma, or condemnation. The Talmud includes pronouncements
and anecdotes intended to exalt a first marriage as faithfulness to
"the wife of thy youth," and to condemn divorce and remarriage;
for example, the laconic "Two divorcées who marry—four opinions in bed" (Pesahim 112a) or "When a man divorces his first
wife even the altar sheds tears" (Gittin 90a). The point is rather
that any negative evaluation and subsequent implications are not
incorporated into the Halakhah. They remain as societal constraints, powerful enough that condemnation was most likely purposely excluded from the legal sphere in order to allow legitimate
avenues to dissolve marriages which were unusually unhappy.

Both biblical law and postbiblical Halakhah permit divorce and
institute no punitive or detrimental consequence to either the
divorcing man or the divorced woman. But the status of divorce is
determined by still two other major considerations which we have

yet to address: First, is there a requirement for certain circumstances or reasons to warrant divorce? Second, how easy is it to effect a divorce? Both issues are embedded in the Deuteronomic text.

Deuteronomy 24 : 1 describes the circumstances of divorce thus: "she fails to please him because he finds some [matter of] indecency [ervat davar] in her." This brief, ambiguous formulation gives rise to a debate between Bet Hillel and Bet Shammai. There are two central questions that call for interpretation:

1. What is the exact nature of the "matter of indecency" (ervat davar)?

2. What is the significance of the clause "because he finds ervat davar in her"? Is it included here merely to explain why she fails to please him but not to exclude other reasons why the woman loses her husband's favor? Or is it here to mandate that only if the husband finds some indecency (ervat davar, whatever that may be) in her may he divorce her, while other reasons do not warrant divorce?

As we shall see in following the talmudic discussion, this is just a simplified formulation of the problems inherent in the Deuteronomic passage on divorce:

Mishnah: Bet Shammai say: a man should not divorce his wife unless he has found her guilty of some sexual misconduct [matza bah dvar ervah] as it is said: "because he has found some matter of indecency in her." Bet Hillel, however, say: [he may divorce her] even if she has merely spoiled his food, since it says: "because he has found some matter of indecency in her." Rabbi Akiva says: [he may divorce her] even if he simply finds another woman more beautiful than she, as it is said: "and it comes to pass, if she finds no favor in his eyes."

Gemara: It has been taught: Bet Hillel said to Bet Shammai: Does not the text distinctly say "thing" [davar]? Bet Shammai rejoined: And does it not distinctly say "indecency" [ervah]? Bet Hillel replied: Had it only said "indecency" [ervah] without "thing" [davar] I should have concluded that she should be sent away on account of "indecency" [i.e., a sexual transgression] but not on account of any [lesser] "thing." Therefore "thing" is specified. Again, had it said only "thing" without "indecency" I would have concluded that [if divorced] on account of "thing" she may remarry, but if on account of "indecency" she should not be permitted to remarry. Therefore "indecency" is also specified.

And what do Bet Shammai make of the word "thing"? [They argue]: It says here "thing" and it says in another place "thing," viz. "By the mouth of two witnesses or by the mouth of three witnesses a thing shall be established." Just as there two witnesses are required, so here two witnesses are required. And Bet Hillel? [They can retort]: Is it written "indecency in a thing"? And Bet Shammai? [They can retort]: Is it written "either indecency or a thing"? And Bet Hillel? For this reason it is written "a matter of indecency" [*ervat davar*] which can be taken either way.

Rabbi Akiva says: even if he simply found another. . . . What is the ground of the difference here [between the various rulings]? It is indicated in the dictum of Resh Lakish who said that "*ki*" has four meanings: "if," "perhaps," "but," "because." Bet Shammai held that we translate here: 'It comes to pass that she finds no favor in his eyes *because* he has found some matter of indecency in her." Rabbi Akiva held that we translate: " . . . *or if* he finds some matter of indecency in her." [Gittin 90a–b]

The Mishnah cites three opinions regarding the circumstances or legitimate grounds for divorce. All three opinions rest on the interpretation of the clause "and it comes to pass that she finds no favor in his eyes because he has found some matter of indecency [*ervat davar*] in her" in Deuteronomy 24 : 1. Bet Hillel and Bet Shammai agree that the grounds for divorce are described by the phrase "he has found some matter of indecency in her" but disagree on the exact meaning of the phrase, specifically the nature of *ervat davar*. The opinion of Rabbi Akiva is different: he interprets the clause in Deuteronomy 24 : 1 to include two separate statements regarding the grounds for divorce. As explicated in the fourth paragraph of the Gemara "Rabbi Akiva held that we translate: 'and it comes to pass that she finds no favor in his eyes *or if* he finds some matter of indecency in her.' " For Akiva's interpretation the exact nature of *ervat davar* is not crucial because the first part of the clause, "she finds no favor in his eyes," stands independently as a description of grounds for divorce, so that a man may divorce his wife even if he merely met another woman he likes better.[3]

The primary concern of the Gemara in our passage is to reconstruct and explicate the nature of the disagreement between Bet Hillel and Bet Shammai. At the core of the controversy is a simple disagreement on the meaning of *ervat davar*. *Ervah* is the biblical term for a prohibited sexual relation (the literal meaning of *ervah* is "nakedness"). It seems most plausible from the context of the Deuteronomy passage, as well as other references to divorce in anecdotal material in the Bible, that the original cause for divorce was adultery. The word *davar* means "thing," or "matter." *Ervat davar* is a construct case made up of the two nouns put together. The crux of the disagreement between Bet Hillel and Bet Shammai is the question of which noun modifies which. Bet Shammai argue that the noun *davar* modifies the noun *ervah*, thus reading the phrase to mean "a matter of *ervah*."[4] Bet Shammai's reading is probably the one closer to the original intent of the Deuteronomic text. Bet Hillel argue that the word *ervah* modifies the word *davar* and should be read here as an adjective, that is, "an *ervah*-like matter." In other words Bet Hillel hold that *ervah* is not used here as a technical term for sexual transgression, but rather in a general descriptive way to indicate something indecent or unseemly.

The Gemara reconstructs the arguments of each side through a fictional dialogue. Bet Hillel begin by challenging Bet Shammai's interpretation, saying: "Does not the text distinctly say 'thing'?" In other words if the text intended to refer to sexual transgression, as Bet Shammai hold, the word *ervah* would suffice since that is precisely the term for sexual transgression. Yet the text states "thing," and since nothing in the biblical text is superfluous, "thing" refers to any other matter as grounds for divorce "even if she has merely spoiled his food."

Bet Shammai respond with the same line of reasoning: "And does it not distinctly say *ervah*?", that is, if any "thing" were intended the word *ervah* would be superfluous. Furthermore if any "thing" is sufficient ground for divorce, *ervah*, sexual transgression, need not be specified since a general "thing" would certainly include sexual transgression. Therefore, according to the reasoning of Bet Shammai, the word *ervah* was specified so that the construct *ervat davar* must mean sexual transgression and nothing of lesser magnitude.

Bet Hillel respond to this argument by analyzing what the implication of the text would be if only *ervah* were stated or if only "thing" were stated. First: "Had it only said '*ervah*' without 'thing' I should have concluded that she should be sent away on account of *ervah* but not on account of any [lesser] thing." Had the text only used the word *ervah*, argue Bet Hillel, it would have been evident that only sexual transgressions are grounds for divorce, which is the position of Bet Shammai. But since the text does not use only the word *ervah*, Bet Hillel argue that it necessarily intends to imply more, that is, to include other things as grounds for divorce. Second, if only the word "thing" had been stated "I would have concluded that if divorced on account of a 'thing' she may remarry, but if on account of *ervah* she would not be permitted to remarry." Clearly one could not argue that the word "thing" is stated in order to exclude sexual transgression as grounds for divorce, since sexual transgression is the most radical violation of the rules and purpose of marriage. Therefore if the text had stated only "thing," a different justification would have been necessary. Stating "thing" alone might imply that the legislation does not apply to divorce due to sexual transgression. One might have then concluded that whereas here the woman may go and marry another man, if a woman is divorced on account of sexual transgression the law is stricter and she is forbidden to remarry. That is not the case in the Halakhah, since the law does not forbid a woman divorced on account of sexual transgression to remarry, except to the man with whom the sexual transgression was committed.[5]

The conclusion of Bet Hillel from this reconstruction of the implication of using only *ervah* or only *davar* in the biblical text is that both *ervah* and *davar* are necessary to understand this phrase. This seems to defeat the argument of Bet Shammai, who interpret *ervat davar* to mean simply and only *ervah* (sexual transgression). Since Bet Hillel have just shown that both words are necessary, the conclusion is that Bet Hillel's interpretation of *ervat davar* as the generalized "unseemly matter" is the correct one. This is so unless Bet Shammai can prove that the word *davar* has some function in the phrase other than implying that more than sexual transgression is intended.

Bet Shammai have, of course, just such an explanation for the function of the word *davar*. They argue: "It says here 'thing' and it says in another place 'thing,' viz. 'By the mouth of two witnesses or by the mouth of three witnesses a thing shall be established' " (Deut. 19 : 15). The word "thing" functions here as a key word to indicate that the testimony of two witnesses to the sexual transgression is necessary in order to permit divorce on those grounds. That is, the word *davar*, according to Bet Shammai, does not function in any way to modify the word *ervah* directly, but rather to introduce the additional information that the testimony of two witnesses is required.

The presumed retort of Bet Hillel to this argument is to say: If the two words are separate, one referring to the grounds for divorce and the other to the testimony of witnesses, why is the sentence not phrased accordingly? Why does it not state "indecency [*ervah*] in a thing [*be-davar*]"? That is, indecency in an act (*davar*) which is attested to by two witnesses. There is a significance, imply Bet Hillel, to the fact that *ervah* and *davar* are linked together in one unit, as a construct case. But this same argument can be turned against the interpretation of Bet Hillel. If, as Bet Hillel hold, the text refers to either sexual transgression or any other "thing" as grounds for divorce, why is this not indicated clearly by stating "either *ervah* or [another] thing"?

Here Bet Hillel retort with the final argument: "For this reason it is written '*ervat davar*' which can be taken either way." Bet Hillel and Bet Shammai have reached a stalemate: neither side can provide conclusive evidence for its interpretation and neither school can raise an objection to the other school's view that cannot be refuted or turned against its own interpretation. At this point Bet Hillel win the argument. Since their interpretation argues for an inclusive meaning (i.e., both sexual transgressions and other "things") it can include the fact that there is an irresolvable disagreement between Bet Hillel and Bet Shammai without internal contradiction. If Bet Hillel argue that the phrase essentially means

that either sexual transgression or other "unseemly things" are
grounds for divorce, they can incorporate Bet Shammai's insistence that sexual transgression is grounds for divorce. Bet Shammai, on the other hand, argue that only sexual transgression is
grounds for divorce, and nothing else. How then are they to explain the fact that they cannot prove this conclusively? Clearly the
text is ambiguous and open to more than one interpretation! This
argument is analogous to the following hypothetical dialogue between A and B:

A: "Statement X is an ambiguous statement."
B: "No! Statement X is not ambiguous, it can only be interpreted
one way."
A: "The very fact that we disagree proves that the statement is
indeed ambiguous!"

Thus the view of Bet Hillel prevails and the phrase *ervat davar* is
understood in the Halakhah to mean that a man may divorce his
wife for a sexual transgression or any other matter that is distasteful to him.

The principle of Bet Hillel that *ervat davar* signifies any unseemly matter holds as the basis for the law of divorce. Yet there is
a difference between sexual transgression and any other unseemly
thing. Whereas in the case of "other unseemly matters" the husband has the *right* to divorce his wife, in the case of sexual transgression he has an *obligation* to do so. Even if he is inclined to
forgive her and forget her violation, the Halakhah requires him to
divorce her as she is guilty of sexual transgression.[6] In his commentary on Deuteronomy 24 : 1 Rashi states that if there is reason
to suspect the wife of sexual transgression "He is commanded to
divorce her lest he come to like her."

Since the Halakhah is in accordance with Bet Hillel the grounds
for divorce are open-ended: they are a matter for individual dis-
cretion and judgment. The cause for divorce is subjective, since
what to one man is a grave matter to another is only a minor
irritation. The Talmud makes clear that regardless of the nature of
the grounds for divorce, once marital disharmony has gotten to

the point where the husband has made up his mind to divorce his wife, he should do so forthwith. Otherwise he is exploiting his wife and "devising evil" against her.

Rabbi Mesharsheya said to Raba: If a man made up his mind to divorce his wife but she still lives with him and waits on him, what do we do? [He replied] We apply to him the verse: "Devise not evil against your neighbor seeing as he dwells securely by thee." [Gittin 90b]

The biblical formulation of the laws of divorce is brief and open to several interpretations, as we saw from the dispute between Bet Hillel and Bet Shammai regarding the grounds for divorce. Similarly, Deuteronomy 24 is also ambiguous about the procedure of divorce. The whole process is described in a few words: "He writes her a bill of divorce [sefer keritut, literally, "a writ of cutting off"] [the marriage], hands it to her, and sends her away." The mishnaic and talmudic discussion is preoccupied with the exacting details of the writing of a bill of divorce (a get), its precise formulation, and the manner in which it is delivered to the woman. Much of Tractate Gittin is devoted to questions such as: Who is qualified to write a bill of divorce? What is the text of such a writ? Who is qualified to deliver a get? How must the woman accept it in order for it to be valid? What happens when a get is delivered by a messenger coming from abroad? etc.[7]

The laws pertaining to the writing, delivery, and acceptance of a get are very complex and include an astonishing range of possible circumstances. We will not present these halakhot here in detail, but rather merely observe the general principle that divorce requires an elaborate and exacting procedure. It is very important to note the difference in complexity between the laws of marriage and the laws of divorce. As we saw in Chapter 2, there is very little technical detail or procedural requirement standing in the way of a man who wishes to marry: all he needs is a perutah or an object of its worth and the woman's consent. In the case of divorce the opposite is true: many legal requirements which demand accuracy and care stand in the way of a man who wants to divorce his wife. But, ironically, the woman's consent is not necessary, as it is in marriage. The Halakhah seems to counterbalance the fact that the woman's consent is not necessary and that the grounds for divorce are open-ended by legislation which will create at least some impediments to divorce.

In biblical law it appears that divorce was a simple matter, and this may have had the important advantage that an unhappy marriage could be ended easily and without delay. However, it also had severe disadvantages from the point of view of the woman. A woman had no protection against unwanted divorce because her consent was not required. She had no protection against a divorce that seemed unjust because the grounds for divorce included virtually anything which displeased her husband. Finally, a woman could do nothing in the face of a rash divorce, given in anger, because there was no "cooling-off" period created by legal requirements and procedure.

Mishnaic law addressed the vulnerability of women not only through the detailed regulations about the writing and delivery of the get, but also through the ketubah. The ketubah is a marriage document that a groom gives to his bride. It outlines the general obligations of the husband toward his wife ("to cherish, honor, feed and support . . . and live together like man and wife"), and lists the financial commitments the husband undertakes toward his wife in case of divorce (or his death). Though the ketubah is written and handed to the woman at the time of the betrothal, the bulk of its text deals with the financial arrangements in case the marriage ends through divorce or the husband's death. The husband agrees in the ketubah to pay his wife three kinds of payments in case of a divorce (the "ketubah sum," the value of the trousseau, and the tosefta, an additional sum), altogether amounting to a handsome payment. The purpose of the payment is to assure the financial integrity of the divorcée, and it may be claimed by the woman against any of her husband's or his inheritors' property.

The importance of the ketubah is that it protects the divorcée against financial disaster. Although the ketubah is given to the bride as part of the marriage ceremony, and was traditionally written artistically and in certain communities illuminated to heighten the joy of the wedding, its legal significance pertains to divorce.[8] Since the *ketubah* obligates the husband to pay his wife considerable sums if he divorces her, it was seen by the rabbis in the Talmud as an important deterrent to rash divorces. The Talmud states that the obligations of the *ketubah* were imposed upon Jewish men so that divorcing their wives would not be a simple, light matter in their eyes. Moreover, to strengthen the protection afforded by the *ketubah*, the Halakhah requires a woman always to keep her *ketubah* with her; if the *ketubah* is lost, the couple may not continue to live together until another *ketubah* is written. If by some accident a woman is divorced and cannot produce her *ketubah*, her husband is still bound by the obligations that would have been included in the *ketubah*, were it to be found.

The *ketubah* and the complex requirements of delivering a *get* afford women some protection against irrational and unjust divorces, but this is only partial protection. The most vulnerable points for a wife remain: she cannot initiate divorce, on the one hand, and may be divorced without her consent, on the other. In the Middle Ages the vulnerability of the woman to divorce with no heed to her wishes was addressed through a total innovation in the Halakhah. Despite the explicit talmudic statement "A woman may be divorced with her consent or without it" (Yevamot 112b), a ruling was introduced which forbade divorcing a woman against her consent. The rule is traditionally ascribed to Rabbenu Gershom Me'or Ha-Golah. However, there is historical evidence that by his time this was already accepted practice among most Ashkenazic Jews.

The *herem* [ban] of Rabbenu Gershom according to the rules of the communities: . . . The law forbids divorcing a wife against her consent and such a divorce is null and void. If a man divorces his wife with her consent and then the divorce is declared void, he may give her a second divorce against her consent, if it is certain that she had not been aware of the irregularity [in the first bill of divorce]. [Meir of Rothenburg (thirteenth century), Responsa, 112d (Prague edition)]

The *herem*, a ban and threat of excommunication against any offender, was a common and convenient vehicle for introducing new legislation in the post-talmudic period. The *herem* permitted the consensus of the community to enter the Halakhah as new legislation. Usually such legislation added new customs and slightly amended previous halakhah and practice. Rarely did it actually contradict the laws of the Talmud. The sanction for such legislation was the consensus of the community, so that anyone violating it was threatened with excommunication.

The legislation prohibiting divorce against the woman's consent is ascribed to Rabbenu Gershom Me'or Ha-Golah together with the prohibition on polygyny. The two are intimately linked. Prior to this ruling the Halakhah allowed a man to dissolve his marriage unilaterally by divorce or alter it radically by taking another wife. Following the ban of Rabbenu Gershom a man can no longer resolve marital problems by such unilateral actions. Marital discord now has to be resolved through negotiations with the woman. Generally a woman could not actually avoid a divorce indefinitely by withholding her consent. A man could ultimately force his wife to give her consent by making their marital life unbearable. However, having the power to refuse a divorce gave the woman at least some control over the terms negotiated for the divorce.

There is actually a certain duplication of functions between the *ketubah* and the ban of Rabbenu Gershom against divorcing a woman without her consent, as Moses Isserles observes in his commentary on the *Shulhan Arukh*:

At the present time in our lands, since one cannot divorce a woman against her consent because of the ban of Rabbenu Gershom, you could have eased the requirements for the writing of the *ketubah*. However, that is not our custom [*minhag*]. [Moses Isserles (Rema), Commentary to *Shulhan Arukh*, Even Ha-Ezer 66 : 3]

Since a woman may no longer be divorced against her will the *ketubah* is not as crucial, for she can withhold her consent to the divorce until a satisfactory financial agreement is reached. However, the *ketubah* did not fall into disuse or become a mere formality even though it was no longer the only guarantee for the woman's rights in case of divorce. The centrality of the *ketubah* in the marriage customs and its antiquity were sufficient to guarantee its perpetuation. One might speculate that after the ban of Rabbenu Gershom the *ketubah* served less a legal function and more a psychological one. It stood at the time of marriage as a testimony to the good intentions and worthiness of the husband. Since marriages were generally arranged and based on family reputation, class, and learning rather than on any intimate familiarity between groom and bride or their families, such testimony and assurance were very important.[9]

The process of change in the laws on divorce which we have examined thus far reveals three major steps that decrease the vulnerability of the married woman to being "sent away" by her husband. The first changes occur in mishnaic and talmudic law. The simplicity of the act of divorce in the Bible is transformed. Divorce becomes a complex legal procedure and this serves to protect women against rash and irrational divorces. The *ketubah* guarantees that the divorcée will not be destitute and also serves as a deterrent against divorcing a wife too easily. Later, in the Middle Ages, the ban of Rabbenu Gershom requires the woman's consent for divorce and thus makes her a negotiating party in the process of divorce rather than a totally passive subject.

Despite the gradual increase in the protection afforded to women, divorce laws maintain women in a position of weakness. The most significant problem in the legal position of women in regard to divorce is that a woman cannot divorce her husband. There are several narratives in the Bible which indicate that biblical society did permit a woman to divorce, or at least to leave, her husband if he failed to fulfill his marital obligations. For example, Judges 19 contains the story of a Levite's concubine (*pilegesh*), who certainly had no more rights than a wife, deserting her husband-master to return to her father's house. Her reasons for leaving are not mentioned but they are apparently not questioned for the husband comes to his father-in-law's house to ingratiate himself and plead to have her back. Another case in 1 Samuel 25 implies that a woman whose husband has deserted her may abandon her marriage and be given by her father to another man. Despite these and other passages which imply some rights on the part of the woman and/or her father to end a marriage, Deuteronomy 24, the explicit legal text on divorce, makes no mention whatsoever of the woman's right to initiate divorce.[10]

The Halakhah for the most part evolves with the assumption that divorce is only an act of the husband. There is some evidence from Genizah material that in the early Middle Ages, at least in North Africa, women had the right to divorce their husbands when the husbands were guilty of such flagrant violations of their duties as desertion and failing to provide food for their wives and children.[11] However, the Babylonian Talmud does not include the possibility of a woman's divorcing her husband and thus the legal tradition which allowed them this power disappeared.

The Babylonian Talmud prescribes only one way for a woman to try to bring about a divorce that she desires, that is, by appealing to a Jewish court to compel her husband to divorce her. The Talmud specifies certain conditions which warrant such court action. These conditions fall into three major categories:

1. When the husband is afflicted by various physical ailments or characteristics which are deemed unendurable for the wife
2. When the husband violates or neglects his marital obligations
3. When there is sexual incompatibility between husband and wife (on this issue, as we shall see, there is a division in the halakhic opinions)

Mishnah: The following are compelled to divorce [their wives]: a man who is afflicted with boils, or has a polypus, or gathers [objectional matter] or is a coppersmith or a tanner, whether they were [in such conditions or positions] before they married or whether they arose after they had married. And concerning all these Rabbi Meir said: although the man made a condition with her [that she acquiesce to his defects] she may nevertheless plead, "I thought I could endure him, but now I cannot endure him." The Sages, however, said: She must endure [any such person] despite her wishes, the only exception being a man afflicted with boils, because she [by her intercourse] will enervate him.

Gemara: What [is meant by one] "who has a polypus"?—Rab Judah replied in the name of Samuel: [One who suffers from an offensive] nasal smell. In a Baraita it was taught: [One suffering from] offensive breath. . . .

"Who gathers." What [is meant by one] "who gathers"?—Rab Judah replied: One who gathers dogs' excrements.

An objection was raised: "One who gathers" means a tanner! ... —
[The definition] is [a matter in dispute between] Tannaim. For it was
taught: "One who gathers" means a "tanner": and others say: It means
"one who gathers dogs' excrements."
    "Or is a coppersmith or a tanner." What is meant by "a copper-
smith"?—Rav Ashi replied: A kettle-smith. Rabbah bar Bar Hana explained: One who digs copper from the mine. It was taught in agreement
with Rabbah bar Bar Hana: What is meant by a coppersmith? One who
digs copper from the mine. [Ketubot 77a]

The Mishnah opens with a list of men who are compelled to
divorce their wives due to a condition which makes them offensive, be it a medical problem or a consequence of their occupa-
tion. The Gemara explicates the details of each condition in an
attempt to understand what makes it offensive. After listing the
conditions, the Mishnah states the general principle that such
men are compelled to divorce their own wives whether the offensive condition arose before or after the marriage. In other words
knowledge of the condition is not sufficient grounds for requiring
the woman to abide it. Apparently the rabbis held that knowing
about these conditions from a distance is not like living with them
every day. The only case in which prior knowledge invalidates a
woman's request for a divorce on one of these grounds is if there is
an explicit statement prior to the marriage that the woman accepts
the man despite his condition. Even in such a case of explicit
agreement there is a minority opinion of Rabbi Meir that the
woman may request a divorce. The woman might have whole-
heartedly believed that the condition was acceptable to her, but
found the reality of it in life unbearable. She may plead: "I
thought I could endure him but now I cannot endure him." The
majority opinion is different, however. Since an explicit declaration was made, the woman must stand by her word and accept her
husband's condition. There is one exception, however, even in
the view of the majority, and that is the case of a man afflicted by
boils, since sexual intercourse aggravates the condition and
would be likely to hamper a normal sexual relationship.
    Two physical conditions are considered too offensive for a
woman to endure: "boils" (a skin disease) and a "polypus" (a

condition the Amoraim speculate caused chronic bad nasal smell). In later Halakhah these conditions are understood more broadly as referring to any physical problem or ailment considered "a serious defect" (moom gadol) because it is offensive to most people. What constitutes such a defect is determined by the rabbi who is faced with an actual problem. Not only diseases cause such defects that a woman has grounds to demand a divorce, but also certain occupations. The exact reason why the occupations mentioned in the passage ("one who gathers, a coppersmith and a tanner") are offensive is already unclear to Amoraim. It appears that they may be occupations which cause one to have a persistent bad odor—at least that seems to be the case of "one who gathers" and a tanner. The general principle, however, is that men who are physically repulsive to their wives, because of either medical or occupational conditions, are compelled to grant their wives a divorce.

The second category of men who are compelled to divorce their wives are those who refuse to fulfill their marital obligations. The marital obligations are primarily two: maintenance and onah.

Rav stated: If a husband says: "I will neither maintain nor support [my wife]" he must divorce her and also give her her ketubah. Rabbi Elazar went and told this statement to Samuel [who] exclaimed: "Make Elazar eat barley! Rather than compel him to divorce her let him be compelled to maintain her!" And Rav [what would he answer]? "No one can live with a serpent in the same basket." [Ketubot 77a]

The husband in this case declares that he will not fulfill his obligation to "maintain and support" his wife (as stated in the ketubah). Rav states that he should be compelled to divorce her. He has violated his commitment in the marriage and thus should be compelled to end it. There is, however, a very strong objection to this view, as stated by Samuel. Samuel first exclaims that Elazar, who reported the opinion of Rav (thus apparently subscribing to it), should "eat barley!" This pronouncement is a bit obscure. It should probably be interpreted "Let Elazar be reduced to poverty and still maintain her!" Samuel held that the man should be compelled to maintain his wife according to his duty, before he is compelled to divorce her. This is an attempt to use the powers of a *Bet Din* to preserve the marriage rather than dissolve it. Indeed Rav's requirement that the husband be compelled to divorce his wife may seem a bit rash, yet Rav's retort indicates that the position is well thought out. The court could compel the husband to support his wife rather than compel him to divorce her, but his refusal to support her is only one manifestation of his general attitude toward her. Clearly the husband is very hostile toward his wife and for her to live with him while the court compels him to maintain her would be like living "with a serpent in the same basket."

Rav and Samuel disagree along the same lines in the case of a man who withholds from his wife her fundamental right of *onah* by refusing to have sexual relations with her. This case is a little more complicated, for whereas no merit can be seen in the act of a man who refuses to support his wife, a man who vows not to have intercourse with his wife may have an acceptable justification. He may forbid himself to have intercourse in order to deprive himself of sexual pleasure as a form of penance or he may wish to go away and study Torah, thus depriving his wife of her sexual rights for the duration of his studies. Rav views a limited period of sexual abstinence for penance or study favorably, provided that the period is brief. He holds that a man may abstain from his marital duty due to a vow if he specifies the length of time (i.e., a week according to Bet Hillel and two weeks according to Bet Shammai).[12] If he does not specify the length of time, he has violated an essential element in his marital obligation and "he must divorce her forthwith and give her the *ketubah*." Samuel holds that a man who makes this kind of unlimited vow may stay with his wife until the end of the permitted period of abstention in the hope that he may find some way to void his vow and thus save the marriage.

Samuel consistently tries to maintain the marriage as long as possible, in the hope that reconciliation and resolution might arise. Rav takes a different basic stance. He feels that when a husband has violated the marital commitment by declaring that he will not support his wife or by vowing to abstain from sex indefinitely, he has already gone too far. The basis for the marriage clearly no longer exists since there is neither goodwill nor intention to fulfill his duties on the part of the husband. Once things have gotten to that point the marriage should be ended immediately by compelling the husband to divorce his wife. The Rabbinate in Israel today generally takes the position of Samuel when it deals with requests for divorce. Couples seeking a divorce are generally urged to attempt to achieve reconciliation, "shlom bayit," and delays are imposed before the husband is allowed to give his wife a get.

The third reason for compelling a husband to divorce his wife is under dispute in the Halakhah: some authorities rule that sexual incompatibility (when the wife says: "He is repulsive to me," ma'is alay) is grounds for compelling a divorce while others refute the notion. The latter authorities hold that the wife is "a rebellious one" (moredet) and treat her accordingly, as we shall soon see. The split in the Halakhah is based on a talmudic passage discussing the nature of the rebellious wife:

What is understood by "a rebellious woman"? Ameimar said: [One] who says: "I like him but I wish to torment him." If she said, however, "He is repulsive to me [ma'is alay]," no pressure is to be brought to bear upon her. Mar Zutra ruled: Pressure is to be brought to bear upon her. [For] such a case once occurred and Mar Zutra exercised pressure upon the woman and [as a result of the reconciliation that ensued] Rabbi Hanina of Sura was born of their reunion. This, however, was not [the right thing to do]. [The successful result] was due to the help of Heaven. [Ketubot 63b]

According to Ameimar there are two kinds of women who refuse to have sex with their husbands. The first is the rebellious woman. This is a woman who basically likes her husband and does not have a problem having sex with him. Rather, she is withholding sex as a means to an end: she wishes to torment him. Later commentaries expand this notion, suggesting that she wishes to punish him for some offense or tries to get something she desires out of him by using sex as a bargaining chip.[13] Such a woman is to be treated severely: she is compelled to revoke her refusal. This is done (as in the case of a rebellious husband) by threats of the Bet

Din, a continuous reduction of her *ketubah* payment as long as she persists in her rebellion, and the Talmud states, her brazenness is announced and condemned in the synagogues every week.[14] (Later commentators generally state that this measure is not actually practiced in their day.)[15] The other kind of woman is the one who refuses to have sex with her husband on the grounds that he is repulsive to her. The reason is presumably some kind of fundamental incompatibility. Such a woman, according to Ameimar, is not compelled to acquiesce to sexual relations with her husband and there are no measures taken against her. Ameimar probably presumes that such a marriage should be ended by a divorce; however, the passage is not explicit enough for us to deduce whether he only assumed that the husband would naturally divorce his wife, or actually held that the husband should be compelled to divorce his wife. This ambiguity is the reason for the subsequent split in halakhic opinions.

Before we proceed with the discussion of subsequent Halakhah we must note the minority opinion of Mar Zutra. Mar Zutra held that even the woman who pleads total disgust with her husband should be pressured to resume sexual activity with him since he felt that even such an extreme situation can be mended and reconciliation achieved. The proof is a case cited where he once ruled in this fashion and the couple did reunite and their reunion resulted in the birth of a son who became a prominent rabbi. However, the opinion of the majority, as reported anonymously in the passage, indicates disapproval of Mar Zutra's ruling. The fact that a prominent son resulted from the reunion was due "to the help of Heaven," that is, to special divine intercession. Such divine intercession cannot be generally relied on in conducting human affairs.[16] Mar Zutra's ruling was wrong as a general ruling even though in the specific case before him it brought beneficial results.

The Talmud then concludes that a woman who is repulsed by the mere thought of having sexual relations with her husband is not to be pressured into resuming her sexual life with him. Rashi, in his commentary on Ketubot 63b, accentuates this ruling. He states: " 'She is not compelled': to protract her [stay in the marriage], but rather he gives her a get and she goes out without her ketubah." Rashi clarifies that one does not make any attempts to prolong the marriage because of hopes that a reconciliation will emerge. Rather, he rules that the husband gives her a get, presumably immediately upon her statement "he is repulsive to me," and that she loses her ketubah payment since she initiated the breakup of the marriage and the husband could not be accused of not fulfilling his duties. It seems that in this matter Rashi follows the general psychological assumptions of Rav: a marriage that has gotten to this point of deterioration is no longer viable. Rashi presumes that a woman would not come forth with this kind of statement and seek the dissolution of her marriage unless things were truly unbearable for her.

Rabbenu Tam takes a different approach, imputing a very different motivation to the woman who states "he is repulsive to me":

> The Kuntres interpreted this passage [as follows]: we do not compel her to remain under him but rather let him give her a get and put her out without her ketubah: That would mean that he is compelled to divorce her. And this does not seem right to Rabbenu Tam for then we would have to worry that she might have set her eyes on another man. . . . And therefore Rabbenu Tam interprets this that we do not compel the husband to divorce her. And, in fact, the Kuntres itself does not explicitly say that you compel the husband to give her a get. [Tosafot on Ketubot 63b]

The Tosafot begins with an analysis of Rashi (the Kuntres). From Rashi's insistence on immediate divorce and his firm statement that the woman is not to be compelled to remain "under him," we would deduce that Rashi holds that should the husband refuse to divorce her (as a spiteful act) he would be compelled to do so. Rabbenu Tam disagrees with this logical extension of Rashi's view. His worry is that this ruling would give women a convenient way to terminate an unwanted marriage if they found another man they desired. A woman in such a position would simply state that her husband is repulsive to her and refuse to have sexual relations with him, and the husband would be forced to divorce her. Rabbenu Tam does not wish to give women such power. Though it appears that Rashi's view does give women a way of forcing a divorce, the Tosafot undermines this possibility by pointing out that Rashi does not explicitly state that the husband is compelled to divorce his wife.

The *Shulhan Arukh* (Even Ha-Ezer 77) and most subsequent authorities followed the opinion of Rabbenu Tam in this matter: while of course they expected the husband to divorce his wife in such circumstances, they did not compel him to do so. But as against this view there is a minority tradition which follows the rule of Maimonides, who held that a man is compelled to divorce his wife if she attests that she cannot bear to have sex with him:

A woman who denies her husband sexual intercourse is called rebellious [*moredet*]. They ask her why she has rebelled. If she says: "I despise him and I cannot bring myself to be possessed [sexually] by him," they compel him to divorce her. For she is not a captive that she should be possessed by one who is hateful to her. And she goes out without any *ketubah* payment at all. [Maimonides, *Mishneh Torah*, Hilkhot Ishut 14 : 8]

Maimonides justifies the forced divorce by pointing out that the woman is fundamentally a free person. She is not a captive who can be forced to have sexual relations against her will. In another place Maimonides refers again to the prohibition against a husband's raping his wife: "He may not rape her [*lo ye'enos otah*] and may not cohabit with her against her will, but only with her consent and out of mutual arousal ["talk"] and joy,"[17] even though he holds that as a general rule a woman should accept sexual relations with her husband when he initiates them and not withhold sex in order to cause him unhappiness or push him to make greater displays of his love for her.[18]

Maimonides goes even further and compels the husband to divorce his wife if he requires her to do certain things which violate her dignity:

A man who makes his wife vow that she would tell others what he says to her or what she says to him of the words of frivolity and jest which a man exchanges with his wife during sexual relations—this one shall be compelled to divorce her and give her her *ketubah*. For, she cannot be asked to be brazen and tell others such embarrassing things. And so also if he makes her promise to make the necessary efforts during intercourse so that she would not conceive, or if he makes her do silly or useless things. Such a man should divorce her and give her the ketubah. [Maimonides, Mishneh Torah, Hilkhot Ishut 14 : 5]

Making a joke at the wife's expense by requiring her to tell others about intimate matters or perform silly and useless tasks is forbidden. It would be a violation of a marital obligation stated in the ketubah: to honor one's wife. The last case is that of a man who requires his wife to try to prevent conception (this is probably not by using contraception but by "natural means": the Talmud reports the opinion of Abbaye that "Women who are harlots turn over after intercourse in order to prevent conception," Yevamot 35b). Though a woman is not legally required to procreate, and therefore in some cases may purposefully try to avert or prevent conception, conceiving and childbearing are considered a "natural right" of women and therefore a husband may not require his wife to avert conception (see Chapter 8 on procreation and contraception).

While Maimonides expands the range of cases where a husband is compelled to divorce his wife, other halakhists often strictly adhere to the definition of grounds for compelling a divorce found in the Talmud. This is true even where the "offensive condition" seems much more severe than those cited in the Talmud. Such is a case discussed by Rabbi Jacob ben Asher, the author of the Tur:

A question was brought before my father the Rosh [Rabbenu Asher ben Yehiel] of blessed memory [and he ruled]: In the case of a man who acts insane [mishtateh] every day and his wife says: "My father was a poor man and because of his poverty he married me to this man and I had thought that I could accept [his behavior] but it is impossible because he is crazy [metoraf] and I am afraid that he might kill me in his rage," we do not force him to divorce her because we only compel those who are cited by the Sages as ones who are compelled [to divorce]. Rather, let her persuade him [tefaysenu] to divorce her or let her accept him and live from his estate.

The woman in the case before the Rosh is not forced to live with a husband who has an offensive physical defect or unpleasant odor due to his work. Rather, he is not responsible for his actions, acting "insane" and apparently having daily tantrums of uncon-

trollable rage. The woman lives in fear for her life. She was forced
into this situation because, being poor, her father could not afford
the dowry necessary to marry her to a decent man. The Rosh
apparently did not question the woman's testimony about her
husband's behavior. Yet he ruled that it is impossible to force this
husband to divorce his wife in order to free her from danger. This
is because the Talmud did not specify dangerous, aggressive, or
"insane" behavior as grounds for compelling the husband to divorce his wife. The best the Rosh can offer the woman is two
options. The first is to use her charms to persuade the husband to
give her a divorce (the same term, *lefayes*, is generally used to
describe the manner in which a husband should persuade his wife
to have sexual relations with him in order that he not do it against
her wishes). The second option is for the woman to accept the
reality of her situation and remain married to her husband but live
apart from him. That is the implication of the Rosh's statement
"let her live from his estate."

The case before Rabbenu Asher ben Yehiel involved a man described as insane and violent. What is the attitude of the halakhic
authorities toward domestic violence in general? Is it considered a
normal part of marital life or a breach of its fundamental principles? There is a range of attitudes in the Halakhah. Some authorities regard wife-beating as wholly unacceptable, and rule, unlike
the Rosh, that a violent husband should be compelled to divorce
his wife (if she seeks a divorce). Others, however, do accept a
limited amount of beating when it is used as punishment for serious offenses, and do not regard wife-beating as a legitimate
ground for compelling a man to divorce his wife.

The Maharam of Rothenburg is one of the most prominent authorities to whom is attributed the view that wife-beating is a
breach of the marital obligation, and who would therefore compel
a husband who beats his wife to divorce her. The Maharam's
ruling is: "a man who beats his wife . . . is compelled to give her a
divorce."[19] Later, the author of *Binyamin Ze'ev* (who lived in the
first half of the sixteenth century in Greece) expands this view by
stating "If we cannot find another solution for the situation, we
compel him to divorce her and give her the *ketubah* payment even

if she had initially accepted the situation knowingly."[20] In other words, even if the woman had accepted being beaten by her husband when she first married him, if she wants a divorce later on her husband is compelled to divorce her and unlike the rebellious wife she does not lose the payment that is her due.

The strongest condemnation of wife-beating is represented in the opinion of Rabbenu Simhah ben Shmuel of Vitri (author of the *Vitri Mahzor*; died 1105) as cited by Joseph Karo in *Bet Yosef*, his commentary on the *Tur*:

> I found in a responsum of Rabbenu Simhah that "it is an accepted view that we have to treat a man who beats his wife more severely than we treat a man who beats a fellowman, since he is not obligated to honor him but is obligated to honor his wife more than himself. And a man who does this should be put under a ban and excommunicated and flogged and punished with various forms of torment; one should even cut off his hand if he is accustomed to it [wife-beating]. And if he wants to divorce her let him divorce her and give her the *ketubah* payment."
>
> Further on he wrote: "You should impose peace between them and if the husband does not fulfill his part in maintaining the peace but, rather, continues to beat her and denigrate her, let him be excommunicated and let him be forced by gentile [authorities] to give her a *get*. . . ." [Joseph Karo, *Bet Yosef*, Even Ha-Ezer 154 : 15]

Rabbenu Simhah views wife-beating as more serious than assaulting a man because in addition to the assault one violates the duty to honor his wife, a duty canonized in the *ketubah*. He mandates severe punishments as the first step in dealing with a wife-beater: a *herem* (ban on social and commercial relationships), excommunication, and corporal punishment. If these threats and measures do not stop the husband from abusing his wife, he is to be compelled to divorce her. Rabbenu Simhah prescribes using the non-Jewish authorities to obtain such a divorce if necessary, since they have power to impose greater punishments than the Jewish courts.

As against these authorities who compel a husband to divorce his wife if he beats her, stand the opinions of some of the most important figures in the history of the Halakhah: Joseph Karo, Maimonides, and Moses Isserles. None of them advocates or accepts severe beating and physical abuse of a wife by her husband, but they all accept limited beatings. Karo rules that "we should not compel a husband to divorce on the basis of such grounds since they were not mentioned [as legitimate grounds] by any of the famous authorities [ha-poskim ha-mefursamim]" (Beit Yosef, on the Tur, Even Ha-Ezer 154 : 15). Maimonides in his Mishneh Torah recommends beating a bad wife as a form of discipline,[21] while Moses Isserles in his commentary on the Tur refines the circumstances when wife-beating is acceptable as a punishment. He rules that under certain circumstances wife-beating does not justify compelling the husband to divorce his wife, but "unwarranted" wife-beating does:

> . . . For, if he is the cause [for the beating] he must divorce her. Only, let the Bet Din warn him first once or twice [not to persist]. But if she is the cause of it, for example, if she curses him or denigrates his father and mother and he scolds her calmly first and it does not help, then it is obvious that he is permitted to beat her and castigate her. And if it is not known who is the cause, the husband is not considered a reliable source when he says that she is the cause and portrays her as a harlot, for all women are presumed to be law-abiding [kesherot]. [Moses Isserles, Darkhei Moshe, Tur, Even Ha-Ezer 154 : 15]

Isserles distinguishes between two kinds of wife-beating: one a form of aggression by the husband ("when he is the cause") and a second, a form of punishment for serious offenses ("when she is the cause"). If a wife persists in cursing her husband and his parents and does not mend her ways after he talks to her nicely, he is justified in beating her in order to punish her and stop her behavior. Should a husband and wife each accuse the other of being the cause of the beating, the court is to discount the husband's testimony. Underlying Isserles's statement that women are generally presumed to be law-abiding (i.e., "innocent unless proven guilty") is a realization that the husband is in a position of greater power in the family and can easily accuse his wife of transgressions of various kinds and justify his beating as a proper punishment. The fact that Isserles favors the testimony of the woman in determining who is at fault in the situation of wife-beating somewhat counterbalances the husband's upper hand in the family.

We have seen that there is considerable divergence in the Halakhah regarding the question of whether wife-beating is a legitimate reason for compelling a husband to divorce his wife. The one extreme in the range of opinions is that wife-beating is not a reason for compelling a divorce, while the other extreme is that wife-beating is a sufficient cause. In the middle is the position of Isserles who distinguishes between acceptable punitive beating and unwarranted aggression for which a man should be compelled to give his wife a divorce. The question of wife-beating in Jewish law and life requires much more research and discussion. Clearly, while there is considerable opposition to wife-beating, the "common wisdom" that Jews do not abuse their wives is incorrect. Those who wish to argue this position often cite the statement attributed to Mordecai ben Hillel (died 1298), author of the influential code *Sefer Mordecai*: "it is not the custom of our people, only of the gentiles." But they do not refer to statements like those by Maimonides or Isserles who favor punitive beating "for a just cause." One indication that wife-beating was not totally taboo in traditional Jewish societies is the fact that recent estimates have placed the number of abused women in Israel today at around 100,000.[22] The blame for this is often placed on the breakdown of traditional family and communal structures. Although this is certainly the critical element, it still seems difficult to argue that a problem of such proportions has no roots in patterns of the past.

The grounds for compelling a man to divorce his wife are, then, offensive physical conditions, violation of marital obligations, and for some authorities sexual incompatibility, and wife-beating. The categories may of course intersect. A man who is repulsive to his wife because of one of the conditions of medical ailment or occupational situation may be so offensive to his wife that sexual relations become unbearable. A man who vows not to maintain his wife or not to have sexual relations with her may in fact be expressing sexual incompatibility and its frustrations.

These categories furnish women with a limited access to the

power that men have in the matter of divorce. Under any of these circumstances a woman may demand that her husband be compelled to issue her a divorce. But how is that done? The power to compel a man to divorce his wife rests with a court, a *Bet Din*. The woman must appeal to the *Bet Din* and ask the court to use its power. This is a problematic procedure for two reasons. First, there is a fundamental problem since "a man can give a divorce only with his full consent" (Yevamot 112b). Second, there is a practical problem of how the court can actually enforce its mandate to compel certain men to divorce their wives. Both issues are addressed in the following talmudic passage:

> . . . Similarly in the case of divorces we say that force is applied to him until he says "I consent." But there too perhaps there is a special reason, viz. that it is a religious duty to listen to the words of the Sages. What we must say therefore is that it is reasonable to suppose that under the pressure he really made up his mind [and agreed]. . .
>
> Rav Judah questioned this [on the grounds of the following *mishnah*]: "A get extorted by pressure applied by an Israelite is valid, but if the pressure is applied by a non-Jew it is invalid. A non-Jew also, however, may be commissioned [by a *Bet Din*] to flog the husband and say to him: Do what the Israelite bids you!"
>
> Now why [should the get be invalid if extorted by a non-Jew]? Cannot we say that in that case also the man makes up his mind under pressure to grant the divorce? This rule must be understood in the light of the statement made by Rabbi Mesharsheya: According to the Torah itself, the get is valid even if extorted by a non-Jew, and the reason why the rabbis declared it invalid was so as not to give an opportunity to any Jewish woman to keep company with a non-Jew and so release herself from her husband. [Baba Batra 48a]

The context of this passage is a rather complex discussion of property claims and transactions under special circumstances of duress. The significance of the text for our discussion is what we can learn about compelling a man to divorce his wife. The idea of compelling someone to an act which should be done by choice is troubling. It is explained by saying that pressure is applied until the man states "I consent." Whereas in the case of selling property all we can say to justify this is "it is reasonable to suppose that under the pressure he *really* made up his mind to sell," i.e., under pressure he had a genuine change of heart (a problematic concept), in the case of divorce we can add the weight of the obligation to heed the rulings of the rabbis. In other words, though initially the husband does not wish to divorce his wife, once ordered to do so by a court he is under legal obligation to follow the order. We can assume, at least for the sake of argument, if not as a believable statement of reality, that the husband would not wish to violate the law by disregarding the orders of the rabbis, and therefore will genuinely consent to divorcing his wife.

The reason the rabbis engage in such a tortured argument is their wish to allow women access to divorce in circumstances of extreme need despite the halakhah that a man must give a divorce of his own volition. Indeed Rav Judah calls for the use of force in compelling a divorce because he apparently has serious doubts that the mere duty to listen to the rabbis and respect their authority will be sufficient to change the mind of a stubborn man.

The mishnah cited by Rav Judah[23] begins by making a clear distinction between a divorce extorted by a Jewish court and one extorted by a gentile court, but then in practice gets around the distinction. The need to insure a way to compel a stubborn husband to divorce his wife overpowers the rabbis' reluctance to open the door to power and authority outside their control. The logical mechanism employed to get around the mishnah's rule is to argue that though a divorce extorted by a non-Jewish court is invalid, a divorce extorted by a non-Jew at the bidding of a Jewish court is valid. The significance of this refinement of the law is that non-Jewish courts held much greater punitive powers than Jewish courts, so their threat was of greater consequence. In the case of an extremely stubborn husband, when the power of a Jewish court to apply pressure, exhort, and make threats did not suffice, "a non-Jew could be commissioned to flog the husband and say to him: Do what the Israelite bids you." It was important then to make a provision for utilizing the power of non-Jewish authorities to compel a divorce in extreme circumstances. Yet it was also necessary to avoid opening up an avenue for undermining the structure of the Jewish community and its institutions. As Rabbi Mesharsheya explains: if a non-Jewish authority could extort a valid divorce this would encourage a woman who was unhappy with her marriage to "keep company with a non-Jew and so release herself from her husband." This would pose a threat both to marriages and to the government of Halakhah through Jewish authorities. The upshot of this discussion is that while a Jewish court can use the "services" of non-Jewish authorities to compel a reluctant husband to divorce his wife, a woman cannot "take the law into her own hands" by befriending a non-Jew and getting him to have the non-Jewish authorities extort a divorce from her husband. Control over divorces remains then in the hands of Jewish courts. A woman who wishes to end her marriage because her husband is offensive to her, or does not fulfill his marital duties, (or is sexually incompatible with her) must appeal to a Bet Din to exercise the power to compel a divorce. The process would clearly be a painful one, so we can confidently assume that it was usually limited to cases of extreme marital disharmony.

Today the need to use the authority of a civil court in extreme cases of husbands' refusing to grant a get remains. In the State of Israel, it is of course not a gentile court. Rather, according to Israeli law the rabbinical courts have the authority to appeal to the civil courts and the police and request the incarceration of a recalcitrant husband. In the Diaspora, the use of civil courts continues to be problematic. In the nineteenth century, following the institution of secular divorce in France, Rabbi Michael Weil of Paris proposed a fundamental solution to the problem by suggesting that any divorce granted by the French courts shall automatically annul the power of the kiddushin so that a get will not be necessary. The suggestion was summarily rejected. In the twentieth century there have been a number of proposals advanced regarding the use of civil authorities to enforce the will of a Jewish court as well as a number of actual trials where a civil court intervened to secure a Jewish divorce.[24] However, none of the proposals or actual cases gained sufficient rabbinical approval or recognition to serve as a general precedent and guideline. In the Diaspora today within the Orthodox world it is not uncommon to use civil authorities to force a stubborn husband to grant a divorce, not by appealing to a court to compel him directly, but by using threats of

other legal actions against him, particularly threats to initiate in-
vestigations of tax evasions, etc. In New York City there is a
women's league which has been established by Orthodox women
in order to bring maximal pressure to bear on husbands who refuse a divorce. The State of New York passed a law in 1983 which
essentially requires a religious divorce as a prerequisite for a civil
divorce. This law is a large step toward greater reliance on civil
laws to enforce Jewish law and resolve the problem of the recalcitrant husband (see Chapter 4).

The talmudic prescription for compelling a man to divorce his
wife in certain circumstances and the medieval ban on divorcing a
woman against her consent are two fundamental changes in the
laws of divorce. The first balances the power of a man to divorce
his wife for practically any cause by allowing a woman with
"good cause" to seek a divorce through a court. The second curbs
the unilateral power of a man to divorce his wife at will by requiring her consent to the divorce. Yet neither innovation fully solves
the problem of inequality of power between men and women in
divorce. Extreme cases are possible and have occurred, where the
power of a court fails to compel a man to divorce his wife even if
the grounds for divorce are indisputably legitimate. Even in Israel
where the rabbinical courts rely on the power of the civil government to impose their decisions there have been a few cases where
a man simply could not be compelled to divorce his wife. The
most celebrated case has been of a husband who, in order to spite
his estranged wife, has been incarcerated in prison for years but
still refuses to give her a *get*.

The ban of Rabbenu Gershom against divorcing a woman without her consent suffers from a similar problem due to the imbalance of powers underlying the laws of divorce. If a woman tries to
match the stubbornness of the recalcitrant husband described
above the *Bet Din* can resolve the problem against her wishes by
suspending the ban of Rabbenu Gershom, that is, either permitting
her husband to divorce her against her consent or to marry a
second wife. In addition, should a woman go on refusing to accept
a divorce, her husband can threaten her with simply leaving her
and establishing a relationship with another unattached woman.

A married man who has children with another woman does not thereby make his children *mamzerim* or bastards (as long as the other woman is unmarried), as does a married woman who has children with another man. Thus the horror of making his children suffer for an illicit relationship does not hang over a man who cannot get his wife to accept a divorce as it does over a woman who cannot obtain a divorce from her husband.

Despite significant changes in the law of divorce which protect women and grant them some power and control over divorce, the overall balance remains greatly unfavorable to women. Women remain very often at the mercy of their husbands, especially when they are the ones who desire a divorce. A husband has the power to delay and even prevent his wife from remarrying by refusing to give her a divorce. As we shall see in the next chapter, a man may deliberately force his wife into the tragic state of the *agunah*, the woman who neither lives a married life with her husband nor has the option of marrying another man. A woman in such a situation can fight for resolution by appealing to rabbis and courts, but she fights against considerable obstacles, all embedded in the original biblical definition of divorce as a unilateral act of the husband.

✳ 4 ✳
THE *AGUNAH* AND THE *YEVAMAH*

The Agunah

THE FATE of the *agunah* is perhaps the most tragic consequence of the laws of marriage and divorce. The *agunah* is a woman whose marriage is in fact ended or suspended, but who legally remains a married woman (*eshet ish*), unable to remarry. The *agunah* is bound (*agunah* means "anchored") to a husband who no longer lives with her but she cannot "acquire herself" and be free to marry another man. There are several circumstances which cause a woman to become an *agunah*:

1. The husband deserts his wife and disappears.
2. The husband dies but there is no valid testimony for his death.
3. The marriage is untenable but the husband refuses to divorce his wife despite the threats and punitive measures of a *Bet Din* (see Chapter 3).
4. The marriage is untenable but the husband is legally incompetent to grant a divorce (usually on account of insanity).
5. A woman becomes a *yevamah* and the *levir* refuses to perform either *levirate* marriage or *halitzah*, or his whereabouts are not known, or he is an apostate.

The problem of the *agunah* is not discussed in the Bible. There is only one use of the term (Ruth 1 : 13) and it does not have the precise legal meaning of *aginut* in later texts. However, in the Mishnah and the Talmud we find ample discussion of the problem, and the responsa literature (especially from the late Middle Ages onwards, as the mobility of Jews increased) is replete with cases of *agunot* (plural of *agunah*).[1] Problems of *agunot* received so much attention in the halakhic literature for two reasons: first and foremost, because of the tragic situation of the *agunah*, who was neither married nor unmarried, and second, because the gravity of the problem often impelled most rabbis to seek the advice and ruling of their prominent contemporaries rather than rule on their own.

The Halakhah had to grapple with a tension between the desire (in fact the *mitzvah*) to find ways of permitting the *agunah* to remarry and the great fear of ruling incorrectly and allowing a married woman to marry another man. The fear of permitting an adulterous marriage by mistake is so great because this transgression is a very grave one, and because the law requires that should the first husband turn up, the woman must be divorced by her second husband but is barred from remarrying her first. She would be forbidden to both men. If she has any children with the second husband they would be *mamzerim* (bastards).[2] One after another the rabbis describe their agony and anxiety in making definitive decisions in cases of *agunot*. They are caught between the hammer of declaring a woman an *agunah* and thus condemning her to spend her life waiting for a husband who will never return, and the anvil of permitting adultery by allowing a married woman to remarry.

The side of leniency in the problem of the *agunah* is succinctly stated by Rabbenu Asher ben Yehiel (1250–1328): "One must investigate all possible avenues in order to release [*le-hatir*] an *agunah*" (Responsa of Rosh 51 : 2). A rabbi ruling on the case of an *agunah* should make every effort to permit her to remarry, and according to another authority, David ben Zimra, should avoid being overzealous in contriving reasons to bar her from remarriage:

And you can see with your own eyes that every wise man [*hakham*, i.e., rabbi] must seek out arguments for releasing [the *agunah*], since it is like a situation of danger [*ke-mekom sakanah*]. . . . And whoever seeks out speculations and exacting details in order to rule strictly and forbid [remarriage] and to make the woman an *agunah*, the rabbis [*hakhamim*] are displeased with him. [David ben Zimra (Radbaz), Responsa, No. 25]

The *agunah* is in a situation of "danger," according to David ben Zimra, not only because of the grave consequences of the state of *aginut*, but also because solving her problem requires urgency. If the *agunah* is not released quickly with the evidence that is available immediately, the chance for resolution decreases dramatically and the woman might eventually commit adultery if she cannot be legally released to remarry. If a woman is in danger of becoming an *agunah* because her husband has deserted her or has disappeared under mysterious circumstances, the longer one waits the less likely it is that his traces would be found. If the husband is thought to be dead but there is no direct evidence of his death, one must seek witnesses immediately, since with the passage of time memory vanishes and witnesses disappear. Finally, the passage of time is a considerable disability for the woman who seeks to be released from *aginut*, for if she comes to a rabbi a long time after the circumstances which caused her to become an *agunah* had occurred, he might well suspect that her arguments for being released and allowed to remarry are very weak. Otherwise, he would naturally reason, why would she have waited so long in the agonized state of *aginut* before coming to request his ruling?

The principle of urging quick resolution of the problems of *agunot* is augmented by permitting testimony of the kind that is unacceptable in most categories of litigation, such as the testimony of a woman, a minor, or words heard in passing in the conversation of non-Jews. This kind of testimony is particularly important in the cases of *aginut* which are due to the husband's death under unclear circumstances. These are the intractable cases of *aginut*, because whereas a deserter may ultimately be found and a reluctant husband eventually convinced or compelled to divorce his wife, a man who has died is gone for good, and if there is no direct testimony to his death, no new evidence is likely to arise. In such cases the Halakhah accepts the testimony of only one witness (normally two male witnesses are required), as well as of persons who are usually ineligible to be witnesses, including the wife herself. Only five women are invalid witnesses for an *agunah* whose husband has died: all are close relatives on the husband's side (his mother, sister, second wife, wife by *levirate* marriage, and daughter by another wife). These women may be hostile to the *agunah* and therefore their testimony is suspect. They may be plotting to get rid of her: if they testify that her husband is dead and she subsequently remarries, then when the first husband reappears she is forbidden to both her husbands. Such plotting is probably more a theoretical than a realistic possibility, but it is sufficient to invalidate the testimony of the husband's closest female relatives.

The woman herself, as we have said, though by no means a neutral party, is a legitimate witness to her husband's death. The reason for this is that were she to give false testimony, the woman would be placing herself in a very risky position. If her husband, whom she had reported dead, ever returns to her, she is an adulteress. The presumption of the Halakhah is that "concerning such matters as are bound to come to light, one does not lie" (Yevamot 93b). One would not testify that a man had died unless it is true, otherwise the "dead man" may one day reappear and uncover the deception.

Against the leniency in accepting testimony which would free an *agunah* and allow her to remarry stands the caution required to prevent adulterous marriages. Permitting a married woman to marry another man meant permitting and assisting in a grave sexual transgression and allowing the possibility of the birth of *mamzerim*. Therefore in cases where the husband was alive no leniency could be found to permit a woman to marry another unless she had a divorce. In the cases of a deceased husband, though the testimony of one witness was sufficient, that testimony had to include *direct evidence* of the man's death. For example, a man seen drowning in a large body of water whose boundaries cannot be seen (*mayyim she-ein lahem sof*) cannot be considered dead unless his body is found. There is a remote chance that he survived and emerged from the water beyond the witness's horizon. Presumption of death, as logical as it may be, is not acceptable as proof of death.[3]

Under normal circumstances, as we have already stated, a woman who testifies that her husband is dead is deemed a reliable witness and is permitted to remarry. Such normal circumstances are defined in the Mishnah by two factors: "When there is peace in the world and peace between him and her" (Yevamot 114b). In peaceful times when families are intact in their communities and a death occurs, the circumstances are known to the woman and to other members of the community. This assures that the woman who states "My husband is dead" most probably has actually seen him dead and is unlikely to lie since other members of the community are involved as well. The second requirement for relying on the wife's testimony alone is that "there has been peace between him and her." If it is known to have been otherwise, one might suspect the woman would testify to her husband's death just in order to be rid of him. Such deception is particularly feared in the case of a couple who traveled away from their own community.

A similar situation of presumed death which may not release an *agunah* is that of death in war:

And if there is a war in the world and she [the *agunah*] comes and says: "My husband is dead," she is not reliable, even if there was peace between them. She would probably rely [in her statement] on the presumption that most of the soldiers died and therefore he must have died too. For example: if the first ones and the last ones were killed and her husband was in the middle, she would say: since these were killed and those were killed, he was killed among them.

Therefore, she is not reliable; even if she says "I buried him." Some say: if she says "I buried him" she is reliable. And if she says "He died in his bed" she is reliable according to everyone's opinion. [Yevamot 114b][4]

In times of war, as described in Yevamot 114b, the rules change. If a woman whose husband went to war states that he had died, her testimony is not considered reliable. This is the case even if there was peace between husband and wife before the war and thus no reason to suspect the woman of deception. The woman is most likely to assume that her husband is dead on the basis of reasonable considerations, but without direct testimony. The situation is illustrated in the example in Yevamot. The soldiers in the battle were arranged in three groups: those in the front, those in the middle, and those in the back. The woman has been given testimony that those in the front and those in the back were killed. Her husband did not return from the war. The logical conclusion is that since he was in the middle he was killed as well. But this is only a logical guess and there is at least a distant chance that he survived. Therefore a woman who testifies that her husband died in war is not reliable. The text goes even further: "even if she says: 'I buried him' she is not reliable." This seems puzzling since it appears that she has direct evidence of her husband's death. The late–seventeenth-century commentary *Bet Shmuel* (by Samuel ben Uri Shraga Feibish) on the *Shulhan Arukh*, Even Ha-Ezer 17 : 48, explains that the woman who says "I buried him" is not reliable because "we suspect that she might be lying since it is not usually possible in a war to linger and bury him." If, alternatively, the body was brought back from the war her testimony is still suspect since disfigurement of battle wounds and the delay between death and burial make identification problematic. Several possible questions about the likelihood of a woman's identifying her dead husband and burying him in the midst of war must have caused the rabbis to reject the testimony of such a woman. But not everyone agreed with this position: "some say: if she says: 'I buried him' she is reliable." Another principle in judging whether or not the testimony of a woman is reliable is advanced by Rabbi Judah ben Ila'i, who judges by the mood and appearance of the woman:

Rabbi Judah says: In all cases she is not reliable unless she comes forth crying and her clothes torn. They said to him: Both this one and that one shall marry. [Yevamot 114b][4]

Rabbi Judah suggests that the testimony of a woman that her husband died should only be accepted if there are clear signs that she is mourning him: she is distraught and her clothes are torn as a sign of bereavement. If she does not show such signs one would naturally suspect her testimony. If the woman shows no sorrow it would seem that there was no peace between husband and wife during the marriage and that invalidates her testimony. However, the majority rules that outward signs of bereavement are not legally required. Whether she comes to testify crying or not, in mourning or not, she would be allowed to remarry on the strength of her own testimony.

As we have seen, while the requirements concerning the witnesses are lax because of the danger of *aginut* (Yevamot 93b), the standards demanding direct evidence of death remain firm, and these are sometimes impossible to meet. The problem of obtaining direct evidence of death is particularly severe in cases of death by war, highway robbery, and other types of attack such as a pogrom. Death under such circumstances often meant that the widow became an *agunah*. This has become a problem of greater and more tragic proportions in recent history due to the Holocaust. An unprecedented number of deaths occurred with no one surviving to bear direct testimony. Many women who by extraordinary luck survived the Holocaust became *agunot*. Because of the "Holocaust *agunot*" there has been increased interest in finding new solutions to the problem, and uncovering solutions proposed in earlier halakhic sources.[5]

The Mishnah, perhaps reading the problem of the *agunah* into the Bible, states that already during the time of the Monarchy a solution to the problem of wartime *agunot* had evolved: "Anyone going out to the wars of the House of David would give his wife a writ of divorce" (Ketubot 9b). The chance of being killed in war with no direct witness surviving was such that a man would divorce his wife before going to war in order to preempt the threat of her becoming an *agunah*.

Rashi and Rabbenu Tam, in their commentaries on Ketubot 9b, differ in their interpretations of this "prebattle divorce." Rashi argues that the *get* given by men on their way to war was a conditional divorce: it was written out but not officially given to the woman. If the husband did not return from the war and was presumed dead, an agent appointed by the husband prior to his departure or a *Bet Din* could "activate" the divorce by formally delivering it into the woman's hands. This notion of a conditional *get* is problematic. First of all, in principle a *get* is an instrument to dissolve a marriage which is no longer tenable and not a safe-guard against future misfortunes for a happily married couple. Second, a *get*, once written, should be delivered to the woman as promptly as possible since a man is not allowed to continue married life with a woman he has decided to divorce. There are also many complications in the details of execution. Since an agent must be appointed there is always the danger that the agent himself will die or disappear and then the woman would be an *agunah* just the same. As for the possibility of appointing a *Bet Din* (rather than a specific individual) as an agent for this purpose, there are many doubts raised in the halakhic literature as to whether a *Bet Din* can function as a *shaliah*, a personal agent.[6]

Therefore Rabbenu Tam prefers a different interpretation of the passage in Ketubot. He argues that the *get* in question was a full-fledged one, but a promise was made between husband and wife that if the husband returns from the war they would remarry. Rabbenu Tam's solution is not without problems either. First, if the husband is a priest he may not remarry his wife since she is, formally speaking, a divorcée, and priests are forbidden to marry divorcées. Second, if when the husband returns one of the parties does not honor the promise to remarry, the divorce, which initially was not in earnest, holds without any conditions and the rejected spouse has no recourse.

The conditional divorce and the divorce before going out to war are two possible ways to avert the threat of a woman's becoming an *agunah*, but both of them are legally problematic and have not been accepted as regular measures for preventing *aginut*. Other suggestions have been proposed but they are also burdened by complications. One suggestion is to institute marriages limited in time: to stipulate in the *ketubah* that the marriage is effective for so many years. If by the end of the stipulated period the husband is not present to renew the marriage, the woman is automatically unmarried and will not become an *agunah*. This idea does not sit well with the fundamental notion of *kiddushin*: that a couple marries with the hope of lifelong commitment and only divorces when the marriage is untenable. Another suggestion is stipulating in the *ketubah* that the marriage would be annulled if the husband is absent for a certain amount of time. This notion relies on the ruling which permits the rabbis to annul a marriage which is inappropriate (Yevamot 110a), but as we have already stated in our discussion of annulment of marriage, that is itself a difficult procedure to sustain.[7]

The Conservative movement in America attempted to deal with the problem of *agunot* due to the husband's disappearance or refusal to grant a divorce through the instrument of the *ketubah*. An addition to the *ketubah* proposed in 1954 by Saul Lieberman had the couple mutually agree to submit to the authority of a *Bet Din* to determine the terms for the dissolution of the marriage (if this is not accomplished by mutual consent) when it deems this appropriate according to Halakhah. The proposal met with severe criticism from Orthodox quarters. Though the addendum has been maintained in Conservative *ketubot*, its validity and enforceability remain questionable.[8] Another preemptive measure was proposed and ratified by the Conservative Rabbinical Assembly in 1968. This measure involves an ante-nuptial agreement (*tenai be-kiddushin*) which makes the marriage conditional upon certain defined circumstances (i.e., the husband is present, supports his wife, etc.). This solution, like the *ketubah* addendum, suffers technical halakhic problems and is no help to women who marry in the usual ceremony without these special precautions.[9]

Another non-halakhic approach to resolving problems of *aginut* has been to appeal to civil courts. There have been several cases in the United States where an *agunah* petitioned a civil court to compel her husband to give her a *get*, arguing that the *ketubah* can be viewed by a civil court as a contractual agreement between husband and wife. The husband who abandons his wife and divorces her by civil divorce violates his obligation to preserve the marriage or to dissolve it "according to the laws of Moses and Israel."[10] The most radical step in this direction has been the recent legislation in the state of New York (passed in August 1983) which states that no civil divorce will be granted unless the person seeking the divorce has removed all barriers to his former partner's remarriage. This "neutral" formulation is clearly aimed at the problem of the *agunah*, making it impossible for a man to get a civil divorce unless he gives his wife a *get*, releasing her and permitting her to remarry. This new legislation, as well as previous court cases, have created considerable controversy from two opposite sides of the fence. On the one side are those raising questions about the validity of such an approach from the point of view of Halakhah, questioning both the courts' interpretation of the *ketubah* as well as the validity of a *get* ordered by a non-Jewish authority. On the other side are those opposed to use of civil legislation and civil courts because they feel that sanctioning a religious ceremony and Halakhah in this way violates the Constitution.[11] The fact that despite the controversy the New York state legislation was strongly supported by both the Orthodox and Conservative leadership points above all to the gravity of the problem and the inability of the Jewish community at the present time to solve it halakhically.

The most far-reaching solution to *aginut* ever proposed is in effect to eliminate *kiddushin* altogether and resort to a system of cohabitation (*pilagshut*). Cohabitation, somewhat like common-law marriage, institutes family life just like marriage. Since according to Halakhah the children of such a marriage are as legitimate as those of a proper marriage, and their rights are the same, no grave problems would ensue. The woman is the one who needs the protection of proper *kiddushin* since the obligations outlined in the *ketubah* automatically apply to the husband when *kiddushin* is effected. But this problem could be solved by a contract or agreement that would state the woman's rights. This solution of abolishing *kiddushin* actually suffers fewer halakhic problems and complications than the other solutions which have been proposed. However, it violates the fundamental precept of marriage by betrothal "according to the laws of Moses and Israel," so it is inconceivable that it would be adopted.[12]

The different halakhic solutions proposed for the problem of the *agunah* have two features in common: first, they are all preemptive measures, and second, they have all been rejected, if not ignored, by most halakhic authorities. The first fact indicates that the problem of the *agunah* could at best be prevented by measures taken at the time of marriage. Once a woman has become an agu-

nah there are certain circumstances where there is absolutely no valid halakhic way of releasing her and permitting her to remarry. The only possible remedy for such circumstances would be a revolutionary change in the Halakhah, giving women, or Jewish courts the power to divorce a man without his consent. Barring such radical change in the Halakhah, women who are *agunot* face two options: a long, tortuous struggle to find a halakhic authority who will, after all, find some way to release them (usually a technical point allowing invalidation of the original betrothal), or by opting out of the observant Jewish community, thereby sacrificing the Halakhah in favor of personal fulfillment in remarriage.

Problems of *agunot* will continue to be discussed, and hopefully resolved, on a case-by-case basis. Since the cases of *agunot* are addressed one by one and usually out of the public eye, it is difficult to ascertain what the dimensions of the problem actually are today. The formal position of the Ministry of Religions in Israel has been that "there is hardly an *agunah* in the State of Israel today who has not been released in accordance with the Halakhah" (Z. Warhaftig, deputy minister of religions, *Proceedings of the Knesset* 11 : 1550). How reliable this testimony may be is unclear since it is in the interest of the Ministry of Religions to minimize the extent of the problem. The few cases of *agunot* that have come under scrutiny since the establishment of the state have caused public scandals and an outcry for legal steps to end the tragedy of the *agunah*, including demands to replace the rule of Halakhah with civil marriage.[13] In other Jewish communities there is no instrument for conducting a complete and systematic survey.

Given the complexities in the laws regarding the release of the *agunah* and the difficulties we have mentioned in all the solutions thus far proposed, it seems that the only way the problem of the *agunah* can be eliminated is by a far-reaching, radical *takanah*. Such a *takanah* would probably be more radical than the *takanot* of Rabbenu Gershom against polygyny and divorce without the woman's consent. It would in fact have to rule in favor of some form of annulment of *kiddushin* after a specified period of absence of a husband or for divorce against or without the husband's consent.

The first option would make the power of *kiddushin* conditional upon the husband's presence as a marital partner; the second would alter the male-centered unilateral nature of divorce. Such radical changes in the Halakhah seem impossible at the present time since the internal divisions in the Orthodox and general Jewish world prevent the kind of consensus that would be necessary to legitimate such momentous legislation. Meanwhile the price to be paid is the individual tragedy of each woman who becomes an *agunah*.

The Yevamah

The *yevamah* is the widow of a man who died childless and was survived by a brother. The widow is bound to the brother: he must either marry her or release her by means of *halitzah* or by his own death. If the surviving brother, the *yabam* (levir), neither marries the *yevamah* nor performs the ceremony of *halitzah*, she becomes an *agunah*.

The law of levirate marriage is biblical. It is stated in Deuteronomy and is also reflected in two narratives: the story of Judah and Tamar (Genesis 38) and the Book of Ruth. The story of Tamar illustrates the plight of the *yevamah*: first she loses her husband Er before bearing a child. Onan, her brother-in-law, then marries her but performs "coitus interruptus," spilling his seed on the ground because he knows that the progeny would not bear his name but rather the name of his deceased brother. As punishment for his act God kills Onan. Widowed again with no children, Tamar must now wait for the third brother, Shelah, to grow up and perform levirate marriage. With the passage of time Judah, Tamar's father-in-law, apparently forgets her and fails to marry her to his son Shelah. In desperation Tamar disguises herself as a prostitute and presents herself to Judah who, unaware of her identity, has intercourse with her. When the truth of her identity comes to light, Judah is remorseful. Though Tamar had in fact committed incest, Judah states: "She is in the right, rather than I. This comes of my not giving her to my son Shelah to be his wife" (Gen. 38 : 26).

The Book of Ruth contains the story of the Moabite woman Ruth, who loses her husband prematurely having had no children with him. She returns to Judah with her mother-in-law Naomi, and there eventually marries Boaz, a relative of Naomi's (on her deceased husband's side), though *not* a brother of Ruth's dead husband. The account in the Book of Ruth differs from the Deuteronomic legislation in both detail and attitude toward *halitzah*, giving rise to some scholarly controversy as to whether it really is an account of levirate marriage as Deuteronomy understands it. We need not enter into the discussion of this problem. The importance of the Book of Ruth is its impact on the popular image of the righteous woman who accepts her fate as a *yevamah* and in the end makes good, marrying a generous and wealthy levir. For the halakhic discussion the important text is Deuteronomy 25, where the details of the law are formulated:

[5]When brothers dwell together and one of them dies and leaves no son, the wife of the deceased shall not be married to a stranger, outside the family. Her husband's brother shall unite with her and take her as his wife, performing the levir's duty. [6]The first son that she bears shall be accounted to the dead brother, that his name may not be blotted out in Israel. [7]But if the man does not want to marry his brother's widow, his brother's widow shall appear before the elders in the gate and declare, "My husband's brother refuses to establish a name in Israel for his brother; he will not perform the duty of a levir." [8]The elders of his town shall then summon him and talk to him. If he insists, saying, "I do not choose to marry her," [9]his brother's widow shall go up to him in the presence of the elders, pull the sandal off his foot, spit in his face, and make this declaration: Thus shall be done to the man who will not build up his brother's house! [10]And he shall go in Israel by the name of "the family of the unsandaled one." [Deut. 25 : 5–10]

Levirate marriage is considered by Deuteronomy the duty of the surviving brother(s) in order to perpetuate the family of the deceased. Yet the brother who does not wish to perform his duty and marry the *yevamah* has a way out. The ceremony of *halitzah* (literally, "undoing a shoe") is an undoing of the bond between the levir and the *yevamah*. The levir rejects his duty and the woman is released and freed to marry another man. Because the levir is shirking his duty, the ceremony is degrading: the *yevamah* shames the levir by spitting in his face. Although *halitzah* legitimately releases the levir from levirate marriage, in Deuteronomy it is viewed as shameful.

The Mishnah elaborates the question of responsibility. The Bible briefly refers to the deceased husband's brother, but what if there are a number of brothers? What if there are brothers who cannot or do not wish to marry the *yevamah*? What if two brothers wish to marry the *yevamah*?

It is a *mitzvah* for the eldest to perform *yibum*. If he does not want to do it you go to all the other brothers, and if they do not want to do it either, you come back to the eldest and say to him: The *mitzvah* is incumbent upon you! Either perform *yibum* or *halitzah!* If he relies on waiting for a minor to grow up, or for a grown one to return from abroad, or for a deaf-mute or for one who is mentally incompetent [*shoteh*], you do not listen to him, but say: The *mitzvah* is upon you, either perform *yibum* or *halitzah!* [Yevamot 39a][14]

The chronological hierarchy of brothers applies when a levirate marriage must be performed: the eldest has the highest degree of obligation (and right) to perform *yibum*. However, any brother may perform *yibum*, and once the deed is done there is no room for questions (Yevamot 24a). Yet if no one wishes to marry the *yevamah* the duty returns to the eldest brother and he must release her by *halitzah*. He may not keep the woman in limbo for any protracted period by saying she should wait to be married by a brother who is not immediately able to marry her. Therefore he may not ask her to wait for a brother who is under thirteen to mature, or for one who is away to return in order marry then. Though the text here suggests that it is preferable that the woman be married to one of the brothers, if the choice is between waiting a long time for levirate marriage and immediate *halitzah*, the latter is preferred.

Indeed when we examine the talmudic references to *yibum* and *halitzah* we see that there are actually contradictory views about which act is preferable. Whereas in the Bible it is clear that *yibum* is a *mitzvah* and *halitzah* a shameful way out, in the Talmud we find dispute about the matter:

The mitzvah of yibum supersedes the mitzvah of halitzah: this was the case at first when the intention was to fulfill the mitzvah. But now that people's intentions are not the fulfillment of the mitzvah, the Sages said that the mitzvah of halitzah supersedes the mitzvah of yibum. [Bekhorot 13a][15]

The text here suggests that in principle yibum is preferable to halitzah since in "olden days" when people acted for the sake of fulfilling the commandments, rather than because of greed or sexual interest in the widow, yibum was preferred. However, in practice it suggests that halitzah is preferable since people's motives are suspect.

The controversy over which act is preferable continues in post-talmudic Halakhah. Rashi, who represents the view that halitzah is preferable to yibum, goes so far as to say that to perform levirate marriage not for the sake of the mitzvah alone is tantamount to commiting a sexual transgression:

Whoever performs yibum not for the sake of performing a mitzvah violates the prohibition against [relations with] his brother's wife. [Rashi, Commentary on Bekhorot 13a]

Under normal circumstances one is prohibited from having sexual relations with his brother's wife: it is an incestuous relation (Lev. 18 : 16). For the levir who marries his brother's wife with "impure" intentions, according to Rashi, it is as if he committed such a transgression.

As against Rashi's view we have the opinion of Maimonides who favors yibum over halitzah and argues that the underlying intentions of the levir are irrelevant:

And what is said here about yibum and halitzah, namely, that the yevamah is not permitted to him unless his intention is to perform the mitzvah through his intercourse, but that if he marries her for her money or her beauty it is as if he committed a sexual transgression [paga be-ervah]: this is not true. The prohibition of ervah has been removed in regard to her as soon as the brother had died without children and he is permitted to [marry] her even if his intention is not for the sake of the mitzvah. Therefore, the law in my opinion is that the mitzvah of yibum supersedes the *mitzvah* of *halitzah* at all times, and that is the Halakhah. [Maimonides, Commentary on the Mishnah, Bekhorot 13a]

For Maimonides there is no reason to prefer *halitzah* over *yibum* since the question of intention is irrelevant and the fear of sexual transgression without basis. Maimonides makes an unequivocal ruling in favor of *yibum*, regardless of the circumstances. Any levir who wishes to marry his *yevamah* would be encouraged to do so, according to Maimonides. But as we have already seen, not all halakhic authorities share this view.

Indeed there is a split in the Halakhah between two traditions: the Sephardic tradition which follows Maimonides' preference for *yibum*, and the Ashkenazic tradition which upholds Rashi's view that *halitzah* supersedes *yibum*.[16] Rashi allows for choosing *yibum* over *halitzah* only if it is really clear that the man's intention is to marry the *yevamah* for the sake of the *mitzvah* or if both man and woman express their sincere wish to marry. Rabbenu Tam goes further than Rashi and rules that even if both man and woman want to perform levirate marriage it is not permitted, unless it is known without a doubt that their act is purely the fulfillment of the commandment *le-shem shamayim* ("for the sake of Heaven") (cited in *Tur*, Even Ha-Ezer 165 : 1). Following the views of Rashi and Rabbenu Tam, Ashkenazic rabbis frowned on *yibum* and considered the man suspect of illicit sexual wishes. As against this view, Sephardic Jews considered *yibum* as a worthy act of a brother toward the wife and the memory of a deceased childless brother.

The divergence between Sephardim and Ashkenazim in regard to *yibum* and *halitzah* was not allowed to stand in the state of Israel. The Rabbinate ruled that *halitzah* supersedes *yibum* (in part because polygyny is also forbidden in Israel), in effect outlawing levirate marriage. If a levir refuses to perform *halitzah*, insisting instead on *yibum*, a court may compel him to perform *halitzah* and use imprisonment to enforce its will (*Takanot Ha-Rabbanut* 5713 [1953]: Section 17). A similar situation exists in the United States where polygamy is illegal. Sephardic rabbis in the United States heed the law of the state (*dina de-malkhuta dina*): they do not permit levirate marriage and require *halitzah* in all cases.

Despite the difference between Sephardic and Ashkenazic traditions of levirate marriage, women in all communities were subject to the threat of becoming *agunot* if they were to "fall before a levir." The *yevamah* bound to a levir can find herself "in limbo" due to one of the following situations:

1. The levir is under the age of thirteen and therefore not yet competent to perform either *yibum* or *halitzah*. The *yevamah* would have to wait until the levir reaches adulthood.

2. The levir is not mentally competent to participate in *halitzah* (he is either insane or a deaf-mute) so that the woman becomes an *agunah*. The only solution in the case of an insane levir is remission of his mental illness and in the case of a deaf-mute that he take her by levirate marriage (by intercourse) and then divorce her.

3. The levir refuses to perform either *yibum* or *halitzah* out of maliciousness or contempt for Jewish law (as was the case with apostates).

4. A brother is known to exist but his whereabouts or his fate are unknown, and the woman's situation is like that of the *agunah* whose husband has disappeared.[17]

Because of the problems with a levir who is a minor, an apostate, incompetent, or whose residence is unknown, the Talmud prescribes that if another brother is present and available he is immediately forced to grant the *yevamah* her freedom through *halitzah*. Problems with levirs are particularly severe in communities of immigrants where only part of a family resides. After the expulsion of the Jews from Spain, for example, this became an issue in many communities in which Spanish Jews resettled. Such was the case in Eretz Yisrael where a considerable influx of immigrants arrived. In Safed, one of the major towns in Eretz Yisrael from the sixteenth century onward, special precautions were taken. Anyone who wished to marry a local woman and was not himself a native of Safed was asked "Do you have any brothers? For in this town they do not give a woman to someone who is a guest and has brothers" (Responsa of Moses Galanti, No. 17). Thus anyone who might leave a woman a *yevamah* with the levir out of reach was not allowed to marry in Safed.

In other communities such extreme measures were not taken, but part of the great concern with family lineage and reputation in arranging matches was due to the fear of *yibum* and *aginut*, rather than with desire for status alone. A man whose brother converted or was rumored to be insane or a vagabond was too high a risk for many brides. Such a man encountered considerable difficulties in securing a good marriage. With the Enlightenment and secularization of parts of the Jewish population, another type of problematic levir arose. It was the brother who had become a *maskil* (enlightened) who often refused to perform *halitzah*, regarding it as a degrading, "primitive" ritual.

The problematic status of the *yevamah* and the tragic fate of the *agunah* both result from particular features of the laws of marriage. In practice it was not uncommon for the *yevamah* to become an *agunah* since it was often very difficult for her to obtain her release through *halitzah*. In Sephardic communities the *yevamah* was more likely to marry her levir, but even that did not always come about. The source of the problems of both the *agunah* and the *yevamah* is the fact that a woman may be bound, irrevocably and eternally, to a given man even if she has no actual relationship with him. The *agunah* is bound to her husband as long as he has not divorced her or died, even if he is gone from her life forever. The *yevamah* becomes bound to a brother-in-law through her husband's death. Whereas the *agunah* at least exercised some control over her marriage at the initial point, the *yevamah* has no power at all in the turn of events which makes her bound to her husband's brother. Both are stuck in a situation beyond their control. Both are dependent on the judgment of a rabbi to release them from their bonds, but such liberation is not always possible. The effort to release *agunot* and *yevamot* from their condition in accordance with the requirements of the law therefore occupies a considerable place in the halakhic literature.

The problems of the *agunah* and the *yevamah* have been major targets for the critique of Halahkah and traditional Jewish life by secular Jews, and more recently by Jewish feminists. In the State of Israel they have been the cause célèbre of the critics of the religious establishment and those fighting for separation of religion and state, and civil rights. Despite the outcry for reform, a fundamental change within the Halakhah in regard to the problems of the *agunah* and the *yevamah* seems unlikely. The internal divisions between halakhists and a generally conservative mood prevent the formation of the kind of consensus needed for instituting new and radical rulings.

✳ 5 ✳
SEXUALITY AND MARITAL RELATIONS

SEXUALITY poses a great problem for all traditional societies. On the one hand the sexual drive is vital for the creation of a family and a social structure. On the other hand it poses a great danger to those very institutions. Sexual temptation and sexual incompatibility are the strongest forces which threaten family stability and marital harmony. Adultery, prostitution, incest, and homosexuality are problems which trouble every culture and society, as is the possibility of the dissolution of marriage through divorce or abandonment.

All Western religious traditions walk a tightrope between legitimation of sexuality and ascetic denial of the libidinal drive. The rabbis recognized this very tension in statements such as "Let us be thankful to our forefathers, for if they had not sinned we would not have come into this world" (Avodah Zarah 5a). Judaism achieves its balance primarily through the legitimation of sexuality in the confines of marriage, which is the primary instrument for harnessing the "constructive" side of the sexual impulse and restraining its "anarchic" aspect. Within marriage the Halakhah permits a fairly wide range of legitimate sexual expression, but it also regiments rather tightly the frequency and appropriate times for sexual activity through the laws of niddah, which proscribe sexual contact during and following menstruation, and through the laws of onah, which prescribe "the times for performing the conjugal duty."[1]

The laws that regulate sexuality are primarily addressed to men. Men are commanded to marry, to procreate, and to perform their conjugal duties at regular times. The main commandment that applies to women is observing the laws of *niddah*, the laws of the menstruant. Other than the general obligation not to consistently and unreasonably refuse sexual relations with the husband, women do not really have "sexual obligations" in marriage. They are not commanded to marry, and they are explicitly exempted from the duty of procreation. Conjugal relations are an obligation of a husband toward a wife, not vice versa.

The imbalance in sexual obligations between men and women is due to the differentiated view of male and female sexuality in the rabbinical sources. Male sexuality is seen by the rabbis as the greater threat to familial and social structures. Male sexuality is active and egocentric, and always in danger of "running wild." It must be restrained through the controls of marriage, procreative duties, responsibility toward the woman, and a powerful taboo on male homosexuality and masturbation.[2]

Female sexuality is seen very differently. This reflects as much social convention as it does the fact that our sources do not relay women's feelings and experiences firsthand, but men's perceptions and conjectures regarding women's sexuality. Women are portrayed as sexually introverted and passive, in contradistinction to the male sexual impulse which the rabbis, as men, experience as active and extroverted: "A man's sexual impulse is out in the open: his erection stands out and he embarrasses himself in front of his fellows. A woman's sexual impulse is within and no one can recognize her [arousal]" (Sanhedrin 7a). Though her sexuality is hidden, it is as powerful as a man's obvious eroticism, or even greater: "A woman's passion is greater than that of a man" (Baba Metzi'a 84a).[3]

The paradox of women's intense sexual desires and their sexual passivity, whether innate or socially imposed, is seen by the rabbis as a great hardship. Indeed that, according to the rabbis, is "the curse of Eve," a curse on the first woman and all women after her:

> And to the woman He said,
>   "I will make most severe
>   Your pangs in childbearing;
>   In pain shall you bear children.

Yet your desire shall be for your husband,
And he shall rule over you." [Gen. 3 : 16]

The first part of Eve's punishment may be parallel to the first part
of the curse of Adam: he is punished in his labor of tilling the soil,
and she in hers, the labor of childbirth.[4] If indeed the eating of the
forbidden fruit from the tree of knowledge involved some kind of
sexual awakening, symbolized in the Genesis account (Gen. 2 : 25;
3 : 7) by the new shame over nakedness, then this is punishment
in kind (*middah ke-neged middah*). The transgression involved
the discovery of sexuality and the punishment makes its consequences painful.

The second part of the curse on Eve is not as plain, yet it is that
part which we need to understand in order to study the place of
female sexuality in and of itself, divorced from procreation. What
is the precise nature of *teshukatekh*, "your desire"? Does the punishment consist in a general condition of the man's lording over
the woman, or is this dominance directly related to the woman's
desire?

The medieval biblical commentators varied in their interpretations of this second part of Eve's curse. The commentaries of
Rashi, Ibn Ezra, and Nachmanides (Ramban) illustrate the variety
in interpretation.

"And your desire shall be for your husband"—[desire] for sexual intercourse. Yet you will not have the boldness to demand it [from him] with
your own words. Rather "he shall lord over you"—all will come from
him and not from you. [Rashi on Gen. 3 : 16]

Rashi defines desire very specifically as the desire for lovemaking
(*tashmish*) and interprets the dominance of the man as specifically sexual as well. The woman's punishment is that she is
unable to act to fulfill her desire; she does not have the boldness to
initiate sex or ask for it. Her husband "shall lord over" her in
matters of sex, "all will come from him"—all initiative will come
from him, not from the woman.

Ibn Ezra interprets this part of the curse differently:

"teshukatekh"—your obedience. And the meaning is: you will obey whatever he commands you, for you are in his domain to do what he wishes. [Ibn Ezra on Gen. 3 : 16]

Ibn Ezra goes against the plain meaning of the word *teshukah*, interpreting the phrase perhaps as an abbreviated one meaning "your desire shall be subject to your husband's desire." However he arrived at it, Ibn Ezra understood the husband's dominance to be general, including all aspects of family life. In the total subjugation to the husband's will lies the woman's curse.

Nachmanides proposes another interpretation:

The correct interpretation appears to me to be that He punished her in that her desire for her husband would be exceedingly great [so] that she would not be deterred by the pain of pregnancy or because he keeps her as a maidservant. Now, it is not customary for a servant to desire to acquire a master over himself, rather his desire is to flee from him. Thus her punishment is measure for measure [*middah ke-neged middah*]; she gave to her husband and he ate at her command and He punished her that she should no longer command him, but instead he should command her, entirely at his will. [Nachmanides (Ramban) on Gen. 3 : 16]

Nachmanides interprets desire, *teshukah*, like Rashi, as sexual desire, "exceedingly great" desire. But unlike Rashi, who sees the punishment in the man's monopoly over initiation of sex, Nachmanides sees the punishment in the woman's general subordination to the man. It is precisely because her sexual desire for the man is so great, in Nachmanides' view, that the woman accepts her status as a servant, contrary to human nature which drives a servant to flee his master rather than seek him. Nachmanides' view fuses the interpretation of "desire" as specifically sexual desire with the understanding of the man's dominance as a reference to all aspects of husband–wife relations. Nachmanides also links the first part of the curse, the pain of childbearing, with the sexual desire addressed in the second part. Like her husband's domination, the pain of labor is a curse which the woman accepts as a consequence of her sexual desire for her husband.

Both Rashi and Nachmanides and perhaps even Ibn Ezra (though he is not explicit), see the woman as caught in a bind between sexuality and subservience. Whether because she cannot initiate sex, or because she "pays" for her sexual desire with total obedience, the woman's curse is bound up with her sexuality. What are the legal implications of this curse?

Rabbi Joshua ben Levi further stated: It is a man's duty to pay a visit to his wife when he starts on a journey; for it is said; "And you shall know that your tent is in peace" (Job 5 : 24). Is this deduced from here? Surely it is deduced from the following: "And your desire shall be to your husband" teaches that a woman yearns for her husband when he sets out on a journey. [Yevamot 62b]

It is a man's obligation to have sexual relations with his wife (the euphemistic "pay a visit") before departing from his house. Interestingly, the preferred proof-text for this principle is not the verse "And you shall know that your tent is in peace," which could easily be construed as a command, but the passage "And your desire shall be for your husband," which is neither an imperative nor addressed to a man. There is a point behind this preference for the text which appears less appropriate for deducing a commandment. The point is to link the woman's curse, her desire for sex and inability to initiate it, with the man's *legal obligation* to "pay her a visit," that is, to initiate sex at a time when he knows she desires it. It appears that the man's duty is to compensate for the woman's curse by initiating sex: this is the duty called *onah*. The curse which brings inhibition of sexual impulse is not to be perpetuated by the husband; rather, it is his duty to counteract it by initiating sex to meet the desires of his wife.

The curse on Eve may be understood as a symbolic formulation of the rabbis' view of female sexuality. Women were thought to have powerful sexual drives but to be temperamentally inhibited in initiating sex. Men do not share this inhibition and thus are commanded to initiate sex on their wives' behalf. Genesis 3 : 16, the curse on Eve, furnishes the reason for the commandment of *onah* but there is also a biblical legal source for this duty.

[7]When a man sells his daughter as a slave, she shall not be freed as male slaves are. [8]If she proves to be displeasing to her master, who designated

her for himself, he must let her be redeemed; he shall not have the right to sell her to outsiders, since he broke faith with her. [9]And if he designated her for his son, he shall deal with her as is the practice with free maidens. [10]If he marries another, he must not withhold from this one her food, her clothing, or her conjugal rights. [11]If he fails her in these three ways, she shall be freed, without payment. [Ex. 21 : 7–11]

In the context of a discussion of the laws pertaining to Israelite slaves (Ex. 21 : 1–11), this passage delineates the status and rights of a female sold into slavery. From this passage which gives the female slave three basic rights—food, clothing, and conjugal rights—the minimal rights of a free married woman are deduced. If these are the rights of a bondwoman, certainly they are also the rights of a free woman. The term for conjugal rights is *onatah* (i.e., her *onah*). The biblical text assumes that the meaning of *onah* is self-evident since it is not elaborated. Yet to the rabbis it is not self-evident, and they furnish several explanations of its meaning and origin.

The term *onah* is given two etymologies in the Talmud. The first one derives the term from the word meaning "season" or "period." Thus *onah* defines the frequency of sexual relations that a woman is entitled to by law. The second etymology derives the meaning of *onah* from the word *innui*, which means "causing pain or suffering." In this interpretation, denying a married woman her sexual rights would cause her pain and suffering. The requirement of *onah* protects the woman from the pain of sexual deprivation. While the first etymology is probably the correct one philologically, the laws of *onah* reflect both elements: they define the required frequency of sex and direct the husband to ensure that his wife gains pleasure from it.[5]

Another talmudic passage goes beyond the simple explanation and etymology of *onah*. In a midrashic interpretation of the three terms describing the bondwoman's basic rights—"*she'erah, kesutah ve-onatah*"—Ketubot 47b–48a attempts to expand our understanding of the qualitative nature of a husband's obligations toward his wife:

Said Raba: The following Tanna is of the opinion that maintenance [*she'erah*] is a Pentateuchal duty. For it was taught: *She'erah* refers to maintenance for so it is said in Scripture: "Who also eat the *she'er* of my people." Her raiment [*kesutah*] is to be understood according to its ordinary meaning [i.e., clothing]. *Onatah* refers to the time for conjugal duty prescribed in the Torah, for so it is said in Scripture: "If thou shalt afflict [*te'aneh*] my daughters."

Rabbi Eleazar said: "*She'erah*" refers to the prescribed times for conjugal duty for so it is said in Scripture: "None of you shall approach any that is his near of kin [*she'er besaro*] to uncover their nakedness." "Her raiment" [is to be taken] according to its literal meaning. "*Onatah*" refers to maintenance, for so it is said in Scripture: "And he afflicted [*innah*] thee and suffered thee to hunger."

Rabbi Eliezer ben Jacob interpreted: [The expressions] "*She'erah kesutah*" [imply]: Provide her with raiment according to her age, viz. that a man shall not provide his old wife [with the raiment] of a young one, nor his young wife with that of an old one. [The expressions] "*kesutah veonatah*" [imply]: Provide her with raiment according to the season of the year, viz. that he shall not give her new raiment in summer nor worn-out raiment in the winter. Rabbi Joseph taught: "Her flesh" [*she'erah*] implies close bodily contact, viz. that he must not treat her in the manner of the Persians who perform their conjugal duties in their clothes. This provides support for [the ruling of] Rav Huna who laid down that a husband who said: "I will not [perform conjugal duties] unless she wears her clothes and I mine," must divorce her and also give her her *ketubah* payment. [Ketubot 47b–48a]

This passage brings as many possible interpretations of the three key words, *she'erah, kesutah,* and *onatah,* as one might imagine. Briefly summarized the variants are:

1. The Tanna (not identified by name): *she'erah* = her food; *kesutah* = her clothing; *onatah* = her conjugal rights

2. Rabbi Eleazar: *she'erah* = her conjugal rights; *kesutah* = her clothing (literal meaning); *onatah* = maintenance (i.e., food)

3. Rabbi Eliezer ben Jacob: *she'erah kesutah* (the two words form one idiom) = clothing appropriate to her age; *kesutah veonatah* (the two words form one idiom) = clothing appropriate to the season

4. Rabbi Joseph: *she'erah* = her flesh: it refers to physical contact during the performance of the duty of sexual relations (*onah*).

Rabbi Eliezer ben Jacob's interpretation of the three words as two idioms indicating clothes appropriate to the age and season is not intended to replace the mainstream interpretation of the three words as food, clothing, and conjugal rights. Rather, it seeks to expand our understanding of one of the rights by using the other words as if they were a commentary on the middle word, *kesutah*. The point of this expansion of the word for clothing is to indicate that the essential right for clothing includes the assumption that they will be provided in appropriate ways to meet the wife's needs as they vary with age and season.

The same principle of interpretation is used to expand the meaning of *onah*, conjugal rights. Rabbi Joseph applies the word *she'er*, which can mean meat or flesh, to the word *onah*. "Her flesh [*she'erah*] implies bodily contact" during intercourse. The word *she'er* sheds light on the quality of the conjugal rights assured in *onah*; conjugal rights are to be performed in intimate bodily contact. A man may neither perform his conjugal duties in his clothes nor require his wife to be clothed. If he demands that "she wear her clothes and I mine," he must divorce her for he has violated his obligations in marriage.

Nachmanides in his commentary on Exodus 21 : 11 goes even further, arguing that all three terms refer to conjugal rights, and leaving the rights of a woman to food and clothes to be based on a rabbinic ruling, not on this biblical passage:

So therefore, *she'erah* [means] bodily closeness, and *kesutah* [means] her bed covers as it says "It is the only covering he has, what else would he sleep in?" (Ex. 22 : 26); *onah* [means] that he come to her at the time for lovemaking. . . . we shall interpret "He shall not diminish her flesh [*she'erah*]" to mean: he shall not deprive her of her flesh, that is to say, the flesh which is appropriate for her which is the flesh of her husband who with her becomes one flesh (Gen. 2 : 24). And the point of the passage in Exodus is that if he takes another he shall not diminish the closeness of flesh, the covers of her bed and her times of lovemaking following the "rule for daughters." And the reason is lest the other one be sitting on an opulent bed where they "become one flesh" while with the first one he sleeps as if she were a concubine, by chance and on the ground like a man coming to a prostitute. And therefore the scripture prevents him from this and thus the rabbis said "*she'erah* implies close bodily contact, viz. that he must not treat her in the manner of the Persians who perform their conjugal duties in their clothes." And this is the correct interpretation because usually the scriptures refer to intercourse [mishkav] in euphemisms and brevity, and therefore discuss these matters with allusions: she'erah kesutah ve-onatah refer to the three matters pertinent to the union of a man with his wife. And let this be the clear basis for the Halakhah and let the woman's food and clothing be based on the rabbis' rulings. [Nachmanides (Ramban) on Ex. 21 : 11]

According to Nachmanides Exodus 21 : 11 establishes the quality of onah, mandating physical intimacy, appropriate surroundings, and regularity.

But before we examine further the quality of the sexual relations which a woman is entitled to by the virtue of her onah, let us consider the basic mishnaic definition of onah which uses quantity as a defining yardstick: The passage which prescribes the frequency of onah appears in the context of a discussion of exceptions to the rule regarding onah:

Mishnah: If a man forbade himself by vow to have intercourse with his wife Bet Shammai ruled: [she must consent to the deprivation for] two weeks; Bet Hillel ruled: [only for] one week.
    Students may go away to study the Torah, without the permission [of their wives for a period of] thirty days; laborers [only for] one week.
    The times for conjugal duty prescribed in the Torah are: for men of independence, every day; for laborers, twice a week; for ass-drivers, once a week; for camel-drivers, once in thirty days; for sailors, once in six months. These are the rulings of Rabbi Eliezer.

There is a disagreement between Bet Hillel and Bet Shammai concerning the maximum period of deprivation from onah that a woman may be subject to; Bet Hillel hold one week, Bet Shammai two. Though Bet Hillel and Bet Shammai differ in the length of time they allow for abstention and in their reasoning, the actual practical difference which results is not great. Both allow only a very limited period of abstention to fulfill a vow.

One acceptable reason for depriving a wife of her conjugal rights is the study of Torah. Students who are professionally dedicated to the study of the law may depart without their wives' permission, thus depriving them of their rights of onah. This passage states that they may only depart for the duration of one month, but another tradition holds that they may go away for up to three years. Though the latter tradition is accepted as Halakhah there is strong opposition to it. The opposing sentiments are recorded in statements and anecdotes which follow our passage in Ketubot (61b–62b) telling about students who went away to study for long periods with tragic consequences, such as their death or their wives' "losing the powers of procreation."[6] Laborers may only go away for one week to study because for them study of the law is not a full-fledged professional commitment, but only a short-term involvement in performing the *mitzvah* of Torah study. Subsequent discussion in the Talmud develops this principle further, ruling that a man may go away for a brief period in other circumstances where the purpose of his journey is performing a *mitzvah*.

Now that we have understood the exceptions, let us return to the general rule regarding *onah*. The Mishnah provides a basic timetable for the frequency of sexual relations. This timetable is adjusted according to a man's profession so that he should be able to practice his trade and also fulfill his marital obligation. Thus a camel driver who must travel in caravans for long periods is only obligated to perform the duty of *onah* once every month and sailors only once every six months. An ass driver who goes on shorter trips from town to town must return home once a week to perform his duty of *onah*. Laborers are obligated to perform their duty twice a week: their work is taxing and might require them to stay away from home a few nights every week. The *Shulhan Arukh* reiterates the Talmudic distinction between laborers who work in their own town and perform their duty of *onah* twice a week, and those who work in a different town and are obligated in the *mitzvah* only once a week (Orah Hayyim 240 : 1). Students of the Torah are obligated to perform their marital duty once a week, and the preference is for performing it on Friday night. Who are the *tayalim* (men of independent means) whose duty of *onah* is every night? "Said Rabin: they are like the decadent residents of Eretz Yisrael who wallow in food and drink and are therefore robust and have great strength for sex" (Ketubot 62b).

The fact that the duty of *onah* is linked to a man's profession reflects two assumptions in the rabbinical worldview. First, it reflects the great importance of the duty of *onah*, for it is necessary to restrict it in order to permit a man to practice his trade. The "ideal situation" from the woman's point of view is one where the man is not hampered by the demands of work, and performs the duty of onah every day. The second assumption is that a man is expected to have one trade all his life. In fact a man is defined by his trade. When a woman chooses to marry a camel driver she knowingly chooses not only a certain class and defined socioeconomic expectations, but also a certain kind of sex life.

In addition to the regular times prescribed by Rabbi Eliezer for onah, the Talmud adds other times when a man should initiate sexual relations with his wife: before he goes away, since "a woman yearns for her husband when he sets out on a journey" (Yevamot 62b), and "near her menstruation" (Pesahim 72b), because the woman knows that she is about to enter a period of abstention and thus desires sex.[7] The importance of the woman's desire is recognized in the requirement of keeping the duty of onah during pregnancy as well. Since during pregnancy there is no possibility of further procreation, and a man may also assume that the normal sexual relationship is subdued, the Halakhah prescribes the duty of onah with a pregnant wife as well. As against later popular notions which held sex to be detrimental especially toward the end of the pregnancy, the rabbis held that "during the first three months intercourse is hard on the mother and on the fetus, during the middle three it is hard on the mother and good for the fetus, and during the last three, good for both" (Niddah 31a).

Given the precise definition of the "times of onah" in the Mishnah and the Talmud, a fundamental question arises: are these times intended as a maximum or a minimum? In other words, is, let us say, twice a week for laborers the most often one may have sex and is more frequent intercourse thus a violation of the law? Or, conversely, is twice a week the minimum that a laborer owes his wife, but if both she and he wish they may have sex more often?

The Talmud already reflects a tension between these two possible interpretations of the prescriptions of onah. On the one hand there is the attitude exemplified by Raba's statement "it is a man's

duty to please his wife with a good deed" *beyond* the requirements of "the periodic visit" (Pesahim 72b). In other words the
times prescribed in the Mishnah set the minimal obligation and
going beyond the "prescribed times" when the wife indicates her
desire is an integral part of the *mitzvah* of *onah*. On the other
hand a more ascetic attitude crops up in a pronouncement like
"let not students of the law [scholars] be with their wives too
frequently like roosters" (Berakhot 22a). This attitude tends to
view the times prescribed in the Mishnah as a maximum: not as a
binding legal limitation, but rather as a statement of what is decent and proper for men of spiritual and moral worth.

The conflict between the latter, ascetic view, and the former,
more permissive view of sexuality intended for the woman's pleasure continues and sharpens in the post-talmudic development of
the Halakhah. The most elaborate and forceful defense of the view
of *onah* as a minimalist standard is Abraham ben David's work,
Ba'alei Ha-Nefesh. Abraham ben David of Posquieres (Rabad)
lived in France in the twelfth century and composed *Ba'alei Ha-
Nefesh* as a guide for the pious life. He devoted a whole chapter,
"Sha'ar Ha-Kedushah," to sexuality and marital conduct.

The *onot* [plural of *onah*] set by the rabbis were determined in general, as
they estimated the woman's notion of what she would be satisfied with
according to her husband's ability and pleasure. If, however, he sees that
she is asking him for that act and that she has a need for it, seeing this as
she attracts his attention by adorning herself in front of him, then he is
commanded to please her in this matter of *mitzvah*. [Abraham ben David,
Ba'alei Ha-Nefesh, "Sha'ar Ha-Kedushah"]

According to Rabad, the times for *onah* prescribed in the Talmud
are only a general estimate; they are to be construed as the minimum standard for frequency of sex, the rabbis' guess of what
women wanted. The obligation of *onah* includes the requirement
that the husband be responsive to his wife when she tries to hint
at her desire. Rabad's assumption that she would do that indirectly "by adorning herself in front of him" parallels what we
have seen Rashi argue in his interpretation of the curse of Eve:
when she desires sex a woman hints at it, not possessing the

boldness to ask for it directly. It is the husband's obligation to counter her timidity by acting "to please her in this matter of *mitzvah*" when she signals her inclination.

As against the attitude of Rabad, both the *Tur* and the *Shulhan Arukh* open the discussion of the conduct of sexual relations with a similar statement: "If a man is married, let him not be with his wife too frequently, but only at the frequency prescribed according to the law of *onah* in the Torah" (*Shulhan Arukh*, Orah Hayyim 240 : 1; and *Tur*, Orah Hayyim 240 and Even Ha-Ezer 25). Karo, however, does instruct a man to be attuned to his wife's sexual needs during other times: on the night of the immersion in the *mikveh*, before departing for a journey (unless the journey is for performing a *mitzvah*, in which case the man is exempt!), and "when his wife is nursing and he recognizes that she is trying to seduce him and attract him by adorning herself in front of him so that he should pay attention to her." The nursing mother can easily be ignored by her husband, similarly to the pregnant woman. Because of her involvement with her infant as well as, perhaps, the effect of the postpartum recovery, a husband may assume that his wife is "asexual" during this period. Karo mandates that if she indicates her sexual interest the husband must be sensitive and responsive.

If we examine the representative opinions of Rabad and Karo on the prescriptions on *onah* we will find that the conflict between "minimum" and "maximum" is perhaps not as sharp and simple as it seems. Both Rabad and Karo emphasize the husband's obligation to be attuned and responsive to his wife's needs. They seem to have similar views of female sexual needs as legitimate, present throughout the life cycle, and in need of protection. Both start with the same assumption, that the laws of *onah* come to correct the natural imbalance between men and women in sexual temperament and power. The difference between the two lies in their view of male sexuality. Both of them regard the male sexual impulse as one which would be better controlled and restrained than given full satisfaction. However, Rabad so emphasizes the need to respond to the woman's sexual desires that he is willing to "ignore" the somewhat negative "side effect" of increased sexual activity for the man. Karo focuses more of his concern on restraining the man's sexual desire and fulfillment. Thus in order not to encourage scholars to spend too much time with their wives "like roosters," he defines the prescriptions of *onah* as a maximum. He seems to assume that going beyond these prescriptions would generally be a way of satisfying the man's (illegitimate) needs, while as a rule the woman is satisfied with the prescribed frequency.

We find the same concern for women's sexual needs in the writings of a contemporary halakhic authority, Moshe Feinstein. Feinstein holds that the sexual needs of contemporary women are greater than those of their predecessors because the general environment is more imbued with sexuality and temptation. Therefore he rules that the times prescribed by the Halakhah for scholars should be increased in his own day in order to meet the increased needs of contemporary women. He does not interpret the Mishnah's prescription as a strict maximum, and thus does not see great halakhic problems in increasing it. Rather, he sees it historically, as a reasonable estimate for its own time of what is proper between husband and wife:

As to the innovation of recent authorities in our day, that students of the law [scholars] should perform the duty of *onah* twice a week: I too support this view. Furthermore, let me add that the main point of the *mitzvah* of *onah* is [suiting it to] what the woman desires and wants. Because of the promiscuity of this generation and the jealousy for another woman's lot a woman feels desire and erotic passion more often than once a week. Therefore, her husband is obligated in this respect because of the very essence of the duty of *onah*. Even if the husband does not perceive his wife's desire, one should attribute that to her embarrassment and her modesty, since it is because of these that the rabbis legislated set times. Therefore, the later authorities have ruled correctly that one should counsel and even obligate scholars to perform *onah* twice a week. [Moshe Feinstein, *Responsa Iggrot Moshe*, Even Ha-Ezer 3 : 28][8]

Feinstein rules for increasing the frequency of *onah* in order to meet the increased sexual needs of contemporary women.

When we turn to the second aspect of the duty of *onah*, the quality of the sexual act, we find a parallel tension between the desire to restrain and curtail sexuality, and the wish to leave a

certain freedom to husband and wife in intimate matters. While
the Halakhah leaves considerable latitude for personal proclivi-
ties, the ascetic tendency remains a powerful psychological
inhibition.

Let us examine the sources for the principle that the man's
obligation in *onah* is to please and satisfy his wife.

If a man is newly married, he shall not join the army nor is he to be
pestered at home; he shall be left free of all obligations for one year to
cheer the wife he has taken. [Deut. 24 : 5][9]

A new marriage is one of the circumstances justifying an exemption from army service. The reason cited by the biblical text is to
give the man the opportunity to cheer or rejoice with his wife. The
biblical text does not distinguish between the man's joy and his
wife's pleasure. Rashi, on the other hand, is very insistent on the
distinction. The point of the biblical legislation, according to his
interpretation, is that the man should bring joy and sexual pleasure to his wife:

"and he shall cheer his wife"—as the translation of Onkelos [the Aramaic
translation] has it: he shall cheer his wife. And whosoever translates "he
shall rejoice *with* his wife" is wrong, translating *ve-samach* instead of
ve-simach. [Rashi on Deut. 24 : 5]

Ve-samach means "and he shall rejoice"; the text, however, has
ve-simach, which means "and he shall cause [someone else] to
rejoice." Rashi makes it clear that the point is for the husband to
bring pleasure to his wife; his own pleasure is only a consequence, not a motivation. So it is with the obligation of *onah*: a
husband is to initiate sex in order to bring pleasure to his wife. His
enjoyment of sex is merely a welcome "side effect."

Sefer Mitzvot Katan, a medieval popular compilation of *mitz-*
vot, makes the direct link between the Deuteronomic legislation
and the commandment of *onah* in Exodus:

"To cheer his wife"—as it is written "and he shall cheer his wife whom
he has taken." The negative [*mitzvah*] is "Her *onah* shall he not dimin-

ish" (Ex. 21 : 11). And behold how great is this positive *mitzvah*. . . . even when his wife is pregnant it is a *mitzvah* to bring her joy in this manner if he feels she is desirous. [*Sefer Mitzvot Katan*, Positive Commandments No. 285]

Deuteronomy 24 : 5 and Exodus 21 : 11 are complementary aspects of *onah*: the former requires that the purpose of *onah* be the sexual pleasure of the woman; the latter prohibits diminishing the prescribed rights.

A man then fulfills two obligations when he initiates sex and intercourse: procreation and *onah*. What is conspicuously missing is his own sexual pleasure as a motivation. Rabad, in his chapter on sexuality in *Ba'alei Ha-Nefesh*, recounts four purposes, or intentions [*kavanot*], which make sex legitimate and desirable:

These are the four *kavanot* for which that act is appropriate:
The first one is for procreation (and it is the most befitting) and the *mitzvah* of *onah* which he is commanded not to subtract from.
The second one is for the constitution of the fetus for our rabbis have said: The first three months it is hard on the woman and the fetus, the middle three it is hard on the woman and good for the fetus, the last— good for both of them. And this *kavanah* is also deduced from the *kavanah* of procreation.
The third *kavanah* . . . [is that] she desires him, and he recognizes that she is trying to seduce him and that she adorns herself in front of him in order that he notice her. And all the more so, when he embarks on a journey, certainly, she desires him then. There is reward paid for this *mitzvah* which is the *mitzvah* of *onah*.
The fourth is that he intends to restrain himself through it, so that he does not desire something prohibited when he sees that his passion increases and he is desiring that thing and is in danger of becoming ill. In this there is also reward, but not as much as in the first, because he could have ruled his passion and curbed his desire. [Rabad, *Ba'alei Ha-Nefesh*, Sha'ar Ha-Kedushah]

Briefly summarized, the appropriate motivations for sex are:

1. Procreation and the prescribed times for *onah*
2. Improving the health of the fetus
3. *Onah* beyond the prescribed frequency

4. Restraining the man's passion and directing it to a woman permitted to him, as well as preventing illness due to unreleased sexual impulse

The man's own desires and sexual needs are last on Rabad's list of acceptable *kavanot*. Even when the man's desires are taken into account, as in the fourth *kavanah*, it is not his sexual pleasure which Rabad accepts, but the prevention of sinful thoughts and physical hazard. As for the man's desires, Rabad counsels "he could have ruled his passion and curbed his desire."

It would be erroneous to conclude that male sexual desires were totally ignored. Rather, they were assumed to be an ever-present motivation for sex that did not need to be anchored in law. It was the woman's sexual needs that had to be formulated into law to ensure their fulfillment. Male sexuality had to be controlled and limited by the legal system, by harnessing it to ulterior ends: procreation and *onah*.

How far does the acceptance of female sexual pleasure extend? Is any sexual practice which gives the woman pleasure legitimate according to the law of *onah*? When we examine the Halakhah we find a tension between the view that any sexual practice which increases sexual pleasure is legitimate as long as there is no "destruction of seed" (*hashhatat zera*—ejaculation outside the vagina), and a restrictive view which frowns on any sexual practices other than intercourse in "the missionary position."

Rabbi Yohanan ben Dahbai said: The Ministering Angels told me four things: People are born lame because they [their parents] overturned their table, dumb because they kiss "that place," deaf because they converse during intercourse, blind because they look at "that place." . . . Rabbi Yohanan said: The above is the opinion of Rabbi Yohanan ben Dahbai, but our Sages said: The Halakhah is not as Rabbi Yohanan ben Dahbai, but rather, a man may do whatever he pleases with his wife. . . . A woman once came before Rabbi and said: "Rabbi! I have set a table for my husband but he has overturned it." Rabbi replied: "My daughter, the Torah has permitted you to him, what then can I do for you?" [Nedarim 20b]

The passage begins with the opinion of Yohanan ben Dahbai, who frowns upon erotic play and sexual contact in ways other than intercourse in the "missionary position." "Turning the table" most probably refers to the woman's being on top during intercourse (or, alternatively, to penetration from behind). Yohanan ben Dahbai does not argue that "turning the table," kissing and looking at the genitals, and "conversing during intercourse" are prohibited by the Halakhah explicitly. Rather, he cites the secrets of the angels (which are not halakhically authoritative pronouncements!) according to which people who engage in these practices give birth to children with defects correlated to the nature of their sexual practices. Though Yohanan ben Dahbai's view is cited, it is rejected by the rabbis: the Halakhah is rather that "a man may do whatever he pleases with his wife" as long as he does not violate the prohibition on spilling of seed. An example is cited to prove this: when a woman came to Rabbi Judah Ha-Nasi and complained that her husband had "turned the table," Judah sent her home empty-handed, stating that such sexual practices are permitted by the Torah.

Despite the halakhic determination that one is free to engage in any sexual practices and positions of intercourse provided there is coitus, a strong aversion to "unnatural" practices remains. Thus we find in another passage the following description of various positions of intercourse and their ill-effects: "He who has intercourse standing up will be afflicted by a seizure; if seated—by *shilshul* [diarrhea?]; she on top and he below—this is the way of brazenness; she below and he above—that is the way of [proper] intercourse" (Gittin 70a). A passage in Niddah addresses the question of position from a different point of view: rather than deriding "unnatural" positions it seeks to explain why the traditional position is natural:

Why is it that during intercourse a man faces downward and a woman faces upward? This one looks at the place from whence he came—the earth, and this one at the place from whence she was created—the man's rib. [Niddah 31b][10]

We find a similar tension in the views regarding foreplay, talking during sex in order to increase arousal, and prolonging the sexual act. Thus one passage exalts the man who performs inter-

SEXUALITY AND MARITAL RELATIONS

course briefly and without seeking to increase arousal and pleasure, while another states: "A man should not converse with his
wife when he comes to her, but words of eros are permitted in
order to arouse her and increase her passion" (Nedarim 20a).
Similarly: "Rabbi Eliezer says: Let a man seduce his wife during
sexual relations. Rabbi Judah says: let him bring her pleasure during intercourse" (Tractate Kallah no. 19).

Though these pronouncements are contradictory in some re-
spects, they do have a common denominator: the legitimate goal
of the sexual act is bringing pleasure to the wife because of the
mitzvah of *onah*. Male pleasure is not an acceptable goal. Thus
those opinions that do permit seductive talk and foreplay do so
only as a way of arousing the woman. For a man to arouse himself
is not only presumed to be unnecessary, but is also seen as sinful.
The *Shulhan Arukh* briefly summarizes this ascetic attitude toward male arousal and sexual pleasure:

If his intention is to restrain himself through her so that he does not come
to where he might commit a transgression, since he sees that his sexual
impulse [*yetzer*] is growing and he desires that thing [it would be legiti-
mate] though better to postpone and repress his desire. For "man has a
small member: he who keeps it hungry is satisfied, he who satisfies it is
hungry." But, a man who does not have a real need for it [sex], but
arouses his passion in order to then fulfill it, that is the doing of the evil
inclination [*yetzer ha-ra*], and soon enough this desire will make him
stray to what is forbidden to him. And about this case our rabbis have
said: he who purposefully arouses himself and causes an erection should
be put under a ban. [*Shulhan Arukh, Orah Hayyim* 240 : 3]

The *Shulhan Arukh* recognizes the strength of the male sexual
impulse. Karo does not reject it completely, of course, but he does
favor all attempts to curb it. Thus if a man sees that he cannot
possibly restrain his impulse, releasing his passion by sexual relations with his wife is legitimate. However, it is more pious to
conquer the impulse and subdue it. Certainly anyone who purposefully arouses himself when he could have abstained from sex
is committing a sinful act. One should always seek to tame the
passions and perform the sexual act as a commandment and not as
a climactic fulfillment of sexual arousal.[11]

As against the forbidding attitude toward sexual arousal which we see exemplified in the *Shulhan Arukh*, we find other sources which view sexuality and arousal more favorably. This attitude is best seen in *Iggeret Ha-Kodesh*, from the thirteenth century (traditionally ascribed to Nachmanides but probably written by the kabbalist Joseph ben Abraham Gikatilla, c. 1248–1325). Though not a halakhic text, *Iggeret Ha-Kodesh* was a popular treatise and exercised considerable influence on the way pious men related to sexuality.[12] The author's favorable view of sexuality and his emphasis on teaching proper ways of initiating sex stems first and foremost from his kabbalistic notion that human intercourse is an imitation and a part of a divine process of unification of different aspects of God.

Intercourse is holy and clean when done when it is proper and the time is right and the intention right. Anyone who says that there is a taint and ugliness in intercourse, God forbid [such a view]! For intercourse is called knowing . . . and this is its hidden meaning. For a drop of seed, when it is brought out in holiness and purity brings down with it knowledge and wisdom from the brain. And it is well known that if it were not an act of great holiness intercourse would not have been called knowing. . . .

And it is clear that just like the hands, when they write a Torah scroll they are dignified and excellent and elevated but if they do an act of wickedness they are despicable and ugly. So also were the tools [organs] of intercourse to Adam and Eve before they sinned.

And this is the secret of knowledge which we are telling you about. Man is contained in the secret of wisdom, reason and knowledge. The man is wisdom, the woman is the secret of reason and pure intercourse is the secret of knowledge, therefore intercourse is an elevated and great thing when it is proper. . . .

But when a man's intention is not pure, that same seed which he brings forth is only a smelly drop in which God has no part. . . . [Nachmanides (?), *Iggeret Ha-Kodesh* (*The Holy Letter*), Chap. 2, "The First Way—The Essence of Intercourse"]

The author of *Iggeret Ha-Kodesh* uses a kabbalistic model to describe the fusion of the corporeal and the divine to make human acts, specifically intercourse, "holy and clean," "an elevated and great thing." With the proper intention, intercourse, the union of man and woman, becomes a union of wisdom and reason, and creates knowledge. "Man is contained in the secret of wisdom, reason and knowledge. The man is wisdom, the woman is the secret of reason and pure intercourse is the secret of knowledge. . . ." This model is represented schematically in the accompanying diagram.

<u>WOMAN</u>   <u>MAN</u>
REASON (Binah)   WISDOM (Hokhmah)
                    INTERCOURSE
                    KNOWLEDGE (Da'at)

Wisdom (Hokhmah), Reason (Binah), and Knowledge (Da'at) are the names of three of the *sefirot*, the emanations of God in the kabbalistic system, which mediate between the Ein Sof (the infinite, unknowable God) and the created world. The Kabbalah understands creation as both the dramatic event which gave birth to the world and the dynamic process which sustains it. The creation is described graphically as an unfolding of divine emanations which lead from the limitless God (Ein Sof) to the material world. The *sefirot* are the emanations which are conceptualized as unfolding one from another, and manifesting different aspects of God. The *sefirot* Binah (Reason) and Hokhmah (Wisdom) come together and create the lower *sefirot* through intercourse which is called "knowing" in the Bible, thus continually sparking the process of creation. According to the kabbalistic doctrine of *Iggeret Ha-Kodesh*, when a man and a woman have intercourse with the proper intention they recreate and participate in the divine process of "begetting" the world. The proper conduct of sex is critical because it mirrors the divine process through human actions.

The second important factor in the author's favorable attitude toward sexuality is his notion of a "female seed," similar to male sperm, which is released during intercourse. If this female seed is released before the male seed, the conception of a male child is favored. In order to encourage this "female semination," the author instructs his reader in ways of arousing his wife.

We have already told you in the previous chapters the things which you need to know in the matter of intercourse and we want to include with them the things we will say in this chapter. And you, place them like a seal upon your heart! . . .

Therefore, you ought to engage her first in matters which please her heart and mind and cheer her in order to bring together your thought with her thought and your intention with hers. And you should say such things some of which will urge her to passion and intercourse, to affection, desire and lovemaking, and some which will urge fear of heaven, piety and modesty. And tell her of pious, good and righteous women and how they bore sons who were honest, pure and worthy of the divine crown, scholars of the Torah, of worship and of great teachings. . . .

And one should converse with her in the middle of the night or close to its last third for the rabbis said . . ."In the third part of the night a woman converses with her husband." And you shall not possess her against her will nor force her because in that kind of a union there is no divine presence [Shekhinah] because your intentions are opposite to hers and her wish does not agree with yours. And do not quarrel with her nor beat her for the sake of having intercourse. The rabbis say in Tractate Yoma: "As a lion smashes and eats and has no shame, so a boor beats and possesses and has no shame."

Rather you should attract her with charming words and seductions and other proper and righteous things as I have explained. And do not possess her while she is asleep because the two intentions are not one and her wish does not agree with yours. But rather arouse her with such things as we have said.

Finally, after you check yourself and see that you are properly ready for intercourse act so that your wife's wish agrees with yours. And now, when you have intercourse with her do not hasten to arouse your passion until the woman's mind is ready and engage her in words of love so that she will begin to give forth seed first and thus her seed would be like matter and your seed like form, as it is said "when a woman gives forth seed and bears a male child," . . . [Nachmanides(?), Iggeret Ha-Kodesh, Chap. 6, "The Fifth Way—Concerning the Quality of Intercourse"]

A man is encouraged to talk to his wife and "engage her in matters which please her heart and mind and cheer her." Any talk which will "urge her to passion and intercourse, to affection, desire and lovemaking" is appropriate because it serves the intention of arousing the woman so that intercourse will occur in mutual desire. The importance of agreement and mutual desire is paramount. The man must be sure to "bring together your thought with her thought and your intention with her intention," and avoid any possibility that he might possess her against her will. In order to enact a divine process through intercourse there must be complete harmony and no violence.

The actual act of intercourse is described in the last paragraph. When he is ready for intercourse, the man is instructed once again to "act so that your wife's wish agrees with yours." The man is to tame his passion and arouse the woman's "so that she will begin to give forth seed first." The notion that if the woman is to "give forth seed first" she will bear a son is derived from Leviticus.

The Lord said to Moses: Say to the children of Israel: When a woman gives forth seed and bears a male child, then she shall be unclean seven days, as at the time of her menstruation. [Lev. 12 : 1]

The phrase "when a woman gives forth seed," which appears to mean simply "when a woman conceives," has sent many biblical commentators on a search for a physiological explanation of female semination. A theory of female seed, analogous to male semen, was a sensible explanation for the female reproductive system before the discovery of the ovaries. It was entertained in ancient Greek science and first appears in the Jewish tradition in the Talmud and Leviticus Rabbah.

The conjunction in the Leviticus verse of the woman's giving forth seed and bearing a male child led to the popular notion reflected in Iggeret Ha-Kodesh that there is a cause-and-effect relationship here. If the woman "gives forth seed" first, as it appears in the verse, then she will bear a male child. What, in the mind of the author, does it mean for a woman to give forth seed first? A woman has no physiological process parallel to ejaculation, but she does have an orgasm which, like the man's, is a discernible physiological event. If we are to take the instruction that "she will begin to give forth seed first" as something that the man can actually observe and thus assure, the man must wait until the woman has an orgasm. Thus the popular notion of "female seed" leads the author of Iggeret Ha-Kodesh to accept and advocate female arousal, for it was assumed that such arousal would assure the birth of sons (who were traditionally more desirable than daughters in Jewish families, as in all patriarchal societies).[13]

Sexual arousal is generally discussed in euphemisms, if at all. The text of the *Iggeret Ha-Kodesh* is among the boldest descriptions of actual sexual practices in traditional literature, and typically it addresses the man and instructs him in his appropriate conduct. There is practically nothing in the rabbinic literature which instructs women in sexual practices other than general admonitions for piety and modesty. If there was any tradition of sexual instruction for young women, it must have been an oral tradition, passed from mother to daughter but never recorded in written texts. There is, however, one exception: a talmudic passage which in itself is rather obscure but in Rashi's interpretation became a bold statement of instruction to daughters in sexual foreplay. The passage contains statements attributed to Rabbi Hisda as "advice for his daughters." Among these is the oblique statement: "He held a jewel in one hand and a *kora* [according to Rashi's interpretation "a crucible," according to the modern commentary of Adin Steinsaltz "a clump of soil"] in the other. He showed them the jewel and did not show them the *kora* until they were suffering and then he showed it to them." (Shabbat 140b). It is unclear what this passage means. The Soncino translation interprets it as a metaphor describing Rabbi Hisda's pedagogic method in giving his daughters advice. However, Rashi interprets it as a sexual metaphor: the jewel is a breast and the *kora* the vagina.

"Rabbi Hisda said to his daughters"—When your husband caresses you to arouse the desire for intercourse and holds the breasts with one hand and "that place" with the other, give him the breasts [at first] to increase his passion and do not give him the place of intercourse too soon, until his passion increases and he is in pain with desire. Then give him [the genitals]. [Rashi on Shabbat 140b]

According to Rashi's interpretation of this passage, Rabbi Hisda's advice to his daughters is essentially a lesson in prolonging foreplay. Rashi's version of Rabbi Hisda's advice is striking, in its frank discussion of sexual play and in its encouragement of prolonging the sexual act and intensifying its power. As against the general prohibition on men's using foreplay to increase their passion the daughters here are instructed by their father in special techniques for achieving mutual arousal.

The passage with Rabbi Hisda's advice and Rashi's interpretation are unusual. Yet as we have shown in other more normative texts, the arousal of the woman is an accepted part of the sexual act. In the varying issues we have discussed such as frequency of sex, the range of permissible sexual practices and the attitude toward sexual arousal and foreplay, there is a common tension between an ascetic impulse to curb sexual expression and a "permissive" tendency toward relative freedom in the conduct of sexual relations. We have presented both specific legislation and nonhalakhic attitudes. If we attempt to compare these two kinds of material, we find that the range of attitudes in the nonlegal sources from the ascetic pole to the "permissive" pole is considerably greater than the range within the Halakhah. Furthermore the Halakhah is generally on the "permissive" side of the spectrum of opinions. Thus, for example, there are several opinions that argue that "abnormal" sexual practices bring about various illnesses and handicaps on either a man or his progeny, yet the Halakhah rules that a man may do with his wife what pleases him and her. Similarly, there is a strong inclination to limit the frequency of sexual relations and regard the times of onah as a maximum for proper and pious sexuality. However, even the Shulhan Arukh, which holds to such an "ascetic" view, does not regard the times of onah as an absolute maximum, and advocates initiating sex with a nursing mother when she indicates her desire

The tension between the relative freedom in sexual practices permitted by the the Halakhah and a more ascetic general attitude toward sexuality is summarized most clearly in Maimonides' ruling on sexual relations in his Mishneh Torah:

A man's wife is permitted to him. Therefore, whatever a man wishes to do with his wife he may do. He may have intercourse whenever he pleases and he may kiss any organ he wishes. And he may have intercourse in a natural or unnatural manner as long as he does not expend semen to no purpose. And nevertheless, the pious way is not to act lightly in this matter, and to sanctify himself during intercourse, as we have explained in the Laws of Knowledge. And he ought not deviate from the common practice, for this thing [intercourse] is really only for procreation. [Maimonides, *Mishneh Torah*, Issurei Bi'ah 21 : 9]

Maimonides rules that the frequency and manner of sexual relations is left up to a man's taste and desires (barring the spilling of seed). One is free to do as he pleases, kiss whatever part of the body he wishes to kiss, and perform intercourse in "a natural or unnatural manner." That is the law. However, Maimonides expresses his discomfort with the latitude allowed by the Halakhah in his counsel to those who wish to follow the pious way: let them not deviate from the common practices which are those related to the procreative side of sex: emphasizing intercourse, minimizing sexual play for pleasure, and, presumably, conducting intercourse in the traditional "missionary" position.

The Halakhah is concerned with the concrete aspects of sexuality: establishing a marital relationship, the frequency of sexual relations, the times of abstention (*niddah*), and of course, more than anything else, with procreation. The Halakhah confines the sexual drive of a man by harnessing it to the sexual rhythms and needs of his wife. Sexual abstention is mandated by the cycle of menstruation. Sexual activity is directed to fulfilling the *mitzvah* of *onah:* meeting and responding to the sexual needs of the woman. The "quiet," introverted sexuality of the woman circumscribes the active, extroverted sexuality of the man. It becomes the center and the regulating mechanism of the intimate marital relationship.

⊰ 6 ⊱

NIDDAH

Laws of the Menstruant

LIKE many other cultures, both in the ancient Near East and in the world at large, Judaism contains a taboo on contact with a menstruating woman. Undoubtedly the taboo is so common since many cultures share the same basic psychological components: fear of bleeding, discomfort with genital discharge, and bewilderment especially on the part of men, at the mysterious cycle of bleeding and its connection to conception and birth. Despite the lack of understanding of the precise physiology of menstruation and conception, many societies came to associate menstruation with death because the lack of menstruation meant conception and life.[1]

In Jewish law the menstruant woman has a defined status: she is a *niddah*, one who is "ostracized" or "excluded." The actual laws which define this status are very complex and they rest on the foundation of the two different contexts in which the menstruant woman figures in biblical law: the laws of purity and impurity, and the sexual prohibitions. The laws of purity and impurity include many instances of contamination besides the case of the *niddah*, such as contact with a corpse, leprosy, seminal discharge, contact with certain insects, and more. All these laws have the same intent: to exclude an impure person (or object) from the divine residence in the Temple. The destructions of the two Temples, first in 586 B.C.E. and again in 70 C.E., removed the concrete locus and justification of the laws of impurity. This historical change made way for the ascendency of the second context and meaning of the laws of *niddah* in the Bible: the sexual prohibitions.

147

After the destruction of the First Temple, an evolution in the laws of *niddah* had already begun to take place. The justification for these laws was shifted from the realm of purity laws to the arena of sexual taboos. This transformation became even more pronounced in the mishnaic and talmudic literature which developed after the destruction of the Second Temple. The transformation also meant a shift from the sphere of public, cultic life to the sphere of family life.

Following this transformation the impurity of a *niddah* retained its legal significance for her intimate relationship with her husband, but lost its importance in the arena of the woman's contact with other members of her family and with strangers. However, while the Halakhah requires segregation of the *niddah* only in her own home and mostly "in the bedroom," many communities preserved a significant measure of segregation in public life as well. Customs of segregation and exclusion prevailed particularly in the realm of the synagogue worship, perhaps because the synagogue was perceived as a symbolic substitute for the Temple.

The laws of *niddah* include innumerable strictures and precautions. Questions about possible violations of these regulations and their exacting details are very prominent in the halakhic literature. The impact of the laws of *niddah* on people's lives was profound since they imposed a set pattern of sexual activity, mandating periods of abstention and physical distancing between husband and wife. Furthermore, by virtue of the fact that purification and resumption of sex normally coincided with ovulation, the laws of *niddah* favored procreation.

The specific laws concerning the *niddah* are derived, as we have said, from the laws of impurity which appear in Leviticus, a book primarily focused on the canons of worship and ritual. The laws of purity were a cornerstone of the ritual practice of the Temple (and local temples prior to the centralization of the cult in Jerusalem). Purity should be understood as a state which permits a person (or object) to approach the place of divine presence such as the Temple. Impurity is a state, caused by numerous factors (listed in Leviticus 11–15), which bars a person from approaching or touching anything connected with God's residence.[2]

The laws of *niddah* are introduced in the context of laws pertaining to bodily excretions which cause a state of impurity. Chapter 15 of Leviticus opens the list of such conditions with the case of a man who has a genital discharge presumably due to some illness. Further on in the chapter we learn that healthy emissions also cause a state of impurity, although of shorter duration.

[16]When a man has an emission of semen, he shall bathe his whole body in water and remain unclean until evening. [17]All cloth or leather on which semen falls shall be washed in water and remain unclean until evening. [18]And if a man has carnal relations with a woman, they shall bathe in water and remain unclean until evening. [Lev. 15 : 16–18]

In the case of a man a genital discharge can be a healthy discharge of semen (either in intercourse or other ejaculation) or an unhealthy one (*zav*). The healthy seminal discharge causes impurity (or uncleanliness—the words are used interchangeably here) which lasts for the duration of the day and which requires washing. An unhealthy discharge causes a state of impurity which lasts for seven days following the cessation of the discharge and the ritual bathing (Lev. 15 : 13). In both cases whatever object is touched by the discharge becomes impure as well, but in the case of an unhealthy discharge the state of impurity is "contagious": anyone or anything which the person with the discharge touches becomes impure as well. Finally, whereas the healthy discharge required only bathing for purification, after an unhealthy discharge one must offer sacrifice at the Temple in order to regain the normal state of purity. Essentially, the treatment of an unhealthy discharge (*zav*) amounts to a system of isolation of victims of venereal disease.

The laws regarding female discharges are analogous though there are some differences in detail. A woman may have a normal discharge of blood when she menstruates (*niddah*), or she may have an abnormal, or unhealthy, discharge of blood (*zavah*). Parallel to the distinction between the laws of impurity for a man with a healthy seminal discharge and one with an unhealthy discharge are the differences in the impurity incurred by the *niddah* and the *zavah*:

[19]When a woman has a discharge, her discharge being blood from her body, she shall remain in her impurity seven days; whoever touches her shall be unclean until evening. [20]Anything that she lies on during her impurity shall be unclean; and anything that she sits on shall be unclean. [21]Anyone who touches her bedding shall wash his clothes, bathe in water, and remain unclean until evening; [22]and anyone who touches any object on which she has sat shall wash his clothes, bathe in water, and remain unclean until evening. [23]Be it the bedding or be it the object on which she has sat, on touching it he shall be unclean until evening. [24]And if a man lies with her, her impurity is communicated to him; he shall be unclean seven days, and any bedding on which he lies shall become unclean.

[25]When a woman has had a discharge of blood for many days, not at the time of her impurity, or when she has a discharge beyond her period of impurity, she shall be unclean, as though at the time of her impurity, as long as her discharge lasts: she shall be unclean. [26]Any bedding on which she lies while her discharge lasts shall be for her like bedding during her impurity; and any object on which she sits shall become unclean, as it does during her impurity: [27]whoever touches them shall be unclean; he shall wash his clothes, bathe in water, and remain unclean until evening.

[28]When she becomes clean of her discharge, she shall count off seven days, and after that she shall be clean. [29]On the eighth day she shall take two turtledoves or two pigeons, and bring them to the priest at the entrance of the Tent of Meeting. [30]The priest shall offer the one as a sin offering and the other as a burnt offering; and the priest shall make expiation on her behalf, for her unclean discharge, before the LORD.

[31]You shall put the Israelites on guard against their uncleanness, lest they die through their uncleanness by defiling My Tabernacle which is among them.

[32]Such is the ritual concerning him who has a discharge and him who has an emission of semen and becomes unclean thereby, [33]and concerning her who is in menstrual infirmity: anyone, that is, male or female, who has a discharge, and also the man who lies with an unclean woman. [Lev. 15 : 19–33]

The text of Leviticus 15 is burdened with detail so that it seems rather confusing at first. The following systematization should help clarify this legislation.

1. For both a man and a woman there are two kinds of discharges which cause impurity: a normal discharge and an abnormal one. For a man the discharge in question is a seminal discharge; for a woman it is a flow of blood.

2. A normal discharge causes a shorter period of impurity than an abnormal one. A normal menstrual period is presumed to last seven days.

3. The person suffering the discharge carries the "highest" degree of impurity, which we shall call "primary impurity."

4. The impure person communicates his or her impurity to other persons or objects, who then may be said to carry a "secondary impurity."

5. A person who touches an impure object (carrying "secondary impurity") contracts impurity as well if the object was touched by a man with an unhealthy discharge or a woman with either a healthy or unhealthy discharge. This may be called a "tertiary impurity."

6. A special case is that of contact through intercourse. In such intimate contact between a man and a woman each one necessarily contracts impurity of the primary level. In addition, a man who has intercourse with a menstruating woman touches the blood itself and therefore becomes impure for the same duration as the *niddah* herself. Communication of impurity through intercourse is discussed in the text only in reference to normal discharges. Presumably intercourse was avoided during an abnormal discharge because of fear of contagion. If one had intercourse inadvertently during a period of abnormal discharge, one observed a period of segregation, offered a sacrifice in atonement, and hoped for the best.

A special case of impurity for a woman is after giving birth. A woman who has given birth is also a *niddah*, but the period of her impurity depends on the gender of her offspring. Leviticus 12 : 1–8 legislates that a woman who gives birth to a son is a *niddah* for seven days, like the menstruant woman. Yet she waits an additional thirty-three days of purification before she may bring a sacrifice to the Temple and regain her purity. For the birth of a girl, the mother is a *niddah* for fourteen days and then must wait an additional sixty-six days before she is purified. In all, after the birth of a son a woman is impure for forty days, after the birth of a daughter for double the time. The reason for the lengthy postpartum period of impurity is biological: bleeding often continues for four to six weeks after giving birth. But the reason for the doubling of the impure period after the birth of a girl is unclear. Perhaps it reflects, as has been suggested by some,[3] the disappointment with the birth of a girl, but this would necessitate seeing the state of impurity as partially punitive, which does not seem to fit the intentions of Leviticus. One conjecture is that underlying this legislation is the sense that the birth of a female, who will one day herself menstruate and give birth, is seen as "doubly bloody" and doubly impure.

The *niddah* going through her normal menstruation is impure only for seven days. After the seven days she bathes herself, washes her clothes, and regains her purity. The importance of establishing a standard period defined as "normal menstrual bleeding" is understood if we realize that prolonged bleeding, even if it comes when menstruation is due, is considered abnormal bleeding. With such a standard established, the distinction between normal menstruation and the abnormal bleeding of a *zavah* can easily be applied by referring to the length of the bleeding period. But in regard to *timing*, the distinction is more difficult to maintain. Any alteration in the regular cycle of menstruation could be considered abnormal. Therefore even in cases of a mere delay in menstruation, where there is no disease or abnormality, the woman would consider herself *zavah*. Once the pattern has been upset, there would be difficulty in reestablishing what is the normal monthly menstruation and what is abnormal bleeding. In addition, it was necessary to distinguish between uterine blood which caused impurity (whether for the *niddah* or the *zavah*) and bleeding originating in the bladder or vaginal walls which, like external bleeding from a wound, did not cause impurity (Niddah 17b).[4]

While the Levitical text makes a seemingly clear-cut distinction between a woman with normal menstrual bleeding and another with abnormal blood flow, further considerations in the Mishnah and Talmud reveal the difficulty in maintaining the distinction. The Talmud reports of the special skill and expertise which some rabbis developed in "examining blood" and deciding whether it is normal or abnormal, and whether it causes impurity or not. Yet the Talmud also reflects the gradual disappearance of this expertise (Niddah 20a–b). The custom of relying on expert examination was gradually abandoned and was replaced by combining the strictures of both sets of laws: the rules for the impurity of the *zavah* and the *niddah*. Women, according to Niddah 66a, turned to themselves: they relied on their own strictness rather than on the examination of bloodstains by an expert rabbi:

Rabbi Zera stated: The daughters of Israel have imposed upon themselves the restriction that even where they observe only a drop of blood the size of a mustard seed, they wait on account of it seven clean days. [Niddah 66a]

Thus postbiblical Halakhah imposed a much stricter code on the *niddah*. Whereas in biblical law the *niddah* was impure for a maximum of seven days, in rabbinic legislation she was impure for up to fourteen days: a maximum of seven of menses, and a subsequent period of seven "white days," free of bleeding.

Having clarified the legislation in Leviticus 15 concerning the *niddah* and the *zavah*, and having shown that the distinction between the two states was abandoned in practice in the talmudic period, we now turn to the central issue in the laws of *niddah*: the prohibition on sexual relations. In Leviticus 15 this issue is dealt with rather briefly. A man who has intercourse with a *niddah* contracts the same impurity ("primary impurity") which affects the woman. He "shall be unclean for seven days and any bed that he lies on shall be unclean" (verse 24). In Leviticus 18, however, sex with a *niddah* appears as a taboo, listed among the sexual transgressions: "You shall not approach and uncover the nakedness of a woman in her menstrual impurity (be-niddat tum'atah)." (Leviticus 18 : 19, see also Leviticus 20 : 18)

In Leviticus 15 intercourse with a *niddah* is treated as a special instance of contact with an impure person and communication of impurity. There is no particular gravity attached to it, let alone indication that it is considered an offense or a sin. This "neutral" treatment fits with the general tone of Leviticus 15, where impurity is an objective, if undesirable, state which one should seek to avoid and should remove by following proper ritual. The state of impurity in and of itself is no transgression, only approaching the Temple in such a state is. God cannot tolerate the presence of an impure person within his domain and anyone approaching the Temple while impure is in imminent danger. The Israelites must follow the laws of purity and avoid the Temple while impure as a measure of self-protection, "lest they die." Similarly, Numbers 19 : 20 threatens: "And anyone who becomes impure and does not undergo purification, that person shall be cut off from the community for he has defiled the Temple of God."

While the state of impurity in general and the state of the *niddah* in particular are not associated with sinfulness or condemnation in Leviticus 15, in two late books in the Bible, Ezekiel and Ezra, the term *niddah* appears as a metaphor for moral impurity and debasement. Ezra, in his attempt to convince the people of Judea to send away their foreign wives (purify the race), reminds them of God's warning that they must not mingle with the local population whose immoral sexual practices have defiled the land. "The land which you are coming to inherit is *eretz niddah* [a land which is like a *niddah*], defiled by the peoples of the land in their abominations, who filled her from end to end in their pollution. And now, do not give your daughters to their sons nor take their daughters for your sons" (Ezra 9 : 10–11). Ezekiel uses the term *niddah* in a similar way to condemn the immoral ways of his people: "And the word of God was upon me saying: Son of man! the house of Israel are sitting on their land and defiling it in their ways and their plots; like the impurity of the *niddah* is their way before me" (Ezek. 36 : 17). Both Ezekiel and Ezra were priests: they are probably displaying the particular sensitivity of the priestly tradition to matters of purity and impurity, since the laws of impurity were closely associated with the Temple and its ritual. Both texts quoted here also reveal a link between the term *niddah* and the notion that the land itself becomes impure. This connection goes back to the phrasing and conceptualization of the sexual prohibitions in Leviticus 18 and 20. In Leviticus 20 : 21 the term *niddah* is extended to refer to a forbidden woman: a brother's wife who may not be approached because of the prohibition on incest.

Leviticus 18 lists all the sexual transgressions including incest, adultery, homosexuality, bestiality, and sexual relations with a *niddah*. All these practices are attributed to the peoples who have surrounded the Israelites, "the practices of the land of Egypt in which you had dwelled and those of the land of Canaan into which I bring you" (Lev. 18 : 23). These sexual practices have, according to this Levitical text, defiled the land in which those people lived until they could no longer be tolerated upon its face:

[24]Do not defile yourselves in any of those ways, for it is by such that the nations which I am casting out before you defiled themselves. [25]Thus the land became defiled; and I called it to account for its iniquity, and the land spewed out its inhabitants. [Lev. 18 : 24–25]

The sexual transgressions enumerated in Leviticus 18 are perceived as so intolerable that the very land upon which they are committed becomes defiled and rejects its inhabitants. Underlying this passage is a notion of an organic harmony of land and people which is destroyed when the people violate elementary sexual taboos. All the sexual prohibitions are grave offenses to be punished severely: "Anyone doing one of these hateful things, whatever it may be, must be cut off [*ve-nikhretu*] from his people" (Lev. 18 : 29).

There is, then, a striking contradiction between chapter 15 and chapters 18 and 20 of Leviticus: in the former text intercourse with a *niddah* causes a state of impurity but there is no hint that it is considered a sin, while in the latter it is an offensive sexual transgression. Anyone who violates the sexual proscriptions listed in Leviticus 18 and 20 is threatened with *karet*, being "cut off from his people." *Karet* appears in the biblical text as capital punishment inflicted by God (or at least there is no explicit mandate or specifications for a court's carrying out this punishment). In postbiblical sources *karet* is defined as punishment at the hand of heaven, presumably premature death. Though not in practice punishable by society, an offense punishable by *karet* is considered a very grave one indeed.[5]

How do we resolve the contradiction between the two treatments of sexual relations with a menstruant woman? The traditional solu-

tion is simple—Leviticus 15 considers accidental intercourse with
a *niddah* while Leviticus 18 and 20 refer to intentional relations:

"If a man sleeps with her"—without evil intention, only unwittingly does
he lie with her, her menstrual blood coming when she is with him. And
this is the explanation [for the contradiction in this passage] since there is
[a punishment of] a *karet* upon the one who lies with a *niddah* on purpose and such is also the law for [intercourse with] a *zavah* even though
it is not mentioned here. [Ibn Ezra, Commentary on Lev. 15 : 24]

If a person commits a transgression without intention, by accident, he or she is not liable for it. Leviticus 15, according to Ibn
Ezra, envisions such a case for a man who has intercourse with a
niddah. In fact, Ibn Ezra explains, the man initiates sexual relations with the woman before her menstruation and it is during the
act of intercourse that the flow of blood unexpectedly begins. Due
to exactly this possibility the rabbis instituted an unclean premen-
strual day. That is, the state of impurity begins *before* the actual
flow of blood is discerned. For women who had regular menstrual
periods, knowing the exact timing of the cycle was therefore very
important. Women who could not accurately predict the onset of
their menstruation had to take the precaution of examining themselves before every act of intercourse. The examination was performed by inserting a soft cloth into the vagina and checking for
bloodstains. The procedure is elaborated in great detail in Tractate
Niddah (especially Chapter 2), which also takes care to provide
for women not competent to examine themselves. Such women,
"the deaf-mute, the imbecile, the blind, and the mentally de-
ranged," are to be guided in the examination and prepared for the
purification in the *mikveh* by "competent women" (Niddah 2 : 1).

Ibn Ezra shows that the contradiction between Leviticus 15 and
Leviticus 18 and 20 can be harmonized through traditional techniques of interpretation, by identifying a difference between the
texts. The difference he finds, intentional act vs. error, justifies
different halakhic rulings. However, a literal reading of the biblical text leaves this explanation somewhat unconvincing. If indeed
accidental intercourse is what is intended in Leviticus 15, why is
this not mentioned explicitly? In the cases of other grave offenses,

such as capital crimes, the biblical text is careful to distinguish between premeditated murder and accidental manslaughter (Numbers 32). One might argue that the case of capital crime involves the threat of blood vengeance and is also much graver than our case, so that the distinction is made there but not in the case of intercourse with a *niddah*. However, another proof is more compelling. Leviticus 4 outlines the general law pertaining to crimes committed accidentally. While the offender is not as liable as he or she would be if the crime were committed knowingly, a sacrifice is still required to atone for the offense—a special sacrifice mandated for accidental transgressions (*shegaga*). Leviticus 15 makes no mention, however, of a sacrifice required for the unintentional transgression of intercourse with a *niddah*. It is not reasonable to assume that such a detail would be omitted, especially since sacrifices are mentioned in relation to the purification of the man who recovers from an abnormal genital discharge (verse 14) and a *zavah* who has recovered from abnormal bleeding (verse 28).

The evidence seems compelling that we have a definite discrepancy between the law cited in Leviticus 15 concerning intercourse with a *niddah* and the law stated in Leviticus 18 and 20. A historical explanation (rather than harmonization) of the discrepancy must postulate that one text precedes the other, one overrides the ruling of the other. Yet what might explain a change in the law, and which text supersedes? A textual analysis seems to yield no immediate answer since both texts are ascribed to the Levitical author and there is no compelling reason to read one text as later than the other. Other grounds must then be found for distinguishing between the texts and interpreting the change in the law.

Let us return to Leviticus 15. In this chapter the justification for the preoccupation with the details of impurity and its transmission is the divine presence among men: "You shall put the Israelites on guard against their uncleanness lest they die through their uncleanness by defiling My Tabernacle which is among them" (verse 31). The presence of the Temple (or numerous local temples) is vital for the laws of purity: it gives them a geographical locus. There is a specific territory which one may not enter in an impure state. Leviticus 15 must be understood as a text closely related to the presence of a Temple.

The laws of impurity and the laws of the *niddah* hinge on the presence of a "holy territory" where impurity is not tolerated. In 586 B.C.E. the Temple was destroyed and the religious and political elite of Judah was exiled from its country. The awareness of the territorial presence of God began to diminish. Placing sexual relations with a *niddah* among the sexual transgressions in Leviticus 18 and 20 may possibly be a response to the destruction of the first Temple. Leviticus 18 and 20 enumerate the sexual prohibitions, the laws which guarantee "sexual order" and establish the structure of family and society. When the prohibition on sex with a *niddah* appears in this set of laws, the vital core of the laws of *niddah* is shifted from the sphere of the Temple to the orbit of the family. Thus the power of the laws of *niddah* is preserved despite the disappearance of the Temple.

The evidence for this historical explanation of the contradiction between Leviticus 15 and Leviticus 18 and 20 is circumstantial. The material in the biblical text is so scanty that only conjecture is possible. In the biblical text we have only a partial reflection of this historical process in the passages mentioned earlier from Ezekiel and Ezra, who use the term *niddah* as a synonym for sinfulness, rather than a strictly technical term for a state that requires keeping one's distance from the Temple grounds and its vessels. However, in postbiblical sources, sources following the destruction of the second Temple in Jerusalem in 70 C.E., the picture is much clearer. Beginning with talmudic material and continuing through the medieval period, we see the transfer of the focus of the laws of *niddah* from the realm of ritual impurity to the sphere of marital and sexual relations. In the following sources we observe a gradual fundamental transformation in the laws of *niddah*; the meaning and focus of these laws shifts from the fear and control of impurity to the regimentation of sexual relations:

If [a married woman has] four [female servants] she may lounge in an easy chair: Rabbi Isaac ben Hanina stated in the name of Rav Huna: Although it has been said "She may lounge in an easy chair" she should nevertheless fill his cup for him, make his bed, and wash his face, hands and feet.

Rabbi Isaac ben Hanina further stated in the name of Rav Huna: All kinds of work which a wife performs for her husband a *niddah* may also perform for her husband, with the exception of filling his cup, making his bed, and washing his face, hands and feet.

As to "making his bed" Raba explained that [the prohibition] applies only in his presence, but in his absence it does not matter. With regard to "filling his cup" Samuel's wife made a change [by serving] him with her left hand. [The wife of] Abbaye placed it on the edge of the wine cask. Raba's wife [placed it] at the head-side of his couch and Rav Papa's [wife placed it] on his footstool. [Ketubot 61a]

The body of this passage discusses the kind of chores a *niddah* may not perform for her husband, and ways of getting around the legislation. But the context is very illuminating: the discussion appears with a passage which outlines the domestic duties of a wife: "all kinds of work which a wife performs for her husband." Following a general discussion of a woman's duties toward her husband and home we find a more limited exposition of what duties a woman is exempt from if she has one servant (who takes over some of the chores), two servants, etc. The final point is the case of a woman who has four servants (presumably four would be enough to take care of all chores in the house and all services for the husband). If a woman has four servants she may, according to Rav Huna, lounge in an easy chair all day and do nothing. However, she must still do three things for her husband: fill his cup, prepare his bed, and wash his face, hands, and feet. Clearly these three functions are not considered mere "work" or "chores"; otherwise they would not be distinguished from other functions. These acts concretize the special relationship between husband and wife. The filling of the wine cup and the washing of face, hands, and feet exemplify the woman's attending to her husband and honoring him, while the making and preparing of the bed suggest the sexual intimacy inherent in marriage. Since these three functions are a symbolic condensation of the essential qualities of the marital relationship, a wife must perform them even if she has sufficient number of servants to perform all the domestic chores.[6]

It is for this very reason that a *niddah* may perform any domes-

tic duties for her husband except these three, for during the period
of the *niddut* the normal intimate relation between husband and
wife is suspended. It is actually sexual relations that must cease
during the impurity of *niddah*. Yet when sexual relations are
halted, the nature of intimacy between husband and wife is so
fundamentally altered that other signs of intimacy must be
changed as well. So while a *niddah* continues to perform her
normal domestic function and chores, those acts symbolic of sexual relations and intimacy are suspended. However, as we see in
the last part of the passage, various rabbis report the ways their
wives have found of minimizing the changes even in the three
symbolic functions. Raba held that the wife may prepare the bed
so long as her husband is not present. The logic is obvious: if
making the bed is forbidden because it is suggestive of sexual
intimacy and intercourse, this really only holds if the sexual
partner, the husband, is in sight. If he is away, making the bed
loses any erotic overtones or implications and becomes a mere
household chore. The wives of Samuel, Abbaye, Raba, and Rav
Papa had ways of filling their husbands' cups while indicating
through some change of position or manner that things are not
"normal" and that both husband and wife are fully aware of the
special distance and separation of the period of *niddut*. The symbolic gesture of placing the cup in an unusual spot, on a footstool,
for example, becomes a private code between husband and wife. It
indicates more subtly than the complete elimination of this function the altered nature of the relationship between husband and
wife when the woman is a *niddah*.

But where are the precautions against transmitting impurity?
The rabbis here list only three prohibitions; meanwhile the *niddah* may cook, clean, wash, etc., and by touching every object in
the house transmit her impurity to her husband, the rest of the
family members, and any visitor who sits down or eats in her
house. Surely, the rabbis knew every detail of the laws in Leviticus 15, but by their time the transmission of impurity from the
niddah to another person had lost its significance: their only concern with the impurity of the *niddah* is within the sphere of intimate relations with her husband.

Rashi, in a responsum about the laws of niddah, makes the point even clearer: in his day the transmission of impurity had become immaterial so that whatever the niddah touched could be freely handled by others. His statement exemplifies another important aspect of the Halakhah on niddah: some of the strictures of Leviticus 15 are observed after all, even in his day, but not because of concern for impurity. Rather they are followed in order to accentuate the special state of the niddah and the separation from her husband which this state requires:

Vessels which the niddah touches in our day are clean for her husband. For people in this age are made impure by graves, and the tent [house] of a dead person, and a reptile, and carcass, and a corpse, and they will not be purified until our King "shall throw upon us pure water to purify us" (Ezek. 35 : 26). Thus, vessels which the niddah touches are permitted to be touched and used. However, we restrict ourselves and do not eat in the same bowl with her nor the leftovers of her food, nor do we sit on her seat or receive anything from her hand except through another [person]. And we give her vessels and a bowl, sheets and pillows and blankets to use during her days of niddah. When she becomes clean again she launders in water those clothes which have a stain and the rest of the things which she sat in she just rinses in water and that suffices. And this custom is proper in order to prevent the habituation of sin [averah]. However, the prohibition of impurity [tum'ah] does not pertain here. [Rashi, Responsa, No. 336 (Elfenbein edition)]

Rashi's statement begins with a general observation: "Vessels which the niddah touches in our day are clean for her husband." In other words, whereas biblical legislation is clear in describing the transfer of impurity from the niddah to whatever dishes and household articles she touches (Lev. 15 : 20ff) in Rashi's time, "our day," this no longer holds. Rather the vessels which the niddah touches and handles her husband may use with impunity. How does Rashi explain this change? He argues that the laws of purity and impurity are in general ignored in his day. People become impure by contact with any number of "agents of impurity": graves, corpses, reptiles, etc. But this has no practical implications because they do not expect to become purified "until our King 'shall throw upon us pure water to purify us,' " that is, until the days of the Messiah.

Rashi states categorically that in his days impurity is irrelevant and people become impure in various ways without worrying about it. Priests, however, are an exception; they continue to observe at least some of the prohibitions on contact with sources of impurity, and will, to this day, avoid entering a graveyard or a house in which a dead person lies. However, Rashi says, though contracting impurity is not a problem anymore, "we restrict ourselves" and keep separate seating, food and dishes, as well as using special beddings. All of these acts of segregation and separation which he lists are intended "to prevent the habituation of sin, but the prohibition of impurity does not pertain here." In other words the separation is important in order to keep one away from sin, namely, to remove the chance of intimacy between husband and wife. The specific trappings of this conscientious separation of husband and wife are taken directly from Leviticus 15. The details are the same but the purposes have changed: not prevention of contracting impurity but prevention of intimacy and sexual relations.

The crucial point of the restrictions mentioned by Rashi is avoiding contact between husband and wife. That is clear from the fact that the couple may use a stranger to transfer objects between them (the husband may receive an object from her "through another"). If purity were at stake, one person is as "endangered" by contact with a niddah as another. Whether her husband or another man, whoever accepts an object from a niddah would become impure. But in fact Rashi is only concerned with the husband's receiving an object from his wife when she is a niddah.

The same emphasis on the intimate relationship of husband and wife as the focus of the laws of niddah can be seen in a passage from Tractate Shabbat which rules on whether a niddah may use makeup and colorful clothes. Here we see a tension between the desire to eliminate any form of sexual arousal during the niddah period (including the woman's making herself attractive with makeup and pretty clothes), and the need to sustain enough attraction between husband and wife to weather the period of separation without damage to the marital relationship:

The early authorities said that she may not pretty herself with makeup nor put on colorful clothes, until Rabbi Akiva came and taught: If you hold this view you will soon make her unattractive to her husband and eventually he will divorce her. [Shabbat 64b][7]

The early authorities take a hard line and forbid a woman to make herself physically attractive during her *niddah* period. This indicates that not only actual sexual contact is forbidden, but also those things which lead to thoughts of sexual intimacy.

However, this stringent view is overturned by the ruling of Rabbi Akiva. Akiva holds that a woman should be allowed to use makeup and wear pretty clothes during her *niddut* so that her husband should not lose his interest in her during the period of separation. He reasons that if a woman is not appealing to her husband for twelve to fourteen days every month, he might come to disregard her, even despise her and eventually divorce her. This view is in line with Rabbi Akiva's opinion that a man may divorce his wife even if he has merely found another woman more attractive (Gittin 90a), since he regarded physical attraction as a very powerful impulse. He therefore allowed a man to divorce his wife because of his attraction for another woman on the one hand, and on the other hand, tried to prevent such a threat to marriage by permitting a woman to remain attractive to her husband during *niddah*.

Though Rabbi Akiva's permissive rule allowing the *niddah* to wear makeup and pretty clothes was accepted as *halakhah*, it was accepted reluctantly. The midrashic compilation *Avot De-Rabbi Natan* (generally dated to the third or fourth century) states: "The rabbis are displeased with a woman who adorns herself during the days of her *niddah*" (Chap. 2). The *Shulhan Arukh* states in a similar vein: "Only with great reluctance did the Sages allow her to adorn herself" (Even Ha-Ezer 195 : 9).[8]

We find the emphasis on husband—wife intimacy in a twentieth-century guidebook for observant women as well. *Daughter of Israel (Bat Yisrael)*, by Kalman Kahana, is a compilation of *halakhot* to guide women in the observance of family life and purity. In a passage devoted to particularly "modern" problems we find

instructions regarding traveling together in a car or other vehicle
during the woman's menstruation:

> 11. If they are travelling for pleasure they may not sit together in an
> automobile, boat or wagon unless someone else sits between them, or
> they may sit on separate benches. If they are not taking a pleasure trip,
> they may sit on the same seat provided that they take care not to touch
> each other. [Kalman Kahana, *Daughter of Israel*, "The Conduct of Hus-
> band and Wife during the *Niddah* Period"]

When on a pleasure trip the restrictions concerning closeness and
contact between the couple are stricter because a pleasure trip is
more conducive to feelings of intimacy and desire for sexual relations. In the case of a pleasure trip a stranger must sit between the
husband and wife unless they sit on separate benches. Again, the
impurity of the menstruant woman is irrelevant for the stranger; it
is not even mentioned. The significant factor is the possibility of
intimacy. Since on a business, or nonpleasure trip one is less
inclined to desire intimacy, the husband and wife may sit on the
same bench, unseparated by the presence of a stranger so long as
they are careful to avoid actual physical contact.

Another example is Joseph Karo's ruling in his commentary on
the Tur regarding purification by immersion in a *mikveh* (*tevilah*)
after the period of *niddah*:

> It has become the accepted opinion that prompt *tevilah* is not a *mitvah*
> [in itself], and therefore you do not find a woman who immerses [in the
> *mikveh*] when her husband is out of town. Nevertheless, if her husband is
> in town it is a *mitzvah* to immerse promptly. And if she delays her
> *tevilah* in order to annoy her husband she is committing a transgression.
> [*Bet Yosef* on Tur, Yoreh De'ah 193]

Karo reports the general opinion that purification in and of itself
is not a duty: it is only a duty when resumption of sexual relations
depends on it. Therefore he states that you will not find women
who observe the purification ritual after every menstruation if
they cannot engage in sexual relations anyway because their husbands are absent. For similar reasons it is generally the practice
that unmarried women do not go to the *mikveh* for purification.

Thus a woman usually performs her first *tevilah* before her wedding, rather than after her first menses.

Karo adds a note of caution to his statement that *tevilah* is not a
mitzvah: a woman who purposely defers purification in order to
"annoy her husband" (that is, to prevent the resumption of sexual
activity) is committing a sin. Karo's statement hits at a delicate
point, for the laws of *niddah* allow a woman who so wishes to force
her husband to abstain from sexual relations. As long as a woman
has not purified herself in a *mikveh* she continues to be a *niddah*
and is forbidden to her husband by the Halakhah. This allows a
woman to withhold sex from her husband without formally refusing sexual relations and becoming a *moredet* (see Chapter 3 on
divorce). It is difficult to ascertain whether this was a common
practice. However, along with repeated praises and admonitions to
women to observe the laws of *niddah* we find many cases in the
responsa literature where sex during *niddah* is at issue. Often we
can detect the mutual accusations between husband and wife: the
wife charges the husband with initiating sex during *niddah* while
he suggests that she causes this by deferring her *tevilah* and thus
making herself unavailable for sexual relations.

The fundamental impetus behind the shift in the laws of *niddah*
from a focus on purity and impurity to a sexual prohibition was
the destruction of the Temple. Rashi's writing is pragmatic: his
responsum cited above reflects this shift but does not ponder or
explain its reason. A theoretical discussion of the original meaning and justification of the laws of *niddah* and their crucial depen-
dence on the presence of the Temple appears in Maimonides'
Guide to the Perplexed. This is to be expected since the *Guide* is a
philosophical work. The context for this discussion is a passage in
the *Guide* which deals with the rationale of the laws of purity and
impurity and their relation to the divine purpose:

[On the laws of impurity]: Accordingly many purposes are achieved by
means of these laws. One of them is to keep men away from disgusting
things [e.g., the impurity of reptiles, carcasses, etc.]. The second is to
safeguard the Sanctuary. The third is to protect what is generally accepted and customary for, as you shall hear presently, unpleasant restrictions were imposed on the Sabians in cases of uncleanness. The fourth is

to ease unpleasant restrictions and to order things in such a manner that questions of uncleanness and cleanness should not prevent a man from engaging in any of his occupations; for this matter of uncleanness and cleanness concerns only the *Holy Places* and *holy things*, nothing else: "She shall touch no holy thing nor come into the Sanctuary" (Lev. 12 : 4).

As for the rest, there is no sin if one remains unclean as long as one wishes, and eats, as one wishes, ordinary food [which has not been consecrated in the manner of the sacrificial "meal"] that has become unclean.

It is generally known that according to the customs observed up to our day by the Sabians in the lands of the East (I refer to the remnant of the Magians) the menstruating woman [*niddah*] remains isolated in her house; the places on which she treads are burnt; whoever speaks with her becomes unclean; and if a wind that blows passes over a *niddah* and a clean person the latter becomes unclean. See how great the difference is between this and our rule: "All various kinds of work that a wife does for her husband are also done by the *niddah* for her husband except for washing his face," etc. (Ketubot 61a). It is only forbidden to have intercourse with her in the days in which she is unclean and defiled.

. . . for us, we only claim that something is unclean or clean with regard to holy things and the Sanctuary. [Maimonides, *Guide to the Perplexed*, III : 47][10]

Maimonides cites a number of justifications for the laws of impurity, but he emphasizes that the laws concerning the *niddah* aim to keep her away from the Temple and from sacred objects only. They do not intend to interfere with her daily life and work. He cites the example of the Sabians, a people he believed lived during the biblical period and practiced a polytheistic, superstitious religion. In his general theory of the reasons for the commandments Maimonides accords an important place to the Sabian culture. He understands many of the *mitzvot* as intentional "antidotes" to Sabian practice, that is, purposefully designed to contradict Sabian custom in order to wean the Israelites away from this polytheistic culture that surrounded them. In the same vein he explains the laws of *niddah*. The Sabians supposedly imposed total segregation on the menstruant woman and considered any contact with her a contamination and threat. The purpose of the laws of *niddah* in the Bible is to drastically reduce the number of activities from which the *niddah* is barred and to permit her to continue her normal domestic activities. Therefore, according to Maimonides, "it is only forbidden to have intercourse with her in the days in which she is unclean." Most other things are permitted.

The principle which allows this drastic limitation of prohibitions, according to Maimonides, is the place of the Temple in the framework of the laws of impurity. The uncleanness which in the Sabian culture mandated total segregation of the menstruant is limited in Jewish law only to the sphere of the Temple, since "we only claim that something is unclean or clean with regard to holy things and the Sanctuary." In her private domain the *niddah* continued to engage in most normal activities except for intimate relations with her husband.

We have argued that the laws of *niddah* underwent a fundamental transformation. Their connection to the laws of impurity was loosened and they became part of the laws regarding sexual transgressions. This process entailed a movement from the public cultic life to the arena of private family life. The intention of the biblical legislation was indeed to exclude the *niddah* from cultic life in order to prevent her from approaching the Temple. Postbiblical Halakhah shifted the restrictions on the *niddah* to the private realm of husband—wife relations. Thus we find more restrictions on the contact of a *niddah* with her husband than on her contact with any other member of the community.

However, while the Halakhah restricts the *niddah* in her relationship with her husband but not in her interaction with other family members, friends, and society at large, the custom of many Jewish communities did curtail the activities of the *niddah* in the public sphere. For example, it was common for women to abstain from synagogue during their period of *niddut*. This is so despite the fact that the laws of *niddah* proper do not exclude a woman from attending synagogue since it is of no consequence if others come in contact with her and become impure, and since the Torah scroll, the "holy object" in a synagogue, is immune to impurity. Perhaps this custom prevailed because the synagogue is symbolic of the Temple where in biblical times the presence of an impure person was indeed prohibited. Perhaps it is also because the degree of isolation of the *niddah* from public affairs in general was greater in practice than was mandated by the Halakhah.

All persons who are impure read the Torah and recite the Shema, and pray [in the synagogue]. . . . [*Shulhan Arukh*, Orah Hayyim 84 : 1]

Now there are those who have written that a *niddah*, during the days that she sees [blood] ought not to enter the synagogue, nor pray or mention the Holy Name or touch a [Torah] book (*Hagahot Maimoniyot*) and there are those who say that she is permitted [to do] all those things; and that is the [correct] essence [of the Halakhah] (Rashi, on Hilkhot Niddah). But the custom in these countries is according to the first view. And during the "white days" it is the custom to permit even in the places where they are accustomed to rule more strictly. On the High Holidays and Yom Kippur, she can enter the synagogue like other women for otherwise it would cause her great sorrow to remain outside while everyone congregates [in the synagogue]. [Commentary of Rema (Moses Isserles)]

The *Shulhan Arukh* begins with the general legislation that all those who have become impure are permitted to participate in the three major events of public worship: the reading of the Torah, the recitation of the Shema (which is the cardinal declaration of the monotheistic faith), and prayer. Though he addresses the problem of men who are the active participants in public worship, this rule is also applicable to women.

The commentary of Moses Isserles (sixteenth century, Poland) indicates that though the Halakhah does not exclude the *niddah*, the prevailing custom in his community, and others, is to bar women from the synagogue during their state of *niddut*. Isserles first cites the opinion of those who are more restricting: they hold that the *niddah*, during the days of actual menstruation (as opposed to the seven "white days" after menstruation has ceased and before purification), is excluded from normal worship. She may not enter the synagogue, she may not pray or recite any blessing which would force her to pronounce the Divine Name, and she may not touch the Torah scroll. Another commentary on the *Shulhan Arukh*, *Turei Zahav* of David Ha-Levi (died 1667) cites the opinion of Solomon Luria (older contemporary of Isserles) that the *niddah* must be careful "not to look at the Torah scroll when the cantor shows it to the congregation." As against this view Isserles states in the name of Rashi that "she is permitted [to do] all those things." From the halakhic point of view Isserles sides with Rashi's opinion, that the *niddah* may enter the synagogue and participate in all the services in the usual way. However, he states, the custom in the communities of eastern Europe is to exclude the *niddah* from synagogue worship, with but two exceptions. First, the exclusion only applies to the days of actual menstruation, though the laws of *niddah* prohibiting sexual relations apply to the "white days" as well. Second, during the High Holidays, when public worship is of greatest importance, the *niddah* is permitted to attend synagogue "like other women." Interestingly, the justification given for this leniency is not a halakhic or religious one, such as an obligation to participate in the period of atonement, but a personal-psychological one. The *niddah* would experience "great sorrow" if she had to remain outside the synagogue while everyone else in the community gathered inside. To abstain from the synagogue on a regular day when other members of the community are absent, each for his or her own reason, is one thing, but to be excluded on the High Holidays when everyone is present in the synagogue is too painful.

The commentary of Isserles exemplifies what was true for Jewish communities in general: while the Halakhah does not mandate exclusion of the *niddah* from public life and ritual, customs and actual practice did curtail her considerably. This was particularly true for activities connected with public worship and the synagogue, perhaps, as we have suggested, because of the symbolic identity of the synagogue and the Temple. Yet there were even more extreme tendencies in the treatment of the *niddah*. These are expressed most strikingly in a medieval work of unknown origin entitled *Baraita De-Niddah* (or *Baraita De-Masekhet Niddah*). This brief treatise is a pseudepigraphic work, that is, it pretends to have been written in an early period, long before its actual composition, and adopts an archaic style. Its name establishes its claim of antiquity, pretending to be a collection of *beraitot*, texts dating from the tanaitic period (c. first to third centuries) which have been excluded from the Mishnah. The Talmud includes many citations of *beraitot* usually brought in order to explain, support, or challenge rulings or opinions in the Mishnah.

The *Baraita De-Niddah* is a difficult and sometimes peculiar text, and scholars question not only its origin and dates but even its place within the boundaries of normative Judaism. Some have even speculated that the treatise may have originated among the Karaites or other heretical circles.[11] Be that as it may, the *Baraita De-Niddah* made a definite entry into mainstream opinions through the writing of Nachmanides and exercised influence on many later authorities. Nachmanides is the first to quote it in his commentary on Genesis 31 where the case of a menstruant woman is in question. The case is the story of Rachel, who stole the household idols [*terafim*] of her father when Jacob escaped with her and her sister Leah from the house of Laban, his father-in-law. Laban, Rachel's father, upon discovering the escape and the disappearance of the idols, chased Jacob and his family and challenged him. Jacob, who knew nothing of Rachel's theft, denied that he had the idols with him. Laban requested permission to conduct a search and Jacob consented. When Laban entered Rachel's quarters he found her seated on her camel. She begged his pardon not to rise from her seat saying she "has the way of women." Laban agreed and fell for her trick: the idols were stashed in the camel's saddle.

Nachmanides comments on Rachel's apology that she cannot get up, noting, at first, that she has a rather lame excuse.

"Let not my Lord be angry that I cannot rise up before you." I do not understand what kind of an apology this is. Do women in that condition [menstruation] not rise up or stand? Perhaps she said [to him] that her head and limbs were heavy and she was sick on account of her menstruation, for that is common among them, especially those such as Rachel whose birth-giving powers are diminished since they have little [menstrual] blood and menstruation presses heavily upon them.

The correct interpretation appears to me to be that in ancient days menstruants were kept very isolated. They were always referred to as *niddot* [literally, excluded ones] due to their isolation since they did not approach people and did not speak with them. For the ancients in their wisdom knew that their breath is harmful, and their gaze detrimental and has ill effect, just as the philosophers ["scientists"] have explained. I will yet mention their experiences in this matter.

And the menstruants dwelled isolated in tents where no one else entered, just as our rabbis have mentioned in the *Baraita De-Niddah*. "A scholar is forbidden to greet a *niddah*. Rabbi Nehemiah says: Even the utterance of her mouth is unclean. Said Rabbi Yohanan: One is forbidden to walk behind a *niddah* and tread upon her footsteps, which themselves are as unclean as a corpse, and so is the dust upon which the *niddah* has stepped, and it is forbidden to derive any benefit from her work."

Therefore, Rachel said: It would be proper for me to rise before my lord to kiss his hands, but "the way of women is upon me" and I cannot come near you nor walk at all in the tent lest you tread upon the dust of my feet. And Laban kept silent and did not answer her because it was customary not to converse with them at all since the speech of a *niddah* was unclean. [Nachmanides (Ramban), Commentary on Gen. 31 : 35]

Nachmanides explains the puzzling situation, Rachel's apparent disrespect for her father and Laban's acceptance of a seemingly poor excuse, by reconstructing the customs of the period. He gives a historical-anthropological description of the situation: the customs which prevailed "in ancient times" justify Rachel's declining to rise up from the camel and Laban's acquiescence. Since in those days the very footsteps of the *niddah* were unclean and transmitted impurity, Rachel was protecting her father from her impurity by avoiding the ground of the tent. Laban accepted her explanation without comment because it was customary to shun any talk with the *niddah*, since even her speech, though ephemeral, was considered unclean.

But Nachmanides' interpretation and description of the customs of "ancient days" is not a mere detached reconstruction of a distant past. First of all, he derived his description of the treatment of the *niddah* in antiquity from the *Baraita De-Niddah*, as he clearly states. But the *Baraita De Niddah*, though it purports to be a tanaitic text, was most probably treated as relevant in Nachmanides' time, as it was in later periods. The best proof for the regard for *Baraita De-Niddah* is indeed Nachmanides himself. He states: "the ancients in their wisdom knew that their breath is harmful," etc.—"knew," not "thought," and knew "in their wisdom." Furthermore Nachmanides claims support for the wisdom of the ancients, as expressed in the *Baraita De-Niddah*, from "the philosophers," the scientists either of his day or of the Greek tradition. Nachmanides was then sympathetic to the treatment of the *niddah* according to the strictures of *Baraita De-Niddah* and to the attitude toward menstruation and the menstruant woman which underlay those rules. The rules of the *Baraita De-Niddah* are clearly extreme and in some instances in direct contradiction to the Halakhah.

We may have questions about the degree to which the laws of *niddah* limited and curtailed the public life of women in different communities at various times. But there is no doubt that these laws placed profound restrictions on the sexual and intimate relations between husband and wife. First and foremost the laws of *niddah* eliminated sex for up to fifteen days every month, so that the laws of *onah* which prescribe the frequency of sexual activity really only apply to a little bit better than half one's married life. This restriction did not always sit well with every Jew. Violations of the ban on sexual relations with a *niddah* are discussed often in the Halakhah, particularly violations occurring during the "white days," i.e., the seven days between the cessation of the menstrual flow and the purification at the *mikveh* (ritual bath). In fact in *Noda Bi-Yehudah*, the responsa of Yehezkel Landau of eighteenth-century Prague (*Mahadura Tinyana*, Even Ha-Ezer no. 91), we read about a man who was heard by his neighbors shouting and "attacking the rabbis for instituting the restriction of the white days" when intercourse is prohibited. That man is also reported to have convinced his wife that one need not follow those rabbinical strictures. Already in the Talmud we find that the rabbis are aware of the impact the laws of *niddah* have in regulating the "sexual rhythm" of every couple. In the Talmud we find an attempt to point to the positive side of this regulation of one's sex life:

It was taught: Rabbi Meir used to say: Why did the Torah ordain that the uncleanness of menstruation should continue for seven days? Because being in constant contact with his wife [a husband might] develop a loathing toward her. The Torah therefore ordained: Let her be unclean for seven days in order that she shall be beloved by her husband as at the time of her first entry into the bridal chamber. [Niddah 31b]

The explanation is not surprising: familiarity breeds contempt and an imposed separation makes the woman much more desirable to her husband when sexual relations are permitted. The prohibition on sexual relations during *niddah* therefore serves to heighten the desire for sex and its pleasure during the period when it is permitted.[12]

Another significant consequence of the laws of *niddah* has to do with procreation. A woman may resume sexual relations twelve to fourteen days after the onset of her menstruation (depending on the exact length of the bleeding) after immersing herself in the *mikveh*. For most women this coincides fairly closely with the time of ovulation in the monthly cycle. The time of ovulation is for most women the optimal time for conception. The regulation of sexual relations by means of the laws of *niddah* favors conception and procreation. With modern advances in physiological knowledge about conception and fertility, rabbis became aware that some women who seemed infertile could not conceive simply because their ovulation occurred earlier than is normal. In such cases the rabbis usually permitted shortening the number of "white days" so that the woman can be purified in the *mikveh* and resume sexual relations sooner after her menstruation. In extreme cases where ovulation and menstruation coincide, some rabbis have proposed the use of mechanical devices which would allow inserting the semen into the vagina without actual skin-to-skin contact of the genitals.[13]

The laws of *niddah* regulate with precision and severity the sex life of a married couple. They are based on two sources: the taboo on sex with a menstruant, which is not unique to Judaism, and the regulation of all aspects of marital life. Sex is a part of marital life as amenable to regulation as are property rights, mutual obligations for financial support, household chores, etc. That sex is to be regulated stands in contradiction to both the notions of Western Romanticism where sex is a climactic, spontaneous expression of love and desire, and the more contemporary view of sex as fulfillment of erotic needs and pleasures. Yet it is fully congruent with the view of sex in the Halakhah, as expressed in the laws of *onah*. While the laws of *niddah* proscribe sexual activities at certain times, the laws of *onah* prescribe them at other times. The two sets of laws complement each other, creating a regulated rhythm of sexual life. It is as natural to the Halakhah to prohibit sex at certain times as it is to prescribe it at others. Spontaneity, as important as it is in the Western contemporary view of sex, is not a significant matter in the traditional Jewish view of sex. The erotic impulse is channeled and even encouraged by the "sexual timetable" mandated by the Halakhah.

The practical impact of the regimentation of sex is that marital life is made up of periods of total abstention followed by periods of sexual activity when conception is favored. The psychological impact of this system is more complex and hard to define. Undoubtedly the regimentation creates a world in which sexuality lacks spontaneity, and perhaps often lacks feeling. Sexuality is generally "other-oriented," requiring one to follow the dictates of law rather than the impulses of Eros. On the other hand, it is likely that for couples who have a mutually satisfying marriage the enforced abstinence and anticipated resumption of relations can serve to intensify the sexual encounter.

✳ 7 ✳

SEXUALITY OUTSIDE OF MARRIAGE:

Incest, Adultery, Promiscuity, and Lesbianism

JEWISH law assumes that only sexuality within marriage is normative, and all other sexual relations are deviant. Certain sexual relationships such as incest and adultery are considered sexual transgressions (*giluy arayot*). Others, such as sex between unmarried people or lesbianism, are restricted by prohibitions but are not considered sexual transgressions. Leviticus 18 furnishes the most comprehensive list of sexual prohibitions and taboos. The prohibited sexual practices are presented as the evil customs of the Egyptians and the Canaanites. The setting in which the sexual prohibitions are revealed is the period in the desert. The Israelites are warned not to return to the customs of the land from whence they came, or to emulate the practices of the peoples of the land which they are about to enter. The sexual prohibitions are central to the creation of a permanent social order and to the separation of the Israelites from their neighbors. Those two foci remain central in postbiblical legislation as well. We find the rabbis greatly concerned with the danger that sexual deviance, primarily adultery, poses to marriage and societal structure. And we also come across many references to the immoral sexual practices of non-Jews, such as the Hellenistic proclivity toward homosexuality or the "heathens' " indulgence in bestiality.[1]

¹The Lord spoke to Moses, saying: ²Speak to the Israelite people and say to them: I the Lord am your God. ³You shall not copy the practices of the land of Egypt where you dwelt, or of the land of Canaan to which I am taking you; nor shall you follow their customs. ⁴My norms alone shall you observe, and faithfully follow My laws: I the Lord am your God.

⁵You shall keep My laws and My norms, by the pursuit of which man shall live: I am the Lord.

⁶None of you shall come near anyone of his own flesh to uncover nakedness: I am the Lord.

⁷Your father's nakedness, that is, the nakedness of your mother, you shall not uncover; she is your mother—you shall not uncover her nakedness.

⁸Do not uncover the nakedness of your father's wife; it is the nakedness of your father.

⁹The nakedness of your sister—your father's daughter or your mother's, whether born into the household or outside—do not uncover their nakedness.

¹⁰The nakedness of your son's daughter, or of your daughter's daughter—do not uncover their nakedness; for their nakedness is yours.

¹¹The nakedness of your father's wife's daughter, who was born into your father's household—she is your sister; do not uncover her nakedness.

¹²Do not uncover the nakedness of your father's sister; she is your father's flesh.

¹³Do not uncover the nakedness of your mother's sister; for she is your mother's flesh.

¹⁴Do not uncover the nakedness of your father's brother: do not approach his wife; she is your aunt.

¹⁵Do not uncover the nakedness of your daughter-in-law: she is your son's wife; you shall not uncover her nakedness.

¹⁶Do not uncover the nakedness of your brother's wife; it is the nakedness of your brother.

¹⁷Do not uncover the nakedness of your wife's daughter; nor shall you marry her son's daughter or her daughter's daughter and uncover her nakedness: they are kindred; it is depravity.

¹⁸Do not marry a woman as a rival to her sister and uncover her nakedness in the other's lifetime.

¹⁹Do not come near a woman during her period of uncleanness to uncover her nakedness. [Lev. 18 : 1–19]

Verses 6–19 of this chapter of Leviticus enumerate the prohibited sexual relationships within the family. The list of prohibited relatives is long and complex, illustrating the centrality of the extended family in biblical life and law. The drawing on page 178 is a schematized diagram of all the prohibited relationships.

The remaining verses in Leviticus 18 describe the prohibited sexual liaisons outside the family framework:

[20]Do not have carnal relations with your neighbor's wife and defile yourself with her.

[21]Do not allow any of your offspring to be offered up to Molech, and do not profane the name of your God: I am the LORD.

[22]Do not lie with a male as one lies with a woman; it is an abhorrence.

[23]Do not have carnal relations with any beast and defile yourself thereby; and let no woman lend herself to a beast to mate with it; it is perversion.

[24]Do not defile yourselves in any of those ways, for it is by such that the nations which I am casting out before you defiled themselves. [25]Thus the land became defiled; and I called it to account for its iniquity, and the land spewed out its inhabitants. [Lev. 18 : 20–25]

Outside the family the prohibitions on sexual relations include adultery, homosexuality, and bestiality for both men and women.

The sexual relations prohibited by Leviticus are referred to as acts of "uncovering the nakedness" of the prohibited sexual party (or her husband). What is meant by "uncovering the nakedness" (ervah)? The word ervah is derived from the same root as erom which appears, for example, in the story of Adam and Eve in the Garden of Eden where at first "the two of them were naked . . . yet they felt no shame" (Gen. 3 : 1) and then, after eating the forbidden fruit, "the eyes of both of them were opened and they perceived that they were naked" (Gen. 3 . 7). But while erom and ervah come from the same root and both mean "nakedness," they are used very differently in the biblical text. Erom refers to physical nakedness with no specific sexual connotations (e.g., the Garden of Eden story: Gen. 3 : 1,7). Ervah refers to nakedness where sexual relations are involved (usually where such relations are taboo). The opposite of giluy arayot ("uncovering the nakedness") is the term kisuy arayot ("covering the nakedness"), which appears in two passages in the Prophets as a synonym for marriage (Ezek. 16 : 8 and Hosea 2 : 11).[2] This opposition of terms indicates the two poles

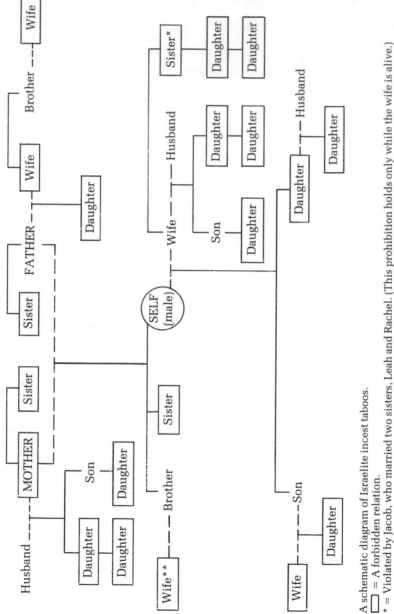

A schematic diagram of Israelite incest taboos.

▢ = A forbidden relation.

* = Violated by Jacob, who married two sisters, Leah and Rachel. (This prohibition holds only while the wife is alive.)

** = If the brother dies, however, "self" is required to take the brother's wife in levirate marriage.

in the biblical and postbiblical notion of sexual mores: legitimate sexual relations in marriage which keep sexual nakedness "under covers" on the one hand, and illegitimate sexual relations, incest and adultery, on the other. Our discussion of illegitimate sexual relations will follow the order in which sexual transgressions are listed in Leviticus 18, focusing on incest, adultery, and lesbianism, the female corollary of homosexuality. We will also examine the question of nonmarital heterosexual relationships.

Incest

The biblical definition of incest is rather broad and includes many relations outside the nuclear family. These are primarily one's aunts, sisters-in-law, stepsisters, mother-in-law, stepdaughters, daughters of a sister-in-law, daughters-in-law, and granddaughters.[3] Essentially these prohibitions cover almost all the females in an extended four-generation family. The one striking exception is relations with nieces. A man is permitted to marry and have sexual relations with his brothers' and sisters' daughters. Such relations are prohibited in most countries today (including Israel), but are not forbidden in the Halakhah.[4]

The most significant feature of the laws of incest is that they are seen from the perspective of a man but are applied equally to men and women. In other words the Bible states the incestuous relations by listing the female relatives which are prohibited to a man, but such relations are violations of the laws for both men and women, and if a man and a woman commit incest they are equally liable and are subjected to the same punishment (Leviticus 20). As we shall see, however, in the case of adultery the law is more complex. It should come as no surprise that the sexual prohibitions are addressed to men; most biblical legislation is. But in the case of sexual transgressions there is a further, more fundamental reason: men are presumed to be the active agents in sexual interactions. Men are the ones with greater physical power and the sanction of social conventions for initiating sex. In the case of incestuous relationships this is a particularly salient point: in the patriarchal family women rely on fathers, brothers, and husbands to be their protectors. The

family is the structure protecting women from sexual exploitation
by outsiders. If an "insider"—father, brother, uncle, or brother-in-
law—himself becomes a threat, seducing or even raping a woman
within his own family, she has little protection.

Maimonides, in his summary of the laws against incest, makes
this very point. The laws against incest are necessary to protect
women from men within their own extended family since it is
those men who have both the power and the easy access to allow
sexual exploitation:

All illicit unions with females have one thing in common: namely, that in
the majority of cases these females are constantly in the company of the
male in his house and that they are easy of access for him and can be
easily controlled by him—there being no difficulty in making them come
into his presence; and no judge could blame the male for their being with
him. Consequently if the status of the woman with whom a union is illicit
were that of any unmarried woman, I mean to say that if it were possible
to marry them and that the prohibition with regard to them were only due
to their not being the man's wives, most people would have constantly
succumbed and fornicated with them. [Maimonides, *Guide to the Perplexed* III : 49][5]

Maimonides argues that the incest prohibitions are necessary because otherwise incestuous relations would be very common. A
man has constant and easy access to the females of his household:
they are under his control and he can summon them easily and
with no fear of reprimand or accusations of impropriety. Thus if it
were not for the severe transgression "most people would have
constantly succumbed [to sexual temptation] and fornicated with
them." Maimonides' objection to free sexual relations within the
extended family is twofold. First, he cites the general aim of limit-
ing sexual activity as much as possible. His second reason is the
taboo on incest: "The second reason derives, in my opinion, from
the wish to respect the sentiment of shame. For it would be a most
shameless thing if this act could take place between the root and
the branch" (*Guide to the Perplexed* III : 49). Similar to Maimonides' image of "root and branch" is a midrashic passage suggesting
that incest is an affront to one's biological origins. In an imaginary
conversation between Amon (an Israelite king who according to

the Midrash had sex with his mother) and his mother, she says: "Could you possibly derive pleasure from that place from whence you came?" Amon answers: "I only do this in order to infuriate my Maker" (Yalkut Shimoni, 2 Kings 24).

Maimonides believes then that the prohibitions of *giluy arayot* are necessary in order to prevent *a natural* tendency to engage in sexual relations with female relatives in the extended family. His point probably reflects accurately a sociological reality in traditional patriarchal society, that every household is likely to include a good number of female relatives outside the nuclear family, either married or single, who could easily become involved in sexual relations with the dominant males of the household. The purpose of the extensive incest prohibitions is perhaps to afford females double protection: by being included in the household they are protected from sexual advances and imposition from outsiders, since the males of the household are their patrons, and through the prohibitions on incest they are protected from insiders.[6]

The Bible includes several anecdotes of incest. Lot's daughters, fearing that all human life had been destroyed in Sodom and Gomorrah, intoxicate their father with wine and then sleep with him (Gen. 19 : 30–36). Judah unknowingly has sexual relations with his daughter-in-law Tamar after she disguises herself as a prostitute (Gen. 38 : 14–29). Finally, Amnon lures his half-sister Tamar into his room by pretending to be sick, and then rapes her (2 Samuel 13). Incest within the nuclear family is almost unheard of in the Bible, except in the case of the daughters of Lot who believed they had seen "the end of world" in the destruction of Sodom and Gomorrah. Similarly, we find no actual cases of incest within the nuclear family reported in the Mishnah and the Talmud. Rather, the primary concern with incestuous relationships is focused on relatives by marriage.

As Maimonides notes in his explanation of incest, the greater danger of incest comes from the relationships of a powerful male relative, such as an uncle or brother-in-law, in the extended family. A passage in Kiddushin identifies another relationship as one "at risk" for incestuous liaison, that of a man and his mother-in-law:

For Rav punished . . . a son-in-law who dwelt in his mother-in-law's house. Only he who dwelt, but not he who merely passed by [his mother-in-law's house]? But a certain son-in-law passed by his mother-in-law's door, for which Rabbi Sheshet chastised him? There his mother-in-law was [already] under suspicion through him. [Kiddushin 12b]

The passage in Kiddushin lists various improper acts, all of which do not involve an actual violation of the law, which Rav punished by flogging [*malkot mardut*]. The last offense listed is that of a man who lives in his mother-in-law's house. This is not actually a violation of any *halakhah*, but it is improper because it may lead to incest. A question is raised: Did Rav only punish a man who actually lived in his mother-in-law's house, but not a man who simply passed by (presumably stopping to greet his mother-in-law, etc.)? The question is posed because of a case where another rabbi, Rabbi Sheshet, did punish a man for merely passing by his mother-in-law's house. However, that was a special case where the man and his mother-in-law were already under suspicion for illicit relations and thus merely passing by was improper. The general rule was that visits were acceptable, but living with the mother-in-law was not. To appreciate the relevance of this ruling to real life we must realize that it was common in the talmudic period for a man in his late teens to early twenties to marry a girl in her early teens. The mother of such a girl was likely to be still quite young herself. Thus it seems plausible that the more mature but still fairly young mother-in-law would be as attractive, if not more so, to the husband than his wife, still in her early adolescence.

In eastern Europe the rule attributed to Rav was not followed. On the contrary, newly married couples most often resided with the bride's parents for several years after their marriage. During this period the husband studied and/or established himself in his trade. The relationship between the young husband and the mother-in-law was more often characterized by conflict than by sexual attraction (the normal adolescent conflict between parents and children often took place with the in-laws instead of with the natural parents because of early marriage). But a few rare cases are reported in the responsa literature where incestuous relationships were suspected between a young man and his mother-in-law or a young bride and her father-in-law.[7]

Cases of incest were very rare, however. The primary concern in the halakhic literature is with the problem of adultery, to which we shall now turn.

Adultery

Adultery is similar to incest in that it is considered a very grave offense in the Bible and in postbiblical Halakhah. However, it is fundamentally different from incest in terms of the strictures it imposes on men and women. The laws of incest prohibit sexual liaisons between specified relations within the family, and they apply equally to both sexes. In other words, just as a man is not permitted to have sex with his mother, daughter, sister, etc., so is a woman forbidden to have relations with her father, son, brother, etc. These prohibitions are reciprocal and parallel. In the case of adultery there is a fundamental difference between men and women. A married woman is forbidden to have sexual relations with all men except her husband: she is "forbidden to the whole world" (asurah le-kulei alma). But a married man is free to have sexual relations with any other woman as long as she herself is single and available (penuyah).

The greater freedom that the man enjoys is a result of his ability to marry more than one woman. Since biblical law allows him concubines as well as wives, there are no punitive measures against a married man who engages in extramarital sex as there are for a married woman. Although the postbiblical Halakhah certainly frowned upon any such extramarital sex, and attempted to curtail it by prohibiting a man to spend time in privacy with women outside his family, such relations remained outside the purview of sexual transgressions (Kiddushin 80b–81b).[8] Of course a man is forbidden to commit adultery with another man's wife as she is to have an adulterous relationship with him: a couple guilty of adultery is equally liable if both are married. But there is inequality in the postbiblical punishment: the adulteress must be divorced by *her* husband, while the adulterer may remain married to *his* wife with impunity.

The punishment mandated in the Bible for adultery is execution: "If a man commits adultery with a married woman, committing adultery with his neighbor's wife, the adulterer and the adulteress shall be put to death" (Lev. 20 : 10). Other references in the Bible imply that in reality there were times where the consequences were less grave.[8] It appears that often the consequence of adultery (or accusation of adultery) was divorce: the husband deserted his wife or sent her away. This is probably the intent of Deuteronomy 24 which rules that a man may divorce his wife by giving her a "writ of divorce" (*sefer keritut*) if he finds in her "a matter of *ervah*."[9]

Biblical law on adultery seems to leave no room for uncertainty and ambiguity. However, there is a major problem in applying the law, the fact that by definition adultery is a very private, often secret matter. It is usually committed with no witnesses or factual proof, yet suspicion of adultery is easily aroused and rumors quickly spread. Such suspicion is a serious threat to marital life and a source of potential violence and danger to the suspected wife. Biblical law makes provisions for dealing with the problem of suspected adultery through the ordeal, a test in which divine judgment determines the guilt or innocence of the suspected wife. This is the ordeal of the *sotah*, the "errant woman," described in graphic detail in Numbers 5:

[12]If any man's wife has gone astray and broken faith with him [13]in that a man has had carnal relations with her unbeknown to her husband, and she keeps secret the fact that she has defiled herself without being forced, and there is no witness against her—[14]but a fit of jealousy comes over him and he is wrought up about the wife who has defiled herself; or if a fit of jealousy comes over one and he is wrought up about his wife although she has not defiled herself—[15]the man shall bring his wife to the priest. And he shall bring as an offering for her one-tenth of an *ephah* of barley flour. No oil shall be poured upon it and no frankincense shall be laid on it, for it is a meal offering of jealousy, a meal offering of remembrance which recalls wrongdoing.

[16]The priest shall bring her forward and have her stand before the LORD.

[17]The priest shall take sacral water in an earthen vessel and, taking some of the earth that is on the floor of the Tabernacle, the priest shall put it into the water. [18]After he has made the woman stand before the LORD, the priest shall loosen the hair of the woman's head and place upon her hands the meal offering of remembrance, which is a meal offering of jealousy. And in the priest's hands shall be the water of bitterness that induces the spell. [19]The priest shall adjure the woman, saying to her, "If no man has lain with you, if you have not gone astray in defilement while married to your husband, be immune to harm from this water of bitterness that induces the spell. [20]But if you have gone astray while married to your husband and have defiled yourself, if a man other than your husband has had carnal relations with you"—[21]here the priest shall administer the curse of adjuration to the woman, as the priest goes on to say to the woman—"may the LORD make you a curse and an imprecation among your people, as the LORD causes your thigh to sag and your belly to distend; [22]may this water that induces the spell enter your body, causing the belly to distend and the thigh to sag." And the woman shall say, "Amen, amen!"

[23]The priest shall put these curses down in writing and rub it off into the water of bitterness. [24]He is to make the woman drink the water of bitterness that induces the spell, so that the spell-inducing water may enter into her to bring on bitterness. [25]Then the priest shall take from the woman's hand the meal offering of jealousy, wave the meal offering before the LORD, and present it on the altar. [26]The priest shall scoop out of the meal offering a token part of it and turn it into smoke on the altar. Lastly, he shall make the woman drink the water.

[27]Once he has made her drink the water—if she has defiled herself by breaking faith with her husband, the spell-inducing water shall enter into her to bring on bitterness, so that her belly shall distend and her thigh shall sag; and the woman shall become a curse among her people. [28]But if the woman has not defiled herself and is pure, she shall be unharmed and able to retain seed.

[29]This is the ritual in cases of jealousy, when a woman goes astray while married to her husband and defiles herself, [30]or when a fit of jealousy comes over a man and he is wrought up over his wife: the woman shall be made to stand before the LORD and the priest shall carry out all this ritual with her. [31]The man shall be clear of guilt; but that woman shall suffer for her guilt. [Num. 5 : 12–31]

The passage begins by presenting two possible situations: the first is a case of a woman who has committed adultery and has kept it secret from her husband although he suspects it. The second is of a husband who suspects his wife of committing adultery though

she is innocent. The common thread between the two situations is
the husband's jealousy and suspicion. Since the woman is suspected of committing adultery by her husband but there are no
witnesses or evidence to resolve the matter, it must be cleared by
deferring to divine judgment, through the ritual of the ordeal. The
suspicion must be cleared or confirmed, because if it is true that
the woman is guilty of adultery, she is forbidden to her husband.

The ritual whereby the woman's guilt or innocence is proven is
described here in detail. The "litmus test" is the effect of the water
of bitterness (water mixed with dust from the Temple grounds and
the ink in which curses are written on the scroll) on the accused
woman. If she is innocent the water will have no effect. If she is
guilty the water will cause her thigh to "sag" and her belly to
"distend" or "swell." There are two puzzling things about this
ordeal of the "water of bitterness." First, it is not clear what "her
belly shall distend and her thigh shall sag" means. Some scholars
have interpreted this to mean an immediate result of the drinking
of the water; others have argued that the effect is understood to be
a consequent miscarriage. "Thigh" is possibly a euphemism for
sexual organs (it is used that way in other places in the Bible, such
as referring to children as the "progeny of your thigh") and its
"sagging" refers to the "dropping" of a fetus in a miscarriage. This
explains the distention of the belly as pregnancy quite nicely,
although the order should be reversed: the curse should be "your
belly shall distend and your thigh shall sag." This is further suggested by the fact that the innocent woman suffers no harm from
the water and is "able to retain seed (ve-nizra'ah zara)." Whatever
the correct interpretation, the biblical text does not give us an
exact, clinical description of the effect of the water; rather, it remains ambiguous and open to interpretation.

More disturbing than the ambiguity about the effect of the bitter
water as a sign for condemning the woman is a simpler question:
What kind of an ordeal is this? It seems far-fetched that water with
some dust and some ink in it could have much of an effect on the
woman who drinks it. When we think of an ordeal we usually
think of one where the chances to be proven guilty are over-
whelmingly favorable. This was the case with the common or-

deals in Middle Eastern traditional societies, such as the ordeal by water practiced in Babylonia where the accused would be thrown into a rapid river, or the ordeal by fire where the accused's tongue would be touched with red-hot iron tongs and guilt would be proven by the presence of a burn. The medieval European judgment by ordeal often required that the accused float in water despite being tied to a stone. All these examples demonstrate that trial by ordeal usually placed great odds against a proof of innocence. How do we understand the trial by ordeal of the *sotah*?

One possibility is that it is not really the actual physical "test" which matters, but rather the devastating psychological reaction to the frightening and humiliating experience. This would take account of the ritualized proceeding, the humiliation of the accused woman by unbinding her hair (a sign of prostitution), and the solemn oath she takes. According to this view, the psychological impact would be so great that a woman with a guilty conscience would reveal her guilt one way or the other.

The other possibility is that the insignificance of the actual physical ordeal is intended in order to practically guarantee that a woman could prove her innocence. This means that the real purpose of the ordeal is not to convict adulterous women who have been skillful enough to hide their transgression, but primarily to afford a way for women to clear themselves of suspicion. Suspicion of adultery in a close-knit community would be almost impossible to dispel, and could easily lead to ostracism and perhaps violent revenge. The ordeal of the "bitter water" allows a fairly simple, safe way for a woman to clear her name with divine approval, sanctioned by the priest and the Temple ritual. If this is the case we have a kind of inverted institution here: the trial by ordeal is transformed from a formidable test weighted toward guilt to an easy one, strongly biased in favor of demonstrating innocence. The ordeal is changed from a measure threatening women to a mechanism for their protection.[10]

The talmudic discussion of the *sotah* is extensive and mostly to be found in a tractate by that name. Tractate Sotah focuses in detail on the ritual of the ordeal, but it does not give us a clue about the plausibility of either of our theories concerning the nature of the ordeal. The primary reason is that the rabbis were not very concerned with the problem of efficacy of the ordeal because it was not practiced in their day, nor at any point in their historical memory. It is even possible that by the time the ritual was recorded in Numbers it was no longer practiced, and that this is the reason for the obscurity of the passage. The talmudic discussion of the *sotah* and her ordeal is therefore totally academic. It is of interest, however, to note how the disappearance of the trial of the *sotah* is explained in the Mishnah and the Gemara:

When the adulterers increased in number the bitter waters ceased. And Rabbi Yohanan ben Zakkai discontinued [the practice] as it is said: "I shall not judge your daughters for their whoring or your sons' wives for adultery [when everyone else is wandering off with whores and offering sacrifice with sacred prostitutes]" (Hosea 4 : 14).

"When the adulterers increased in number": Our rabbis taught: "And the husband shall be guiltless" (Numb. 5 : 31). At a time when the husband is guiltless the waters test his wife, if the husband is not guiltless the waters do not test his wife. . . .

Rabbi Eliezer said: The prophet said to the children of Israel: If you should be strict with yourself the waters will test your wives but if not, the waters will not test your wives. [Sotah 47a–b]

The efficacy of the ordeal of the bitter water depended on the accusing husband's innocence. However, when husbands became as suspect of adultery as their wives, the ordeal lost its efficacy.

The cessation of the ritual of the bitter water is attributed in the Mishnah to the decree of Rabbi Yohanan ben Zakkai, who lived in the generation of the destruction of the Temple (70 C.E.) and established the school at Yavneh after the Roman conquest of Jerusalem. This should be seen not as a historical dating, but as part of a genre in mishnaic and talmudic literature, dating fundamental changes in society and its ethics to the destruction of the Temple.[11]

In the postbiblical period two major elements in the legal procedures related to adultery fell into disuse: the ordeal of the *sotah* to determine guilt or innocence, and capital punishment to deal with the guilty. But adultery remained, of course, an ever-present problem and a grave offense in Jewish law. The deterrent power was gradually transferred from capital punishment to the consequences for the personal status of the adulteress: namely, she was divorced by her husband and forbidden to marry her lover. She remained empty-handed, forfeiting both her marriage and her adulterous relationship:

Mishnah: . . . Just as she is prohibited to the husband [asurah le-ba'alah] so is she prohibited to the paramour [asurah le-vo'alah]; as it is said: "Defiled . . . and is defiled" (Numb. 5 : 29). This is the statement of Rabbi Akiva. Rabbi Josiah said: Thus did Zechariah ben Ha-Katzav use to expound: Rabbi said: The word "defiled" occurs twice in the scriptural portion, one referring [to her being prohibited] to her husband and the other to the paramour. [Sotah 27b]

The mishnah in Sotah 27b cites two traditions, one in the name of Rabbi Akiva and one attributed to Rabbi Judah Ha-Nasi. Both traditions cite the repetition of the word "defilement" in Numbers 5 as the proof-text for the halakhah that the adulteress is forbidden to both her husband and her lover. Initially this rule prohibiting the woman to both her husband and her paramour is introduced only in reference to the period between the first announcement of suspicion by the husband and the determination of guilt or innocence by the ordeal of the bitter water. However, the rule is then expanded: it becomes not a temporary "separation order" but a permanent consequence.[12] The double-edged prohibition of resuming relations with both husband and lover becomes the punishment for adultery, replacing execution which had disappeared from actual practice sometime during the second Temple period. The adulteress was in practice cut off from her community by this measure: she was divorced by her husband, could not marry her paramour, and obviously had very little chance of finding another man who would marry her. Other punitive measures were imposed in different communities according to their own customs. Some of these measures were flogging for rebelliousness (malkot mardut), a ban of excommunication on the adulterous couple, enforced exile from the community, and in North African communities, public humiliation through shaving the heads of the couple and parading them through the streets.[13]

Promiscuity

The problem of adultery is so important in the Halakhah because of the great emphasis placed on the exclusive sexual allegiance of a married woman to her husband, the severe punishment for adultery in the Bible, and the grave consequences to the lives of the children born from illicit relationships (they are bastards or *mamzerim*).[14] However, the problem of adultery is only one manifestation of the general problem of sex outside of marriage.

We have seen that in biblical law a married man who has sexual relations with an unmarried woman is not guilty of any offense since he could theoretically marry the woman. The Talmudic prohibition of private, intimate contact with a woman other than one's wife (*yihud*) and the medieval ban on polygyny considerably restricted this freedom for men. Still, a man who had such extramarital sex, if he did not try to marry the woman, had not committed a sexual transgression. He was certainly condemned, and perhaps even flogged in some communities but his offense remained of much lesser magnitude than a sexual transgression.

How does the Halakhah view the unmarried woman (called *penuyah*) who has sexual relations? As long as she is not betrothed or married, a woman may have sexual relations with one or more men without violating any explicit sexual prohibition. Sexual relations outside the framework of marriage are not adultery for a single woman, just as they are not for a single or married man. If a single woman has an exclusive sexual relationship with a man whom she could legally marry, that relationship is construed as a "common-law marriage," and should she switch her alliance without a divorce, she would be considered an adulteress.

However, the Halakhah does not accept such nonmarital sexuality, but rather condemns it and labels it "promiscuity" (*zenut*). The definition of *zenut* is problematic for it is used in the rabbinical sources in several different ways. First, it is a term connoting professional prostitution. Second, it refers to sexual relations of an unmarried woman which are not aimed at effecting marriage, but rather are done for pleasure. Third, zenut is often used as a descriptive term to condemn any kind of illicit sexual alliance, including adultery.[15]

The primary importance of the meaning of zenut for the Halakhah is in regard to the special laws of marriage for priests, since the priests are forbidden to marry certain women permitted to all others, among them a woman called a zonah (Lev. 21 : 7). It is with this prohibition in mind that the rabbis discuss the meaning of the term. As it turns out, the rabbis themselves disagree about the definition of zonah:

> "Zonah" implies, as her name [indicates, a faithless wife]; so Rabbi Eliezer [said]. Rabbi Akiva said: "zonah" implies one who is a prostitute. Rabbi Mattiah ben Heresh said: Even a woman whose husband, while going to arrange for her drinking [i.e., the ordeal of the sotah], cohabited with her on the way is rendered a zonah. Rabbi Judah said: Zonah implies one who is incapable of procreation. And the Sages said: Zonah is none other than a female proselyte, a freed bondwoman, and one who has been subject to any meretricious intercourse. . . .
>
> Rabbi Elazar said: An unmarried man who had intercourse with an unmarried woman with no matrimonial intent, renders her thereby a zonah. Rabbi Amram said: The Halakhah is not in agreement with the opinion of Rabbi

The passage in Yevamot includes six different opinions on what the word zonah means. Rabbi Eliezer equates a zonah with an adulteress. Rabbi Akiva holds that a zonah is a professional prostitute. Rabbi Mattiah ben Heresh has a much stricter view: he holds that a woman merely suspected of adultery by her husband becomes a zonah if she has intercourse with her husband, because there is the possibility that as a result of the impending ordeal she will be found guilty and forbidden to her husband. Rabbi Judah interprets zonah to mean a woman incapable of procreation who thus carries on sexual relations with no procreative intent. Rabbi Elazar hold that a single woman who has sex with a single man not for the sake of effecting betrothal (kiddushin via intercourse) is considered a zonah. The Sages do not accept Rabbi Elazar's strict view: sexual relations between a single man and a single woman not for the purpose of kiddushin, while frowned upon, do not make the woman a zonah.

The problem of sexual relations between a man and a woman who are both free of marital ties is complicated. The rabbis wish to discourage such "free" sexual relations on the one hand, but on the other hand there is no specific sexual transgression involved in such circumstances. The biblical prohibitions which form the basis of the sexual code in the Halakhah only prohibit incestuous and adulterous relations. The rabbis attempt to resolve this dilemma in two ways. As a general rule they apply the principle *Ein adam oseh be'ilato be'ilat zenut*, meaning that one does not generally cohabit with promiscuity (*zenut*) in mind, but rather for the praiseworthy purpose of effecting *kiddushin*. Thus a man and a woman who carry on a full sexual relationship are really presumed married, rather than acting promiscuously. However, when circumstances indicate, the rabbis reverse this rule and render sexual relations a mere act of *zenut*, rather than an act of betrothal. Such is the case when the man acts improperly, taking a woman who had been engaged to another, refusing to follow the sexual act with proper *kiddushin* with money or a deed, or failing to follow through on his action and live with the woman as husband and wife.[16] Secondly, the rabbis forbid a man and a woman to spend time together in privacy unless they are married or blood relatives. This "preventive" approach prohibits the circumstances which would permit sexual relations outside of marriage to take place.

The problem of *zenut* in the sense of promiscuity is ever-present in the Halakhah and the halakhic and religious authorities struggle against it in order to keep sex within the confines of marriage. Contrary to popular notions that sex outside of marriage is a product of the modern sexual revolution, halakhic codes and responsa indicate its presence in traditional Jewish society. How common sex outside of marriage was is a complicated, perhaps intractable historical problem, but there is no doubt that it is not a new phenomenon.

Lesbianism

As against adultery and *zenut*, lesbianism is an almost unheard-of form of "sexual deviance" in traditional Jewish society. Lesbianism is not mentioned in the Bible at all. Homosexuality is enumerated in Leviticus 18 and 20 among the sexual transgressions as a *to'evah*, "an abhorrence," but it seems that sexual relations between women were not even entertained as a possibility. The Talmud includes two references to lesbianism, and both make it very clear that it is not considered parallel to male homosexuality. The term used in the Talmud for women engaging in sexual acts is *mesolelot*. It is not clear what the literal meaning and derivation of this term is. The context suggests, as we shall see, some kind of sexual act. Rashi, in his commentary on the Talmud, gives an explanation: "Like in intercourse of male and female, they rub their femininity [the genitals] against one another" (Rashi on Yevamot 76a). From another Talmudic passage where the word *mesolelet* (the singular form) is used to describe a mother fondling her son (Sanhedrin 69b) we draw a similar interpretation of the term: it refers to genital contact which is sexual in nature but does not involve penetration as in the act of intercourse between man and woman.

The first talmudic passage which discusses a lesbian act is concerned with a technical question: Does sex between women constitute an illicit sexual act which would then make a woman ineligible to marry a priest and receive the benefits due to the priest's family (the tithe)?

Raba said: The Halakhah is not in accordance with . . . [those who stated] in the name of Rav Huna: "Women who are *mesolelot* are disqualified from the priesthood," [This is so] even according to Rabbi Eliezer who held that a bachelor who has intercourse with a single woman thereby renders her a *zonah*, because that [opinion of Rabbi Eliezer] is [only stated] in reference to [sex] with a man but not in regard to [sex] with a woman [where] it is mere licentiousness. [Yevamot 76a]

Raba disputes the opinion attributed to Rav Huna that women involved in a sexual act (*mesolelot*) are disqualified from the priesthood. Since women are not eligible for the priesthood altogether we must understand this to mean that those called here *mesolelot* are not eligible to *marry* into the priesthood. Or if already members of a priest's family (by birth or marriage) such women are disqualified from eating the terumah (the tithe which the priests collect to support themselves). Rabbi Eliezer is reported to have been unusually strict in his views about sexual relations outside of proper marriage. He ruled that sex between a single man and a single, available woman, when it is done for the express purpose of sexual pleasure and not betrothal, makes the woman a zonah. However, Raba, who presents the argument in this passage, states that this opinion of Rabbi Eliezer's is not relevant to the case of women who are mesolelot. Rabbi Eliezer's opinion (which, as we have seen, was rejected by the rabbis) holds for the case of a single man and a single woman, but here we are dealing with something else, sexual relations between two women. If a woman has sexual relations with another woman, the violation is less severe than if she has sex with a man: "with a woman it is mere licentiousness." "Licentiousness" (pritzut) is a lesser offense than "prostitution" (zenut) and carries no punishment or legal ramifications. Raba's reasoning is not fully detailed in this passage but it is implicit in his reliance on the opinion of Rabbi Eliezer. Even Rabbi Eliezer, who took a very severe view of sex between an unattached man and a single woman, did not consider lesbian acts to constitute a legal violation of the sexual prohibitions. The reason is inherent in the difference between the sexual acts: in the case of a man and a woman there is actual penetration in the act of intercourse. Sexual arousal and satisfaction between women occurs without intercourse and does not qualify as a "sexual act" in the technical legal sense.[17] Thus sexual acts between women are viewed by Raba as improper, but they do not carry any legal significance or consequence.

Another passage in the Talmud mentions lesbian acts and similarly rules that such acts do not constitute a sexual transgression:

Samuel's father did not permit his daughters to go out with [ornamental] threads [on the Sabbath], nor sleep together. . . .

"He did not permit them to sleep together": Shall we say that this supports the opinion of Rav Huna? For Rav Huna said: "Women who are mesolelot [commit lesbian acts] with one another are disqualified from the priesthood." No. It was in order that they should not become accustomed to a foreign body. [Shabbat 65a–b]

The custom of Samuel's father to forbid his daughters to sleep together in the same bed was not intended to prevent lesbianism, but rather to accustom them to sleep alone. Being accustomed to "a foreign body" presumably would condition them to want to sleep together with a man, perhaps without regard to marriage, or more likely, in violation of the requirement to sleep separately during the period of *niddah*.[18]

The only two references to lesbianism in the Talmud therefore agree that lesbianism does not constitute even an act of promiscuity which would disqualify a woman from marriage to a priest. It is merely licentiousness, a condemnable act but with no legal or punitive ramifications. Maimonides adopts this position, but argues that although the sexual act itself is not a punishable sexual transgression, the rebelliousness it reflects is:

Women are forbidden to engage in lesbian practices [*mesolelot*] with one another, these being "the doings of Egypt" (Lev. 18 : 3) against which we have been warned, as it is said: "You shall not copy the practices of the land of Egypt. . ." (Lev. 18 : 3). Our Sages have said: "What did they do? A man would marry a man, or a woman a woman, or a woman would marry two men." Although such an act is forbidden, the perpetrators are not liable for a flogging, since there is no specific negative commandment prohibiting it, nor is actual intercourse of any kind involved. Consequently, such women are not disqualified from the priesthood on account of prostitution, nor is a woman prohibited to her husband because of it. It behooves the court, however, to administer the flogging prescribed for rebelliousness since they performed a forbidden act. A man should be particularly strict with his wife in this matter and should prevent women known to indulge in such practices from visiting her and her from visiting them. [Maimonides, *Mishneh Torah*, Issurei Bi'ah 21 : 8]

Lesbian acts do not constitute a sexual transgression or *zenut* because: (1) there is no explicit prohibition in the Bible; and (2) there is no actual intercourse. Yet Maimonides' concern about the danger of lesbianism is evident, and he prescribes two actions against it. One measure is preventive: it is a man's duty to supervise his wife and forbid any contact and association with women known as lesbians. The second measure urges a court dealing with a case of lesbianism to apply the punishment for rebelliousness.

Both in Maimonides' *Mishneh Torah* and in the Talmud we find lesbianism excluded from the corpus of sexual prohibitions, as opposed to male homosexuality which is explicitly forbidden in Leviticus 18 : 22 and in subsequent halakhic sources.[19] Perhaps even more striking than the "permissiveness" of all the sources regarding lesbianism is the paucity of material about it: only two references in the Talmud, both of them in unrelated contexts, and only one brief statement in the *Mishneh Torah*. What explains this paucity of material?

The answers can only be speculative. It seems that there are three major possibilities. It may be that lesbianism did not really exist as a recognizable social or legal problem. Possibly women accepted their role as sexual partners in marriage as so self-evident, so powerfully reinforced by the society and culture, that other sexual practices were not entertained. A second possibility is that legal problems regarding lesbianism indeed arose (such as: Is lesbianism grounds for divorce without consent? Does a woman divorced because of lesbian practices forfeit the *ketubah* payments?) but were resolved without written record, suppressed because they were too embarrassing. A third possibility is that lesbianism existed in the lives of women but remained unknown to the men who made the decisions in matters of Halakhah.

This raises a fundamental question about our access to the real life of women. The Halakhah concerning women only reflects what was known to men about the lives and problems of women, either by observation or report. But whatever in the actual daily life and experience of women remained unknown to the men who determined Halakhah remains hidden for us as well. Here, as in the case of the real-life nature of normative sexual relations between husband and wife, the true historical reality of women's experience is silent.

We have examined four categories of sexual deviance: incest, adultery, promiscuity, and lesbianism. While each is different in detail and legal ramifications, they have an underlying basis in common: they are conceived of within a patriarchal marital structure and male terms of reference. The greatest concern with incest in the Halakhah is focused on the possible sexual alliances between powerful men and dependent women within the extended family. As Maimonides points out, the close proximity of men and women in the family and the dominance of men combine to make incest a "natural inclination." Were it not for laws against the incestuous relationship, their natural inclination would lead the men to frequent sexual relations with their female relatives. The laws of adultery too reflect the power relationships between the sexes. Marriage is an exclusive relationship between a man and a woman, but it is a one-way exclusiveness. The married woman is the exclusive sexual partner of her husband, forbidden to all other men. The married man, on the other hand, is not precluded by his marriage from relationships with other women provided those women are single, although such promiscuity is condemned for both sexes. Should an adulterous relationship occur, both partners, man and woman, are equally guilty of a sexual transgression. Finally, we see the same pattern in the treatment of lesbianism. Sexual acts between women are not considered a violation of the law because no act of intercourse takes place. The male sexual experience of heterosexual intercourse is the standard for defining what is a sexual act, and thus what is a sexual transgression. All these categories of deviant sexual relationships are judged by the same yardstick of "normative sexuality." Normative sexuality in Jewish law is heterosexual, initiated by the male, and confined within marriage.

✵ 8 ✵
PROCREATION AND CONTRACEPTION

PROCREATION is a primary aspect of family and society in the Jewish tradition. It is the cornerstone of marital life, though not its exclusive purpose; companionship, fulfillment, and avoidance of sin (illicit sexual acts and fantasies) are of equal importance. For men procreation is a positive commandment, but for women it is only an act of choice and free will. In fact the Halakhah displays a determined effort to exclude women from the legal duty to bear children, which flies in the face of an intuitive assumption that men and women have equal parts in procreation.

The exemption of women from the *mitzvah* of procreation makes the use of contraception a possibility for women. Moreover, the Talmud includes explicit references to women who use a contraceptive device. However, the legal ramifications of the references to contraception are a matter of interpretation and controversy in the halakhic tradition. Since the Talmud describes contraception in somewhat ambiguous language and without a clear prescriptive formulation, the halakhic literature which evolved encompasses a wide spectrum of opinions and highly complex and subtle argumentation.[1]

The very first statement addressed to Adam and Eve in the Bible is the commandment of procreation: "Be fruitful and multiply and fill the Earth and subdue it" (Gen. 1 : 28).[2] What could be more natural than to assume that this is a commandment incumbent on men and women equally, since both must participate in procreation as equal partners? Yet the Halakhah rules otherwise. As against the plain meaning of the passage in Genesis and the biological facts of procreation, it makes procreation a duty of the man only. The Talmud and later commentaries rely on rather convoluted logic and interpretation in order to exempt women from the *mitzvah* of procreation.

Mishnah: A man is commanded concerning the duty of propagation but not a woman. Rabbi Johanan ben Beroka, however, said: Concerning both of them—it is said, "And God blessed them; and God said unto them: Be fruitful, and multiply."

Gemara: Whence is this deduced? Rabbi Ile'a replied in the name of Rabbi Eleazar son of Rabbi Simeon: Scripture stated, "And replenish the earth, and subdue it"; it is the nature of a man to *subdue* but it is not the nature of a woman to subdue. On the contrary! "And subdue it" implies two! Rabbi Nahman ben Isaac replied: It is written, "And thou subdue it."

Rabbi Joseph said: Deduction is made from the following: "I am God Almighty, be thou fruitful and multiply," and it is not stated, "Be ye fruitful and multiply."

Now, what is the decision?—Come and hear what Rabbi Aha ben Hanina stated in the name of Rav Abbahu in the name of Rav Assi: Such a case once came before Rabbi Johanan at the Synagogue of Caesarea, and he decided that the husband must divorce her and also pay her the amount of her *ketubah*. Now, if it be suggested that a woman is not subject to the commandment, how could she have any claim to a *ketubah*?—It is possible that this was a case where she submitted a special plea; as was the case with a certain woman who once came to Rabbi Ammi and asked him to order the payment of her *ketubah*. When he replied, "Go away, the commandment does not apply to you," she exclaimed, "What shall become of a woman like myself in her old age!" "In such a case," the Master said, "we certainly compel [the husband]."

A woman once came [with a similar plea] before Rabbi Nahman. When he told her, "The commandment does not apply to you," she replied, "Does not a woman like myself require a staff in her hand and a hoe for digging her grave!" "In such a case," the Master said, "we certainly compel [the husband]."

Judah and Hezekiah were twins. The features of the one were developed at the end of nine months, and those of the other were developed at the beginning of the seventh month. Judith, the wife of Rabbi Hiyyah, having suffered in consequence agonizing pains of childbirth, changed her clothes [on recovery] and appeared before Rabbi Hiyyah. "Is a woman," she asked, "commanded to propagate the race?"—"No," he replied. And relying on this decision, she drank a sterilizing potion. When her action finally became known, he exclaimed, "Would that you bore unto me only one more issue of the womb!"

Our passage begins with the statement in the Mishnah of the general principle according to the majority opinion that a man is commanded to procreate but a woman is not. The minority opinion recorded in the name of Johanan ben Beroka is that the duty of procreation applies to both men and women. The Gemara first explicates the disagreement by supplying various traditions of proofs for one position or the other. The question "Now, what is the decision?" is answered with three anecdotes which prove that three different rabbis ruled in accordance with the position that women are exempt from the duty of procreation while men are bound by it.

The initial discussion in the Gemara focuses on the precise meaning of the commandment to procreate as stated in Genesis 1 : 28. The first argument, by Rabbi Ile'a, is based on deduction from the meaning of the last word in the verse: ve-kivshu'hah, "and conquer (subdue) it." Subduing, argues Rabbi Ile'a, is in the nature of a man, not in the nature of a woman. Therefore the whole phrase can only be understood as addressed exclusively to Adam, and to men in subsequent generations. The reply to this argument is obvious: the grammatical form, that is, the use of the plural "and subdue it" (ve-kivshu'hah) clearly implies that two people, man and woman, are addressed in this verse. A peculiar grammatical feature, however, makes this argument reversible. The traditional biblical text is not vocalized, so the consonants could be read two ways: ve-kivshu'hah, which is second person plural; or ve-kivshah, which is second person singular, masculine. Therefore, as Rabbi Nahman ben Isaac points out, the text could be read as addressed to the man only.

Rabbi Joseph introduces a new factor, another text where the formula "Be fruitful and multiply" appears and where it is unquestionably addressed to a man, Jacob, alone (Gen. 35 : 11). Rabbi Joseph's operating principle is a basic one in biblical exegesis: where the meaning or usage of a word or phrase is questionable, its precise meaning is determined by the way it is used in another context in the Bible. The comandment to Jacob is clearly addressed in the second person singular masculine form: *preh* u-rveh, to a man only. The resulting conclusion is that procreation is a *mitzvah* only for men.

The subsequent question "What is the decision?" reveals that the linguistic and grammatical arguments are considered inconclusive. What is conclusive is the evidence of tradition: the way in which rabbis in the past had ruled on legal problems which involved the duty of procreation. The first case cited was determined by Rabbi Johanan in Caesarea, who, we are told, ruled that "in such a case" the husband must divorce his wife and pay her the *ketubah* payment. But what was the case in question? The text leaves that implicit and we can reconstruct it only by following the rest of the argument.

The woman who came to Rabbi Johanan in Caesarea apparently requested that her husband be required to divorce her because she was childless and believed that with another man she might be able to conceive. But if she has no legal obligation to procreate, then remaining married though she has no offspring involves no violation of the law (as it would for a man). She is therefore seeking the divorce for personal reasons and in such a case it would seem that the husband cannot be *compelled* to divorce her, nor must he pay her the *ketubah* payment.[3]

At first it seems that Rabbi Johanan did believe that women are obligated to procreate and therefore awarded the childless woman a full payment of her *ketubah*. But, in fact, he granted her the divorce on the basis of special considerations: Possibly "this was a case where she submitted a special plea; as was the case with a certain woman who came to Rabbi Ammi." The woman in the second case was in the same situation: being childless, she sought a divorce and her *ketubah* payment. Rabbi Ammi turned her down because the commandment of procreation does not apply to her. She made a special plea, that is, an extralegal plea: she needed children to care for her in old age. Rabbi Ammi accepted this reason as sufficient ground for compelling a divorce, even as he held to the view that procreation is not incumbent upon the woman. In other words, the husband was to be compelled to divorce his wife since, while not *obligated* to procreate, a woman has a *right* to bear children. The first two cases can therefore be explained without recourse to a position that obligates women to procreate, though they initially seemed to imply that view.

The following two examples are similar. The woman who came to Rabbi Nahman, presumably requesting a divorce, was first turned away because "the commandment does not apply to you." When she pleaded her need for children to support her in old age ("Does not a woman like me require a staff in her hand and a hoe to dig her grave?"), Rabbi Nahman reversed his decision and accepted her request.

In the last case we have an excellent illustration of the connection between the exemption of women from the commandment of procreation and contraception. Judith, the wife of Rabbi Hiyyah, suffered great pains in the birth of her first two children, who were twins. Subsequently she asked her husband (having disguised herself) for his ruling on the question of procreation. Following his answer that she is not obligated to procreate, she took a drastic contraceptive measure—drinking "a cup of roots," a sterilizing potion. Though Rabbi Hiyyah reacted with an outcry of grief, he did not challenge the legality of her action.

Procreation then is a legal duty of men and a "human right" of women. A man who has been married to a woman for ten years without producing any offspring is required to divorce his wife and marry another in order to fulfill his obligation.[4] A woman in the same situation had the right to request a court to force her husband to divorce her if the husband refused to grant her her freedom of his own accord. Although the biblical phrasing of the commandment of procreation implies a joint obligation of husband and wife, the rabbis go through a number of linguistic and interpretive "exercises" in order to read the biblical text against its plain meaning. Why do they go to such lengths to exempt women from the duty of procreation? I believe that there are two primary reasons. The first is a general sentiment regarding procreation. It seems that the rabbis took it as self-evident that women had a natural desire to bear children. Men, on the other hand, were seen as torn between familial "instincts" and other powerful motivations such as learning and economic activity.[5] For men it

was necessary to mandate procreation as a duty to assure that
other activities did not take precedence. For women it was seen as
unnecessary, and perhaps "unnatural." The second reason may
have been to allow contraception in some circumstances.

The exemption of women from procreation removes one major
hindrance from the way in considering the use of contraception.
But the issue of contraception of course is much more complex.
As we might guess from the case cited above of Judith, the wife of
Rabbi Hiyyah, the presence of suffering and/or danger in childbirth (or during pregnancy) is a major factor in the consideration.
The one explicit passage concerning contraception (which is repeated in three different places in the Talmud) discusses the cases
of three women in special circumstances which seem to entail
unusual danger through pregnancy or childbirth. These three
women are described as using a *mokh* to prevent conception.
Mokh is the term for very fine soft cotton, so what the Talmud
most probably intends is pressed cotton inserted into the vagina,
somewhat like a tampon, to block the cervix or absorb the semen
and prevent pregnancy.

Rabbi Bebai recited before Rabbi Nahman: Three women use the *mokh* in
their intercourse: a minor, a pregnant woman and a nursing woman. The
minor, because she might become pregnant and as a result might die. The
pregnant woman, because she might cause her fetus to become a *sandal*.
The nursing woman, because she might have to wean her child prematurely and that would result in his death.

And what age is the minor? From the age of eleven years and one day
until the age of twelve years and one day. One who is under or over this
age carries on her intercourse in the usual manner.

This is the opinion of Rabbi Meir. The Sages, however, say: The one as
well as the other carries on her intercourse in the usual way and mercy
will be vouchsafed from heaven, as it is said: "The Lord preserves the
simple." [Yevamot 12b][6]

This critical passage reports the minority opinion of Rabbi Meir in
detail and the majority opinion of the Sages in a generalized statement at the end. To begin with, let us summarize Rabbi Meir's
opinion. Rabbi Meir reportedly holds the view that three types of
women use a *mokh* in intercourse in order to prevent conception,

and they do so because pregnancy poses a danger to them. Rabbi Meir does not explicitly state how the women use the mokh, but presumably they insert it before intercourse. As we shall see in our subsequent discussion, the vagueness about the contraceptive technique involved here leads to considerable controversy in post-talmudic Halakhah. The three women in the passage are all at risk if they become pregnant. The minor between ages eleven and twelve (already evidently married) is judged capable of conception but still too young to carry a pregnancy to term and give birth without serious danger to herself. The woman who is pregnant is thought by the rabbis to have some chance of a second conception and pregnancy, so that a second, superimposed fetus could press the existing fetus to the point where it becomes a sandal (apparently related to the word "sandal": "flat as a sandal"). The nursing mother was considered at risk because the rabbis thought that a second pregnancy could adversely affect the production of milk so the nursing infant would have to be weaned. The danger in the latter case is actually not to the mother but to her child. The nursing woman uses contraception in order to protect an existing child. The threat to a suckling child must of course be understood in the context of a culture and economic reality where breastfeeding was the major, if not the exclusive, source of nourishment for several years after birth.

The dangers to the three women in the passage from Yevamot must be understood as a reflection of the rabbis' notions about female physiology. The rabbis assumed that were a nursing woman to conceive, the milk would stop or would be spoiled by the fetus. This notion might have been related to the image of conception suggested in Leviticus Rabbah:

Job said: "Remember that you have molded me like clay. . . . Did you not pour me out like milk and curdled me then like cheese?" (Job 10 : 9). . . . A woman's womb is full of standing blood, and from there it flows out in menstruation. And at God's will, a drop of whiteness goes and drops into her and instantly, the fetus is created. This is likened to a bowl of milk: if you put in it rennet it curdles and stands, if not it remains liquid. [Leviticus Rabbah 14 : 9]

If conception is like the curdling of milk, perhaps the rabbis had the notion that becoming pregnant would curdle the milk in the breasts of the nursing mother.

The notion that a pregnant woman is at risk of conceiving a second time and squashing the first fetus is a peculiar one too. It must be seen as an indication of the rabbis' ignorance of the internal reproductive organs and their amazement at the process of pregnancy and birth. Another passage in Leviticus Rabbah expresses their astonishment that a fetus does not drop out of its mother's womb during pregnancy, that as much as a woman eats there is still plenty of room for the fetus, and that the baby emerges slowly during birth. Here the rabbis recognize that there is room for both food and fetus, but their ignorance of female physiology made them worry about a "super-imposed" fetus.

Rabbi Abba ben Kahana said three things: Normally, if a man takes a purse of coins and turns the opening downward, do not the coins fall out? And the fetus is held within the mother's bowels and God protects him so he does not fall and die. . . .

Said Rabbi Tahalifa of Caesarea: If a man eats a piece of bread and then another, does not the second piece push the first? But a woman, how much does she eat and how much does she drink and yet this does not press the fetus.

Said Rabbi Simon: The bowels of a woman are made compartments upon compartments, knots upon knots, bunches upon bunches. When she gives birth she does not drop the fetus all at once. He was speaking in metaphor: one rope is loosened and then two ropes follow. [Leviticus Rabbah 14 : 3]

The danger to the minor seems the best anchored in physiological reality. It is related to the rabbis' notions about the stages of sexual maturation in females. Legally, women become adults at the age of twelve, but sexual maturation is a gradual, individual process. The passage in Yevamot presumes that just before reaching legal maturity a girl is already sexually developed so that she may conceive. However, she is not sufficiently developed to safely carry a pregnancy to term. In a passage in Tractate Niddah the rabbis attempt to pinpoint the physical signs of sexual matu-

rity. They attempt to correlate external physiological develop-
ments (the breasts and pubic hair) with three stages of sexual
maturation.

Mishnah: The Sages spoke of [the physical development of] a woman in
figurative speech: an unripe fig, a fig in its early ripening stage and a ripe
fig. She is like "an unripe fig" while she is yet a child; "a fig in its early
ripening stage" when she is in the age of her maidenhood. During both
the latter and the former stages, they ruled, her father is entitled to anything she finds and to her handiwork and to the right of invalidating her
vows. "A ripe fig"—as soon as she becomes a *bogeret*, and her father has
no longer any right over her.
    What are the marks [of a *bogeret*]? Rabbi Jose the Galilean says: The
appearance of the wrinkle beneath the breast. Rabbi Akiba says: The
hanging down of the breasts. Ben Azzai says: The darkening of the ring
around the nipple. Rabbi Jose says: [The development of the breast to a
stage] when one's hand being put on the nipple it sinks and only slowly
rises again. [Niddah 48a]

The *mishnah* here consists of two parts: the first is a description of
the three stages of female development, the second a consideration of what is the critical sign of sexual maturation. The first part
describes the three stages of development metaphorically. The
analogy to a fig works as follows: an unripe fig is a female child;
the period of early ripening is a maiden (early puberty); and the
ripe fig is a mature woman (*bogeret*). When she becomes sexually
mature, a woman becomes an independent adult in all other re-
spects as well.
    The significant distinction is clearly between the last stage of
bagrut (maturity) and the earlier stages. The second part of the
mishnah is therefore devoted to a sharper delineation of the last
stage of development. What is the specific physiological sign of
maturation? Here the fig is likened to the breast and the stages of its
ripening are correlated with physiological signs of maturation.
Opinions concerning the "critical signs" of maturity differ and the
mishnah cites four of them. All of the opinions cited in the *mishnah*, however, locate the sign of maturity in the developing breasts.
Only in the elaboration of the Gemara do we get an alternative view:
"Rabbi Simeon stated, [a woman is mature] when the *mons veneris*
grows lower." The emphasis on the breasts may be due to their

development preceding the development of pubic hair and menstruation, or possibly, more simply, to their greater visibility.

The wealth of speculation about the stages and signs of sexual maturity indicates the rabbis' fascination with the problem. Part of this fascination is probably due to the fact that this topic provided a legitimate framework for talking about sex. But the most important factor for our discussion is that early marriage placed women in a hazardous situation since they were to begin sexual activity when their bodies were not fully ready for it. Since the rabbis were not able to determine definitively the signs of sexual maturity, Rabbi Meir, in the passage from Yevamot, advocates that women at risk of premature pregnancy use a contraceptive device to protect themselves.

Having understood the reasons why the rabbis considered the three women at risk, let us return to the core question: the legitimacy of using contraception. The focus of controversy in the interpretation of this passage lies in the very first sentence. Rabbi Meir is quoted as saying "three women use the mokh." A careful reading shows that this is a statement of fact and not a legislative pronouncement. The statement could be interpreted in two ways if it is read as a legal statement:

1. "Three women may use the mokh."
2. "Three women must use the mokh."

Law is concerned only with prohibitions and permissions, so that to be read as a halakhic statement Rabbi Meir's view has to be read one way or the other. The consequences of each reading are critical for the Halakhah concerning contraception. Rabbi Meir's view is a minority opinion: the Sages disagree with him. However, we cannot ascertain exactly what the position of the Sages is unless we clarify Rabbi Meir's position. If Rabbi Meir meant "three women may use the mokh," then it seems that the majority ruled that the three women may not use the mokh. If Rabbi Meir holds that the three women must use the mokh, then the Sages would argue that these women need not (but may) use it. As we shall see in the subsequent discussion the possible interpretations are actually much more complex and varied than the description here.

The split in the Halakhah between the readings "may use" and "must use" becomes evident in the talmudic commentaries of Rashi and his grandson, Rabbenu Tam. Rashi held to the first interpretation: "use the mokh" means "*may use the mokh*":

"Use the *mokh*": [they] are *permitted* to place the *mokh* in the place of intercourse when they have intercourse, so that they would not become pregnant. [Rashi on Yevamot 12b]

According to Rashi, Rabbi Meir holds that the three women *may* use a *mokh* to prevent conception but the majority of the rabbis disagree with him. Therefore, according to Rashi, the majority opinion *forbids* the three women from using contraception, holding that all of them carry on unobstructed intercourse and rely on heaven to protect them from danger.[7]

The consequence of Rashi's position is that according to Rabbi Meir *only* the three types of women may use contraception. If Rabbi Meir holds that the three women *may* use a *mokh*, then we may conclude that he would rule that other women who are not in unusual danger from pregnancy *may not* use contraceptive devices. The Tosafot commentary on the passage begins by showing this conclusion from Rashi's interpretation and then advances Rabbenu Tam's contrary reading of the text:

"Three women use the *mokh*": The Kuntres [Rashi's commentary] interpreted: They are permitted to use the *mokh* but other women are forbidden because of the destruction of seed, even though they are not commanded on procreation. . . . And Rabbenu Tam says that *prior to* intercourse it is definitely *forbidden* to place a *mokh* there for it is not the natural way of intercourse. Like a man who casts his seed upon rocks and trees is he who casts it into the *mokh*.

However, if she places the *mokh* there *after* intercourse there is no reason to prohibit it. . . .

And the woman who places it there afterward is not warned on destruction of seed because she is not commanded on procreation. "Who use the *mokh*" which we read here means "are *obligated* to use the *mokh*." [Tosafot on Yevamot 12b]

As stated succinctly at the end of the paragraph, Rabbenu Tam's position is that Rabbi Meir holds that the three women *must* use a *mokh*. What would the grounds be for such a requirement? Rabbi Meir, according to Rabbenu Tam's interpretation, considers the three women in mortal danger if they become pregnant. He therefore requires them, in accordance with the principle of *pikuah nefesh*, the duty to protect life, to prevent the risk of death to themselves (in the case of the minor) or their progeny (a fetus and an existing child, in the case of the pregnant and nursing woman, respectively.)

If Rabbi Meir holds that the three women must use a *mokh*, as Rabbenu Tam has it, then the Sages who disagree with him merely refrain from requiring those women to use contraception. The implication is then that the Sages *permit* the three women to use a *mokh* while Rabbi Meir *requires* it. If that is the case, the position concerning other women is moot: one might argue that according to the Sages in the majority, the three women may use a *mokh* but others may not. But it is equally logical to hold that all the Sages are concerned with is not requiring the three women to use contraception, so that the three women and all other women are free to do as they choose. That indeed seems to have been Rabbenu Tam's position.

However, there is another major factor: the issue of the time of insertion of the *mokh*. Rabbenu Tam's view is very explicitly stated in the Tosafot (even though it is apparently contradicted by the position taken in his *Sefer Ha-Yashur*, which may well be more accurate historically but was little known to halakhists and is therefore less significant).[8] The *mokh*, he believes, is the kind inserted after intercourse. The reason is that if it is present during intercourse the man deposits his seed into it, and that is equivalent to "casting it on rocks and trees," i.e., to wasting seed, which is a violation of the law. If the woman inserts the *mokh* after intercourse to absorb the semen she is merely preventing the sperm from functioning effectively in conception, that is, contravening the potential of procreation. Since a woman is not required to procreate, preventing the possibility of procreation does not entail a violation on her part.

If we return to Rashi's commentary we discover that there is no explicit attention to the issue of the timing of the insertion. However, the language "place the mokh in the place of intercourse *during* intercourse" suggests an assumption of insertion before intercourse. Thus we have Rashi and Rabbenu Tam at opposite ends of the spectrum. Rashi holds that Rabbi Meir *permits precoital* contraception to the three women (and by extension, to women at risk) while the rabbis, and thus the Halakhah, forbid it. Rashi then would forbid women who are in danger, such as the three women in the talmudic passage, to use contraception. It remains a matter of conjecture whether Rashi would permit women who are in much greater danger to use contraception. Rabbenu Tam argues that Rabbi Meir *requires* women at risk to use *postcoital mokh* but that the Sages do not require it. The majority opinion, according to Rabbenu Tam, would permit (by the virtue of not forbidding) use of postcoital contraception to women in danger as well as to women with normal pregnancies. Precoital *mokh* is forbidden altogether, according to Rabbenu Tam: not, however, by the passage of "the three women," but by the prohibition on *hashhatat zera,* wasteful emission of sperm.[9]

The views of Rashi and Rabbenu Tam are the "openers" for an extremely rich and complex halakhic literature on the subject of contraception. To illustrate the complexity of the problem we will focus on sources which cover the full range of possibilities inherent in this issue, from the most restrictive to the most permissive. We will define as "restrictive" those views which limit the categories of women who may use contraception and the acceptable methods of contraception and as "permissive" the positions which allow greater flexibility to more women in the use of contraception. The most permissive position would combine Rashi's interpretation of the passage as referring to *precoital mokh* with Rabbenu Tam's interpretation of "three women use" as "three women *must* use." This position would require women at risk to use precoital contraception and permit it to all other women. The most restrictive possible view is a mirror image: it would hold Rabbenu Tam's insistence on postcoital *mokh* and Rashi's interpretation of "use" as "may use," and thus would state that Rabbi Meir allows women at risk to use postcoital contraception but the Sages, and thus the Halakhah, forbid contraception of any kind to any woman unless the danger is demonstrably much greater than the danger to the three women.

Let us begin our survey of the possible legal positions as they are actually represented in halakhic literature. The opinion of Moses Sofer (1762–1839), one of the most important Orthodox figures and halakhists in the modern period, is a very clear illustration of the more restrictive approach to contraception. In a responsum concerning a woman whose life had been threatened by pregnancy several times, Moses Sofer forbade precoital contraception:

You asked me concerning a woman who is in danger during pregnancy and nursing and several times has been under great threat, whether she is permitted to use a *mokh* during her intercourse so that she would not become pregnant. . . .

Indeed, by your question it is made clear that the *mokh* would be in place during intercourse itself, and I have not found anyone who would permit that at all. Therefore, I see no reason to enter into a detailed discussion of this. . . .

The law is that during intercourse, in my opinion, [*mokh*] may not be permitted, but after [intercourse] it is possible to be more lenient. But [it must be done] with the husband's permission. [Moses Sofer (Hatam Sofer), Responsa, Yoreh De'ah 172][10]

Following Rashi's interpretation, Moses Sofer indicates that his rule pertains to precoital *mokh*. He forbids it though the danger to the woman is well proven. However, he is willing to be more lenient regarding postcoital *mokh* because, in his view, the talmudic passage does not entertain that possibility so there is no explicit prohibition on it. However, he adds an innovation: the husband must approve of using postcoital *mokh*. This is presumably in order to allow the husband some say in an act which actually could be carried out totally without his knowledge.

The reasoning behind Moses Sofer's ruling here is explicated in another passage in his Responsa where he rules about the possibility of a woman's sterilizing herself by drinking a sterilizing potion:

The permission for a woman to drink a sterilizing potion [*kos ikarin*] . . . pertains to a single woman or even a married woman in the days of the rabbis of the Talmud, when the husband could marry another woman or divorce his wife against her consent. But now that the ban of Rabbenu Gershom Me'or Ha-Golah is in effect, we must conclude that she does not have the right to drink a sterilizing potion without her husband's consent. [Teshuvot Hatam Sofer, Even Ha-Ezer 1 : 20]

A woman in danger of great suffering (as was the case of Rabbi Hiyyah's wife) may, according to Yevamot 65b, sterilize herself with a potion. Moses Sofer argues that the Talmud assumes that this can be done against the husband's wishes (as indicated in the story of Rabbi Hiyyah's wife). As against the talmudic rule, he states that in modern times the woman's independence in making this decision no longer holds since the husband does not have recourse to marrying another woman or divorcing his wife regardless of her wishes. After the ban of Rabbenu Gershom the decision to prevent conception must be mutual to husband and wife since it can irrevocably undercut the husband's right and duty to procreate.[11]

Recently a request was brought before the Supreme Court in Israel that in cases of abortion the husband's opinion must be heard. This request of the ultra-Orthodox party Agudat Yisrael represents the same logic as in Moses Sofer's ruling on contraception. The Supreme Court ruled that the committee which authorizes abortions (made up of two physicians and a social worker) *may*, but *need not*, hear the husband's opinion.[12]

Moses Sofer follows a restrictive path which emerges from Rabbenu Tam's interpretation that precoital *mokh* is forbidden altogether and Rashi's view that the Sages do not permit the three women to use contraception. He does leave a small opening for permitting contraception in the case of extreme danger (greater than that of the three women since there has already been actual hazardous conditions) when contraception is used after intercourse and with the husband's consent.

A more lenient position which is still based on Rashi's interpretation of the talmudic passage is offered by a contemporary of Moses Sofer:

How could the Sages permit her to place herself in danger? This is a violation of biblical law: "You shall protect your lives carefully," and we are enjoined not to rely on miracles. It must be that the danger to the three women is very remote and does not really require safeguards. . . . But where a woman is in clear danger from pregnancy . . . the Sages would agree [with Rabbi Meir] . . . so that she not be separated from her husband. [Shlomo Zalman of Posen: *Hemdat Shlomo* (Responsa) No. 46][13]

It is unthinkable for the author of *Hemdat Shlomo* that the rabbis would prohibit a woman in danger from taking protective measures such as using the *mokh*. If that were the case the rabbis would be permitting, even forcing, a woman to endanger her life, which is a violation of *pikuah nefesh*. Yet he agrees with Rashi's view that Rabbi Meir says "may use the *mokh*" and therefore the Sages mean "may not." The solution to the problem is simple: the three women are only in remote danger from pregnancy and the ruling reported in the Talmud holds for such cases of far-fetched hazard. But "where a woman is in clear danger," such as the woman considered by the Hatam Sofer (a woman who had experienced several pregnancies which threatened her life), the rabbis would agree with Rabbi Meir and permit use of contraception, in order to allow the couple to maintain their marriage: "so that she not be separated from her husband."

Menahem Mendel Schneersohn (1789–1866), the third in the dynasty of Habad rabbis, follows similar logic in his responsum on contraception. But whereas the author of *Hemdat Shlomo* allows the *mokh* only for women in great danger, Schneersohn allows it even where there is lesser risk. Even "ordinary risk" is greater in his eyes than the risk envisioned for the three women in the Talmud.

The Creator so ordained human nature that the three women ordinarily do not conceive. . . . However, in cases of ordinary risk (as in the case before us) the Sages certainly would agree with Rabbi Meir that a *mokh* must be used. The author of *Hemdat Shlomo* permits a *mokh* in case of mortal danger. But, according to the way I see it, *mokh* should be permitted even where risk is only possible, as the text says with regard to the nursing mother: lest she wean and lest he die—which is a double "lest." She may wean and yet it may not hurt him [the nursing child]; or she may, as the Talmud suggests elsewhere, hire a nurse or supplement his diet. But with danger of another kind, even the Sages would agree with what Rabbi Meir says about the nursing mother; for pregnancy to such a

woman (as in the case before us) would be much more likely than to a
nursing woman. [Menahem Mendel Schneersohn, *Tzemah Tzedek*, Even
Ha-Ezer 1 : 89][14]

The initial argument is similar to that of Shlomo Zalman: the three
women are only rarely in danger from pregnancy because they do
not normally conceive: there is a natural contraceptive effect from
their physiological state. According to Schneersohn, Rabbi Meir
requires even these women in remote danger to use a contraceptive device whereas the Sages do not. Schneersohn does not follow Rabbenu Tam's logic to its full extent by allowing the three
women, *and all others,* to use postcoital *mokh.* Rather he seeks
further proof to show that "*mokh* should be permitted even where
risk is only possible." This proof is found in the language of the
talmudic passage which postulates two factors in the hazard to a
nursing mother. The nursing mother uses a *mokh* "lest she wean"
the nursing child and "lest he die." The mother could wean the
nursing child without harm to the child, so that if she conceives
there is only a remote possibility of danger to the child. Danger to
a nursing child is more remote, in Schneersohn's view, than
danger to a minor or pregnant woman who might conceive. Therefore he concludes that the hazard which justifies using contraception covers a broad range, from "mortal danger" to any possible
risk for women who are likely to conceive (i.e., other than the
three women).

   The most permissive positions found in the Halakhah follow, as
we have said, the interpretation of Rabbenu Tam, that "use the
mokh" means "must use the *mokh.*" We are back to a simple
argument: Rabbi Meir requires the three women to use a *mokh* but
the Sages do not. Neither Rabbi Meir nor the Sages would consider forbidding the three women to use a *mokh.* This argument is
clearly laid out in one of the earliest texts on contraception, the
responsa of Hai Gaon, who wrote in the Gaonic period in Babylonia.

In the matter of the three women, the Sages did not forbid them the use of
the *mokh;* they merely said they do not have to [use it]. Most certainly
they are permitted to use it. Women who do not wish to rely on "Mercy

will be vouchsafed from heaven"—they and their husbands should use the mokh and there is no fear at all.

And as to the suggestion of the Sages that one need only supplement the child's diet, you say that someone tried it in this generation and the child was not adversely affected . . . but, when she uses the mokh so that she does not become pregnant she need have no fear [at all] even not [the worry] that supplementation of the diet [might] be necessary. ['Hai (ben Sherira) Gaon, Teshuvot Ha-Gaonim, Yevamot (p. 167)][15]

In Hai Gaon's view all the Sages wish to state is that the three women are not required to use contraception. The three women and others are free to use contraception if they so choose. Hai Gaon's reasoning is based on the final part of the Talmudic passage. He concludes from the Sages' statement "And mercy will be vouchsafed from heaven" that the three women need not use the mokh if they would rather rely on divine protection. But in general women are not required to rely on divine mercy; rather, they "should use the mokh." Hai Gaon assures that even if the husband participates in the decision to use contraception ("they and their husbands should use the mokh"), no transgression (i.e., spilling of seed) is committed.

The possibility of preventing the danger to a nursing child by directly supplementing her diet to replace the mother's lost milk might seem preferable to preventing another pregnancy altogether. However, Hai Gaon rejects it, despite the report that it works in practice, in favor of contraception. Contraception will eliminate all worries, even the minor worry about supplementing a nursing child's diet. His advocacy of using contraception for any woman who is in danger, be it as slight as having to supplement a child's diet, is quite extraordinary.

Yet Hai Gaon's is not a lone permissive voice. Solomon Luria, the Maharshal, living in the sixteenth century, held an extremely permissive view as well. Luria was second only to Moses Isserles among Ashkenazic halakhists who responded to the publication of the Shulhan Arukh with commentaries elaborating the customs practiced by Ashkenazic Jews. Thus he had great stature as an Ashkenazic halakhic authority.

Rashi assumes [that the] three women are ordinarily forbidden [to use a mokh] since *hashhatat zera* is involved. . . . Rabbenu Tam sees no violation [using a mokh] after the act [of intercourse]. . . . Hence the three women [according to Rabbenu Tam's reading] "need not" [according to the Sages] and others too may [use a mokh] . . . but only postcoital. . . . But it seems to me that although Mordecai represented Rivan as holding with Rabbenu Tam [regarding postcoital mokh as the assumed device] and RaN too so holds, still, Rashi's interpretation is the correct one. Precoital mokh is assumed and it is not improper: it is still normal intercourse, for one body derives its natural gratification from the other. It is no different than coitus with a nonchildbearing woman . . . as is evidenced by what Ri concluded from Resh Niddah where precoital mokh is taken for granted. . . . And I wonder at Rabbenu Tam, how it could have occurred to him to interpret otherwise than is obvious from Resh Niddah.

Still, the [other] point made by Rabbenu Tam is correct, that even "other women" may use the mokh and the three women "must" . . . just as Asheri said. . . . It may also be inferred from Asheri's language that precoital mokh is assumed. . . . Resh Niddah implies also that other women may, for it says, "what about women who are using the mokh . . ." not "what about the three women who are [using the mokh]. . . ." That any woman may use the mokh is the correct inference. The law follows the Sages that the three women "need not" but they and others "may." [Solomon Luria (Maharshal), *Yam Shel Shlomo* 1 : 8][16]

In two paragraphs, citing many other authorities, Luria addresses the two central issues regarding contraception: first, whether the contraceptive device is used during or after intercourse, and second, whether the phrase "use a mokh" means "may use a mokh" or "must use a mokh." On the first issue Luria sides with Rashi's presumed interpretation: precoital mokh is assumed in the text on the three women. It is precisely because he assumed precoital mokh that Rashi, in Luria's view, interpreted the Sages as saying that the three women may not use a mokh. Rashi assumed the mokh to be present in the vagina during intercourse, thus making the ejaculation wasteful (*hashhatat zera*). Rashi was right to assume precoital mokh, but he was wrong, in Luria's opinion, in deciding that intercourse in such a case is improper. What makes intercourse proper or improper is not the generative potential, for if that were the case one would be forbidden to have intercourse with a woman who is sterile, not yet capable of bearing children, or presently pregnant. But the Halakhah in fact encourages sexual intercourse with a barren or pregnant wife because of the other "benefits" of sex: fulfilling the *mitzvah* of *onah*, maintaining the happiness of the marriage, and the couple's mutual physical pleasure. Proper intercourse is defined by natural insertion of penis into vagina and the fact that "one body derives its natural gratification from the other" in the act.

Luria then rejects Rabbenu Tam's interpretation that postcoital *mokh* is assumed (despite the concurring authorities which he cites) and agrees with Rashi that the passage about the three women deals with precoital *mokh*. But he does not accept Rashi's view that precoital *mokh* causes *hashhatat zera*, and therefore, as becomes clear in the second paragraph, has no reason to forbid the three women to use it. Indeed in the second paragraph Luria sides with Rabbenu Tam's interpretation: Rabbi Meir says "Three women must use the *mokh*" while the Sages demure, holding that the three women are not required to use contraception. The conclusion is that while the Sages do not require the three women to use precoital *mokh*, they certainly do not object to the use of contraception. Neither do they find it necessary to forbid any other women to use a *mokh*. Rather the Sages, according to Luria's interpretation, hold that "any woman may use the *mokh*."

In line with his permissive position on the use of the *mokh*, Luria also presents an unusually lenient position on the issue of sterilization (*kos shel ikarin*). He permits a woman to sterilize herself when the danger is not to her own body or her children, but rather the risk of giving birth to children who will rebel and go astray from "the path of righteousness," if this has already been the case with existing offspring:

In regard to a woman who has children who are rebellious and offenders, [sorim u-morim] and she is permitted to take a sterilizing potion because she is afraid that she will have more children and they too will not follow the righteous path, I say that she should not drink [it] unless she really suffers with birth like the wife of Rabbi Hiyyah. And yet, if her sons do not follow the right path and she is fearful that she should multiply such progeny, certainly, she is permitted [to drink it]. [Solomon Luria, *Yam Shel Shlomo*, Yevamot 6 : 44]

Luria seems to contradict himself: first he states the presumption that a woman who has evil sons may sterilize herself in order not to bring more children of that kind into the world. Then he says that only suffering in birth justifies self-sterilization, but finally he concludes by affirming again that a woman may sterilize herself lest she multiply her wicked progeny. It seems that Luria is trying to describe a woman in such fear of bearing more wicked children that it causes her tangible suffering. At any rate, what this confusing passage does show is that, for Luria, the use of contraception is generally open to all women who have their own compelling reasons for wanting to avoid bearing more children.

Solomon Luria's position is the most permissive position within the bounds of the halakhic discussion. He combines Rashi's "permissive" position in respect to method of contraception and Rabbenu Tam's leniency in permitting the three women and all others to use a contraceptive device. He concludes that any woman may use a contraceptive device inserted prior to intercourse. He considers as reasonable grounds for practicing birth control not only danger or extreme pain to the mother, but also concern over the welfare of her children, both physical and moral.

Even when we consider the most permissive position of Solomon Luria we must balance it with the value of procreation in traditional Jewish society. His leniency should not be interpreted as either license for or indication of widespread use of contraception. Luria undoubtedly held procreation as a personal and communal goal of supreme importance. Rather, his permissive view must be understood as the most extreme manifestation of a conscientious effort in the Halakhah to provide women with legitimate avenues for protecting their lives, their bodies, and their existing families when continued pregnancy and childbearing was a threat. We must bear in mind that prior to the development of modern medicine pregnancy and childbirth carried a significant hazard. The fear of death in childbirth was by no means far-fetched, nor the concern about the nutrition and welfare of a nursing infant a rare problem. Thus the controversy over contraception in the Halakhah must be seen as a balancing act between the primacy of procreation and the very real hazards of childbirth.

✧ 9 ✧

ABORTION

ELECTIVE abortion has been a highly controversial issue in the last decades. The contemporary debate revolves around the question of whether a woman has the moral and/or legal right to choose to abort the fetus she carries. In Jewish law the question of purposefully induced abortion first arises in the Mishnah: May a fetus be destroyed by the mother or her agent (a physician)? The issue of abortion in the Halakhah remains a hotly debated one today.[1] There is a consensus that the Halakhah permits an abortion when it is necessary in order to save the mother's life. The grounds of contention are the possible other reasons for inducing an abortion: preventing the birth of an illegitimate child, an unwanted child, or a severely handicapped child.

The biblical sources for the discussion of abortion in the Halakhah do not address the issue of elective abortion. The Bible only refers to accidental abortion, yet this reference lays the foundation of the halakhic discussion.

[22]When men fight, and one of them pushes a pregnant woman and a miscarriage results, but no other misfortune ensues, the one responsible shall be fined according as the woman's husband may exact from him, the payment to be based on reckoning. [23]But if other misfortune ensues, the penalty shall be life for life, [24]eye for eye, tooth for tooth, hand for hand, foot for foot, [25]burn for burn, wound for wound, bruise for bruise. [Ex. 21 : 22–25]

The case in Exodus is of an accidental abortion caused by a man's striking a pregnant woman in the course of a fight with her husband. The fetus is expelled from the womb and is lost. If the woman herself suffers no harm, the man who struck her and

219

caused the miscarriage is fined. The husband sets the amount of the fine, since the loss of the fetus is deemed his loss, and the fine is paid under supervision of the judges. If, on the other hand, there is "misfortune," if, say, the woman loses her life as a result of the miscarriage, the case becomes a capital crime and the attacker pays with his own life.

There is a clear distinction in this ruling between the woman and her child: the woman is a living person, a *nefesh*, and anyone who harms her body or kills her must pay in kind. The fetus is not a person in this sense. Destroying it through causing an abortion is not a capital crime and carries no capital punishment. Rather it is a crime of causing loss and destruction, analogous to property damage. The damage is inflicted on the husband, not on the pregnant woman, since he loses his progeny. Why is it the husband who suffers the loss of progeny and not the woman? Because in biblical law, while the woman herself is not quite the property of her husband since she is a person and not an object (harming her is a capital crime and not a crime against property), any of her products, whether through work or pregnancy, are the property of her husband. The text in Exodus 21 indicates that in biblical law a fetus has the status of an object, not of a person. This fundamental principle informs the discussion of abortion in Jewish law even when the abortion is intentional and not accidental.

In Christianity there is a totally different development based on the same source, Exodus 21 : 22. This development hinges on a different translation of the phrase "but no other misfortune ensues" than the one used here, which is based on the traditional Torah text. The Septuagint translates the word *ason* ("misfortune," "disaster") to mean "form," and applies it to the fetus rather than to the mother. Subsequently the text was understood as making a distinction between a fetus that has no form and a fetus with a form. The Church Fathers ruled that a fetus is formless until the fortieth day and becomes formed thereafter. Thus killing an unformed fetus was not a capital crime but aborting a formed fetus was. Even that distinction was abolished in later Christianity because the soul was believed to enter the fetus at the moment of conception, and thus aborting a fetus even prior to the fortieth day meant dooming that soul to hell since it could not gain its salvation by baptism. Beginning with the same biblical source the Catholic church developed an absolute prohibition on abortion, while Jewish law found room to permit it.[2]

The circumstances when abortion is permitted are subject to much halakhic discussion. In the Talmud we find permission for abortion in order to save the life of the mother. The underlying justification for this ruling is that the fetus is not a living person and has no independent status. The fetus is considered a part of its mother's body: ubar yerekh immo, "a fetus is its mother's thigh" (Hulin 58a and Gittin 23b). It has no legal rights such as inheritance and holding of property. Even when it begins its path toward independent life, that is, when the birth process starts, it is still not a nefesh (living person), and it may be destroyed to save its mother:

If a woman is having difficulty giving birth, one cuts up the fetus within her and takes it out limb by limb, because her life takes precedence over its life. Once its greater part has emerged, you do not touch it, because you may not set aside one life for another. [Oholot 7 : 6]

This passage in Oholot (Oholot is a tractate in the Mishnah for which there is no talmudic commentary) is the cornerstone of the halakhic discussion of therapeutic abortion, that is, abortion performed to save the life of the mother and preserve her health. As long as the fetus has not emerged, which according to this text happens when "most of its body has come out," and according to a variant cited in Sanhedrin 72b "when its head has come out," it is not a person and therefore its life is inferior to its mother's life. Once the fetus has emerged it has the same status as the mother and then, even if it threatens the mother's life, it may not be touched. This is because the fundamental principle of capital law in the Halakhah is that one may not set one life over another because "you do not know that your blood is redder than his" (Sanhedrin 45b).

Since the text in Oholot explicitly refers to the principle that "one may not put aside one life for another," it seems absolutely clear that the reason one *may* dismember a fetus in the birth process to save the mother is that it does not yet have such "life." Such indeed is Rashi's explanation: "For as long as it has not yet emerged into the world, it is not a *nefesh* [living person] and one may kill it to save its mother" (Rashi on Sanhedrin 72b). By extension of the same principle, if the fetus threatens the life of the mother prior to the beginning of birth, for example, in the case of severe hemorrhaging or toxemia, its life should be set aside to save the life of the mother.

Most cases of threat to the mother's life occur during the birth process itself, as described in Oholot. The Talmud rules that because the fetus is not a *nefesh* it may be aborted to save the mother's life so long as it has not emerged sufficiently to acquire its own life. In another context the Talmud rules that a newborn is not actually considered viable (*bar kayma*) until it has lived for thirty days (Niddah 44b). Could we perhaps say that even a newborn infant is not a full-fledged life and may be set aside to protect its mother's life? No, because even though the newborn's future life is still in question, the life it possesses now has the same worth as the life of a viable person.

Ben Zion Uziel, who was chief rabbi of Israel in the 1950s, explained this principle in his ruling on abortion:

Because when a child dies within thirty days (being then considered a stillborn and not mourned like a person who had died) it becomes evident only in retrospect that it was stillborn [*nefel*] and that the period of its life was only a continuation of the vitality of its mother that remained in him. But if one should kill it within the thirty days because its life is only a continuation of the mother's vitality, since there is no way of ascertaining whether it indeed was a stillborn or not, that is not a crime for which one is executed, because of the doubt. Nevertheless it is certainly prohibited to kill it, because of that doubt. [Ben Zion Uziel, *Mishpetei Uziel*, Hoshen Mishpat 3 : 46]

Uziel explains that it is only in retrospect, when a newborn dies before it reaches its thirtieth day, that one realizes that it was in fact a stillborn. You cannot justify killing a newborn by the argument that it might have died within the first thirty days anyway.

But Uziel rules in an unusually lenient manner that a person who kills a child within thirty days of its birth is not liable for a capital crime because of the questionable life of the child. He uses this conclusion to justify therapeutic abortion. His ruling is actually of greater significance to another problem which, to the best of my knowledge, has not yet been formally addressed in the halakhic literature: the problem of discontinuation of life-support mechanisms for a premature or severely damaged newborn baby who cannot live independently.[3]

In addition to permitting an abortion to save the life of a woman having great difficulty in childbirth (clearly, life-threatening difficulty and not the natural pain of the birth process), the Talmud permits, even orders, an abortion in another situation: when a pregnant woman is sentenced to execution. As we shall see, this rather peculiar ruling serves as the basis for those halakhists who wish to be lenient and permit abortion in other than life-threatening circumstances. The passage in Arakhin which contains the discussion of abortion in a woman doomed to execution must be understood as a theoretical analysis of principles, not as a reflection of practice, since it is evident that in talmudic times, capital punishment was generally not carried out.

Mishnah: If a woman is about to be executed, one does not wait for her until she gives birth; but if she had already sat on the birthstool [yashvah al ha-mashber] one waits for her until she gives birth. . . .

Gemara: But that is self-evident, for it is her body! It is necessary to teach it, for one might have assumed since Scripture says "according as the woman's husband shall lay upon him" that it [the woman's child] is the husband's property, of which he should not be deprived. Therefore, we are informed [that it is not so]. . . .

"But if she had already sat on the birthstool": What is the reason? As soon as it moves [from its place in the womb] it is another body [gufa aharina]. Rav Judah said in the name of Samuel: If a woman is about to be executed one strikes her against her womb so that the child may die first, to avoid her being disgraced. That means to say that [otherwise] she dies first? But we have an established principle that the child dies first. . . . This applies only to [her natural] death because the child's life is very frail. The drop [of poison] from the angel of death enters and destroys its vital organs, but in the case of death by execution she dies first. . . . [Arakhin 7a–b]

Let us first summarize this rather complex passage in Arakhin. The Mishnah begins with a ruling in the context of laws pertaining to the benefits which the living may derive from the dead (persons and animals). The ruling is that a pregnant woman sentenced to execution is killed immediately unless the birth process has already started. In other words, one does not wait for the pregnancy to be completed and the child to be born, but destroys both the mother and the embryo she carries. The Gemara opens with a question: Is it not self-evident that one does not wait for the fetus to mature and be born since we know that the fetus is considered a mere part of its mother's body? The answer is that it is not self-evident since one might have concluded from Exodus 21 where the fetus is the property of its father that the father may not be deprived of his property because his wife has transgressed and is to be executed. Therefore, explains the Gemara, an explicit ruling is necessary. The only exception to the rule is when the fetus has already begun its descent into the birth canal (when the mother has "sat on the birthstool"). However, this exception has nothing to do with the father's property rights, but rather with the fact that at this point the fetus has become "a separate body" (notice, not yet an independent life!) and is no longer part of its mother's body.

Following the general explication of the passage the Gemara enters a rather grisly discussion of the details of the fetus's fate in the execution. According to Samuel the fetus is not merely a passive part of the woman's body in the execution, but rather one purposely attempts to kill it. His reasoning is that the woman not be disgraced in the execution. How might she be disgraced? Rashi explains that the trauma of the execution could cause the onset of labor and a stillbirth in the midst of the execution. To prevent this the fetus is killed first. The rabbis question this reasoning not on moral-religious grounds but on the basis of their physiological knowledge. Do we not know that when a pregnant woman dies her fetus always dies first because the cause of her death ("the drop from the angel of death") enters the womb first and destroys the fetus? The answer is that this principle holds in the case of natural death from disease, but not in the case of sudden death by execution. Samuel's principle thus remains: one kills the fetus first to avoid the mother's disgrace at her last moments of life.

The passage in Arakhin seems a rather bizarre mixture of cruelty and compassion. On the one hand we have a seemingly heartless, technical discussion of the execution of a pregnant woman and the destruction of her fetus. It seems extremely cruel to the woman who cannot give birth to her child and to the fetus which is not given a chance to be born and live its own life. On the other hand the consideration behind this is in fact a compassion and concern for the woman who has been doomed. The Gemara does not explicate these considerations but they are explained by the commentary of the Tosafot. It would be cruel to the woman if she were not executed immediately in order to wait for the birth of the child, explain the Tosafot, because a delay between sentencing and execution is a form of torture, *innui ha-din*. *Innui ha-din*, delay in carrying out the sentence, is prohibited in Jewish law because it adds unwarranted anguish to the punishment. A person sentenced to execution should not be tormented psychologically by having to await and anticipate his end. Therefore a pregnant woman is executed immediately rather than being made to wait in anguish until the pregnancy comes to its term. This, the Tosafot clarify, only holds when the sentence has already been pronounced. If the woman is known to be pregnant before the trial or the determination of the sentence, the sentencing itself is postponed until after the birth. In such a case, waiting is not *innui ha-din* because the woman can hope for acquittal or a lesser punishment.

The practical importance of the ruling in Arakhin is not of course for cases of execution, but for other cases where the mother is in great distress due to the pregnancy. It is possible to deduce from Arakhin a general principle that a fetus may be aborted to avoid mental anguish (any condition analogous to *innui ha-din*) or disgrace to the mother. Only a few halakhists choose to pursue this logic. The most permissive among them is Jacob Emden:

You asked if it is prohibited to destroy a fetus in the womb of a mother who is known to have been whoring, whether a single woman or a married woman.

I found the responsum in the book *Havat Yair* where the rabbi [Yair Bachrach] was asked about it. . . . And this is his answer: . . . There is no difference between her being single and available, and the fetus being a *mamzer* [bastard] from a married woman. . . . And I, most junior among my peers, say that in my humble opinion there is a big difference in this matter . . . between [a married woman who commited adultery] and a single woman, or, certainly, a married woman who is pregnant from her husband. . . . Indeed, the one asking the question asked about a married woman who had whored and it is a very good question, and I, according to my views, would lean toward permitting her [to abort] if I were worthy of giving a ruling. For, it seems to me that there is room to be lenient since she had committed adultery and "the blood is on her hands." From now on she is doomed to execution according to the law of the Torah. Even though her life is not given into our hands to end, nevertheless she is condemned to death by the judgment of Heaven . . . and if her sentence were in our hands we would have executed her and the fruit of her womb, just as it is in Arakhin where you do not wait for her [to give birth]. And this case is even stronger since there [Arakhin] it is in reference even to a legitimate fetus and here it is a fetus conceived through transgression that is also condemned to death.

It is evident that you do not worry about it [the fetus] and it is killed through [the execution of] its mother. Therefore, it seems to me simple that there is also no prohibition against destroying it. . . .

And even with a legitimate fetus, there is reason to be lenient for the sake of a great need as long as it had not yet moved even if it is not a case of threat to the mother's life, but to save her from it because it causes her pain. And the matter needs further deliberation.

Nevertheless, it is evident that there is still a prohibition *a priori* on destroying the fetus. . . . clearly it is not forbidden when it is done because of a [great] need. . . . Therefore, our ruling is: if there is no reason [that is, in case of legitimate fruit] it is forbidden to destroy the fetus. But in the case before us of a married woman who went astray, I have pronounced my lenient opinion that it is permitted [to abort], and perhaps it even almost has the reward of a *mitzvah*. . . . [Jacob Emden, *Responsa She'elat Ya'avetz*, No. 43]

The case discussed by Emden was first brought to another authority, Yair Bachrach (1638–1702, Germany), who ruled on it in his responsum (no. 31) in *Havat Yair*. It involved a married woman who conceived in adultery. Afterward "she repented and cried out all day and all night without rest to her teary eyes, which flowed tears like a river, and she struck her head against the wall till it bled" and she asked her husband and the rabbi to allow her to repent. She suspected that she was pregnant because her menstruation ceased, and so she went to the rabbi to ask if she may "drink from the potion which will expel the cursed seed." The author of *Havat Yair* first rules that the Halakhah is no different for a *mamzer* (bastard) than for a legitimate child. Bachrach then argues on the basis of talmudic reasoning that "there is total permission for what you have asked [performing an abortion] according to the law of the Torah, were it not for the custom held among us and among them [non-Jews] to prevent breaking the restrictions against prostitution and those whoring after promiscuity." In other words, Bachrach holds that from a strictly legal point of view the woman in question may drink a potion that will induce an abortion. Yet he finally rules against it because of the prevailing customs of Jews and gentiles alike to forbid abortion (for Jews, of course, other than to save the mother's life), in order to hold promiscuity in check.

Bachrach holds that the law which does not forbid abortion (prior to forty days) applies equally to legitimate and illegitimate fruit. But in the end he reverses his lenient position. Emden takes issue with Bachrach's claim that there is no difference between a legitimate child and a bastard. He argues that a woman who conceived in adultery would be sentenced to death according to Torah law, and she and her fetus would be killed. Therefore the fetus is really condemned to death by the law and the mother may then kill it "and we do not worry about his life." Emden's argument seems logical enough, but suffers a major flaw. The fact that the fetus would die with the mother if she were to be executed by a court does not mean that anyone else, including the mother, may kill it. Still, with this argument in addition to the standard ones, Emden feels there is enough reason to rule that "there is no prohibition against destroying it."

Regarding legitimate children Emden also differs with Bachrach and renders, in his words, "a lenient opinion." Though he does not rule that abortion is generally permitted (as does Bachrach), he introduces less than life-threatening circumstances as legitimate grounds for permitting abortion. He allows aborting a legitimate child in a case of "great need," provided that it is done before the fetus begins to move on its way out of the womb. What is such "great need"? Emden does not clarify it beyond referring to the pain caused to the mother. Clearly this could not be the natural pain of birth. On the other hand it is evidently not a threat to life, but a lesser hazard. Perhaps Emden does not explicitly define "great need" on purpose, for this vagueness makes his ruling flexible. Through this general term he allows abortion for reasons of suffering, not only threat of death, and leaves the determination of what constitutes "great need" to each rabbi in every specific circumstance. One set of circumstances may cause pain and great need to one woman but not to others, and furnish grounds for permitting her to abort where others would continue the pregnancy to term.[4]

As opposed to the talmudic rulings permitting abortion in order to save the mother's life and preserve her from anguish and disgrace, there are several passages in the Talmud which tend to prohibit abortion. The clearest of such statements is Rabbi Yishmael's:

Rabbi Yishmael says: "He who spills the blood of man, in [by] man shall his blood be spilled." What is "man in man"? This is the fetus. [Sanhedrin 57b]

Yishmael's statement is an interpretation of the passage in Genesis 9 in which, following the Flood, the sons of Noah are given a set of universal laws. One of these laws pertains to capital crimes and rules that whoever commits murder shall be killed by his fellowmen: "He who spills man's blood by man shall his blood be spilled." The Hebrew is ambiguous since the letter *bet* can mean either "by" or "in." Yishmael interprets the *bet* not to mean "by man" but "in man." He therefore reads the verse in Genesis (against its plain meaning): "He who spills the blood of a 'man in a man' shall be killed." The "man in a man" he understands to be a fetus.

The laws given to the sons of Noah are regarded by the rabbis as universal moral laws governing the gentiles (*Bnei Noah*). According to Yishmael, killing a fetus is prohibited to the gentiles and considered a capital crime. Yet, as Rashi explains in his commentary to Yishmael's statement, "If [a gentile] strikes a woman and her child is expelled, he is executed for this, and among Israel he is not until [the fetus] emerges into the world." The notion that abortion is a capital crime for gentiles but not for Jews was problematic since the Halakhah typically assumes that the laws of Bnei Noah are encompassed within the laws of the Jews which are much stricter and more numerous. The Tosafot solve this problem by arguing that abortion is a transgression for both Jews and gentiles. For a gentile, killing a fetus is a *capital* crime and for a Jew it is not. For a Jew it is a transgression of the category *asur aval patur* (prohibited but not punishable). Despite this formal distinction, as a rule gentile and Jew are both prohibited from killing a fetus but are permitted to do so in order to save the life of the mother. While the prohibition of abortion to Bnei Noah does not interfere with the permission to abort a fetus in order to save its mother, it does express very forcefully the fundamental opposition to abortion.

The view of abortion in the Talmud is therefore two-sided. On the one hand, the fetus is not considered a person and thus may be set aside to save the mother's life and preserve her from disgrace. On the other hand the fetus is a potential person and thus killing it is similar to murder. In fact the universal laws for non-Jews equate abortion with murder. The laws of the Jews do not rule out abortion as murder, but do include the fetus in the same category with all living persons who should be saved at all costs, even if one has to violate the law to do so (Arakhin 7b).

Despite the complexity of the talmudic view of abortion, it would have been reasonably simple for subsequent halakhists if they could rely on the Talmud alone in rendering judgments on abortion. There would be no question about allowing abortion to save the mother's life, and there would be a natural spectrum of opinions about what circumstances constitute the same suffering as *innui ha-din* or the disgrace of a woman about to be executed.

However, a ruling in Maimonides' *Mishneh Torah* confuses and complicates the issue for all halakhists writing from the twelfth century onward:

This, too, is a *mitzvah:* not to take pity on the life of a pursuer [*rodef*]. Therefore the Sages have ruled that when a woman has difficulty in giving birth one may cut up the child within her womb, either by drugs or by surgery, because he is like a pursuer seeking to kill her. Once his head has emerged he may not be touched for we do not set aside one life for another; this is the natural course of the world. [Maimonides, *Mishneh Torah*, Hilkhot Rotze'ah U-Shmirat Nefesh 1 : 9][5]

Maimonides cites the ruling of Oholot Chapter 7 which allows dismembering a fetus in order to save the mother's life, but he brings a totally different justification for it. Whereas in Oholot, and in Rashi as well, the justification is that the fetus is not a *nefesh,* in Maimonides the reason is that the fetus is like a pursuer. The Halakhah permits anyone who sees a person pursuing another in order to kill him (indicated by a weapon in his hand, etc.) to kill the pursuer in order to save the victim. The normal rules pertaining to manslaughter are suspended: one may kill the pursuer without warning and due process. Furthermore, Maimonides states that it is prohibited to take pity on the pursuer and refrain from killing him. He must be killed in order to save the victim. This law is Maimonides' justification for killing a fetus when the birth threatens the mother's life.

The apparent implication of Maimonides' ruling is that it is *only* because the fetus is a pursuer that one may kill it, and *not* because the fetus is not a *nefesh* and thus its life inferior to the life of the mother. This contradicts the discussion in Sanhedrin 72b where the question of the fetus as a pursuer is considered. In the passage in Sanhedrin it is suggested that the fetus be considered a pursuer but this suggestion is then rejected. The reason is that the threat which the fetus poses to the mother is part of nature, unlike murder. Therefore abortion is permitted because the fetus is not a *nefesh,* not because it "pursues" its mother. Yet Maimonides puts forth the "pursuer" argument and thus implies that no other circumstances besides threat to the mother's life warrants abortion, making it difficult to understand and justify the rulings of Arakhin 7a–b, Sanhedrin 72b, and Rashi.

The contradiction between Maimonides' view and the talmudic sources poses difficulties for those writing after him, and indeed much of the halakhic discussion focuses on the problem of the fetus as a pursuer.[6] Furthermore there are problems in the logic behind Maimonides' ruling, for it seems flawed in and of itself. Yehezkel Landau (eighteenth century, Prague), for example, in a responsum on abortion, raises some of the inherent logical problems in Maimonides' pursuer argument:

And the difficulty in the ruling of Maimonides is that he considers the fetus before its head emerges to be a pursuer, and after its head emerges he does not consider him a pursuer for that is "the natural course of the world." And this is peculiar since before the head emerges it is also "the natural course of the world"! Unfortunately, this matter has not been clarified for me and I find no clear way to explain it, and to explain it away with excuses—that has already been done in previous generations. [Yehezkel Landau, *Noda bi-Yehudah* (2nd ed.), Hoshen Mishpat No. 59]

If Maimonides holds that it is only because the fetus is a pursuer that we may kill it and not because it has inferior status, that is understandable. But then, what is the difference between a fetus before its head has emerged and one after? The fundamental point of the law in the Talmud is that there is a difference between a yet-unborn fetus, which is not yet a *nefesh*, and a fetus whose head has emerged and is already a living person. If you abolish this distinction, as Maimonides implicitly does, you are left with no distinctions at all. The fetus after the head has emerged is pursuing its mother just as much as the fetus before birth. Or, as Landau states it, if the fetus after the head emerges is not considered a pursuer because the difficulty of birth is part of the natural course of things, why is this not true for the fetus before the head emerges? Is it not part of the natural course of things that a fetus has difficulty emerging from the womb and thereby endangers its mother's life?

Most authors do not focus on this logical problem in Maimonides. Rather, they are preoccupied with the contradiction between Maimonides' view and the Talmud and Rashi. Two basic approaches emerge: one essentially adopts Maimonides' pursuer argument as the one and only justification for aborting a fetus, while the other tries to "save" the view of Rashi and the Talmud that the fetus is not a *nefesh* until its head emerges, and explain Maimonides' statement as a reference to only a specific aspect of the problem of abortion. The first approach leads to the most stringent rulings on abortion, permitting abortion only in cases where the fetus endangers its mother's life during birth prior to the emergence of the head. The second view allows more lenient rulings because it continues to hold that the fetus before birth is inferior to the mother in its claim on life. This view permits abortion in cases of hazard other than death during birth.

The first approach can be seen in the halakhic writings of Hayyim Soloveitchik (died 1918):

The reason for the opinion of Maimonides here, namely, that the fetus is like a pursuer pursuing her in order to kill her, is that he believed that a fetus falls into the general law of *pikuah nefesh* [avoiding hazard to life] in the Torah since a fetus, too, is considered a *nefesh* and is not put aside for the life of others. And if we intend to save [her] life through the life of the fetus and he were not a pursuer the law would pertain that you do not save one *nefesh* through [sacrificing] another. Therefore, if we were to judge this case according to the general rule of *pikuah nefesh* in the Torah we would not put aside the fetus's life for the mother's life. And it is only because of the law of saving the one who is pursued that there is the ruling that the fetus's life is put aside to save the mother's life. . . . [*Hiddushei Rabbi Hayyim Soloveitchik* to *Mishneh Torah*, Hilkhot Rotze'ah 1 : 9]

Soloveitchik states emphatically that the fetus *is* considered a *nefesh* and therefore is protected by the law of *pikuah nefesh* and by the law which forbids choosing one life over another. Only because the fetus is a pursuer may you save the mother through killing it. Soloveitchik regards Maimonides' rule of the pursuer not as a ruling against the pursuer but as a duty toward the pursued; the victim must be saved from murder.

Issar Unterman, chief rabbi of Israel in the 1960s and 1970s, advanced the same principle as Soloveitchik: the fetus may be killed only because it becomes a pursuer; otherwise killing a fetus "is within the category of murder . . . and without the reason of 'pursuer' it is altogether forbidden to kill the fetus."[7] However, Unterman modifies his strict position by allowing certain circumstances of emotional distress to qualify as pursuit for murder by the fetus. The circumstances are those where pregnancy and birth may cause the mother such distress that she will have suicidal intentions. In such a case the fetus is threatening the mother's life, though the agent of "pursuit" is the mother herself. A fetus that plunges its mother into a suicidal state may be considered a pursuer and thus may be aborted.

As against the strict views of Soloveitchik and Unterman, we find authorities who try to maintain a more lenient position. The most lenient, like Jacob Emden, essentially reject the ruling by Maimonides. They view it as an addendum to the talmudic rule, aiming to strengthen the justification for abortion but not intending to undermine or challenge the reason stated in the Talmud for permitting abortion. Most authorities try to walk a fine line between Maimonides and the Talmud as interpreted by Rashi. Shneor Zalman (Freikin) of Lublin (died 1902), for example, explains that the reason for Maimonides' "pursuer" argument is not to eliminate the reasoning in the Talmud (that the fetus is not a nefesh) but to teach us that the fetus is the type of pursuer that pursues without evil intention. It is like the case of a load on a ship that is about to sink at sea, and may be cast away in order to save the ship and its passengers:

In such circumstances the cargo is the reason for the danger to life and is therefore called pursuer. Even though there is no crime in the cargo that is on the boat at all, and the excess weight is caused equally by the people [nefashot] as by the cargo, nevertheless, the cargo is considered pursuer and it is sacrificed to save the people. [Shneor Zalman of Lublin, Responsa Torat Hesed 2 : 42]

The point of the analogy between the fetus and cargo on a ship is that both are considered pursuers without having evil intentions and without purposeful pursuit. The second similarity is that when compared to the life of a living person (nefesh) both the cargo and the fetus are sacrificed to save the person's life though they did no wrong. The interesting element in this interpretation is that Shneor Zalman uses the pursuer argument to learn something relevant about the fetus, but ultimately relies on the inferior status of its life to justify "throwing it overboard" like the cargo, in order to save the mother's life. In other words, in principle he does not abandon the ruling of the Talmud and Rashi that the fetus's life is set aside because it is not a *nefesh*.[8]

The more lenient position allows abortions in cases of hazard to the mother, other than mortal danger. Such was a case brought before Ben Zion Uziel, who like Unterman was a chief rabbi in Israel.

You have checked with me about a question brought before you where a woman who was suffering some ailment in her ear became pregnant and then became dangerously ill and the doctors told her that if she does not abort her fetus she should become totally deaf in both ears. She and her husband fear God and keep His laws and they ask if they are permitted to follow the doctors' orders and abort the fetus by means of drugs, in order to save her from total deafness for the rest of her life. . . .

We learn in this matter that according to the doctors the fetus will cause its mother deafness for the rest of her life, and there is no greater disgrace than that, for it will ruin the rest of her life, make her miserable all her days and make her undesirable in the eyes of her husband. Therefore, it is my humble opinion that she should be permitted to abort her fetus through highly qualified doctors who will guarantee ahead of time that her life will be preserved, as much as this is possible. [Ben Zion Uziel, *Mishpetei Uziel*, Hoshen Mishpat 3 : 46]

Uziel rules in favor of allowing an abortion in order to save the mother's hearing, even though her life itself is not endangered (he is careful to require abortion by competent doctors lest the abortion itself endanger the mother's life). He bases his ruling on Arakhin, where abortion is permitted to save the woman from disgrace. He holds that "there is no greater disgrace" for the woman than losing her hearing completely, for she will be miserable, and possibly become unattractive and a nuisance to her husband. This could ultimately undermine her marriage and ruin her life. Uziel's view is that because the fetus is not a *nefesh* it may be killed in order to protect the mother. On the other hand, he continues, the status of the fetus does not allow aborting it when there is no good reason, since the fetus has potential life:

At any rate, it is very clear that they did not permit killing a fetus other than when there is a need for it, even if the need is a slim one [*tzorekh kalush*], such as when it would disgrace the mother. But without a need it is certainly prohibited, because it is destruction and prevention of the possibility of life for a *nefesh* in Israel.

Uziel's view is very lenient. Not only does he allow abortion for almost any "need," even a weak cause, but he does not cite murder, or the suggestion of murder, as the reason for prohibiting abortion "without a need." Rather, protection of potential life is the reason for prohibiting abortion without good cause.

Most recently Menachem Elon, chief justice of the Israeli Supreme Court and a highly regarded scholar of the history of Jewish law (author of the three-volume compendium *Ha-Mishpat Ha-Ivri*), published his view on the question of whether or not abortion is considered murder in the Halakhah. As against the position of Unterman, who equates abortion with murder, Elon states: "Other halakhists follow the more generally accepted way of the Halakhah in arguing that killing a fetus does not constitute a violation of the prohibition on murder, but only a transgression against a [lesser] prohibition, which most authorities consider a prohibition according to the rabbis only [not according to the Torah]."[9]

In a volume of responsa composed during the Holocaust, Ephrayim Oshri addresses the question of permitting abortion in order to save both mother and infant from murder by the Nazis. He introduces the volume of responsa by saying: "I wrote outlines of these answers in those days of horror so that they should remain in memory."

In the matter of saving herself by abortion in the Ghetto: I was asked . . . about a woman who became pregnant in the Ghetto if she is permitted to abort in order to eliminate the pregnancy since the Nazis [ha-tme'im] ordered that any Jewish woman who becomes pregnant shall be killed, she and her fetus, and therefore this is a matter of danger to life.

. . . When a specific person has been requested from the community, they may hand him over [so that he shall be killed and the community saved], all the more so here: certainly it is pemitted to kill the fetus in order to save the woman. . . . And since in this case it is clear that both of them would die, definitely one should permit her to perform an abortion. [Ephrayim Oshri, *Responsa mi-Ma'amakim*, Part 1, No. 20]

Oshri cites the ruling that a community may sacrifice one of its members in order to save everyone else, if the person is someone who has been specified and requested by name. If you may do that with a living person, certainly you may do it with a fetus. Since it is clear beyond doubt that without an abortion both mother and fetus will be killed, an abortion is permitted. The situation Oshri discusses pertains to the inhuman tyranny of the Nazis. But a similar problem could arise for medical reasons. It is conceivable that a pregnancy and/or birth would threaten the life of both mother and child. In such a case, as in the case discussed by Oshri, an abortion is mandated.

Contemporary questions to halakhic authorities have often focused on circumstances where there is danger to the future child and not to the mother. Problems of this nature arose with mothers who feared the birth of a child with severe deformities or retardation because the mother used Thalidomide or contracted rubella during the pregnancy. Abortion was sought in order to prevent the birth of a deformed child into a life of suffering. The Halakhah has no room for killing a fetus in order to prevent its future suffering, because handicap or suffering do not infringe on the right to live. However, in a recent opinion Rabbi Moshe Yonah Ha-Levi Zweig of Antwerp ruled that in the case of a Thalidomide baby abortion is permitted before the fortieth day, but afterward may only be performed "for the mother's health" and not for other considerations.[10] A possible way out of this problem is to rely on the view of Emden and others that anguish to the mother constitutes a "great need" and can justify abortion. Thus Rabbi Yehiel Jacob Weinberg, an authority who lived in Switzerland, published a ruling in 1966 permitting a woman who contracted rubella during her first trimester to abort the fetus because fear that it will be born "without some organ or without any intelligence . . . causes her pain."[11]

An even more extreme case is that of a fetus known to have Tay-Sachs disease, for not only is such a fetus doomed to great physical suffering, but its life expectancy is very short (three to four years). Thus the mother can expect great suffering if she bears such a child, and the child is ultimately not viable since the disease is terminal and incurable. Because of these considerations, Eliezer Waldenberg (1917——), a prominent rabbi in Jerusalem, has ruled that aborting a Tay-Sachs fetus is permitted:

One should permit . . . abortion as soon as it becomes evident without doubt from the test that, indeed, such a baby [Tay-Sachs baby] shall be born, even until the seventh month of her pregnancy. . . . If, indeed, we may permit an abortion according to the Halakhah because of "great need" and because of pain and suffering, it seems that this is the classic case for such permission. And it is irrelevant in what way the pain and suffering is expressed, whether it is physical or psychological. Indeed, psychological suffering is in many ways much greater than the suffering of the flesh. [Eliezer Waldenberg, *Responsa Tzitz Eliezer*, Part 13, No. 102]

While Waldenberg argues very strongly for permitting abortion to a woman faced with the tragedy of giving birth to a Tay-Sachs baby, other contemporary halakhists have opposed this, as they maintain that only direct physical threat to the mother's life is legitimate grounds for abortion.

Not unlike Catholics and fundamentalist Protestants, Orthodox Jews are faced with the challenge of mores from their surrounding environment regarding abortion that have changed radically in the last decades. In North America and Europe wide sections of the population consider abortion a legitimate option for a woman who does not want the child she carries, regardless of her reasons. Despite repeated challenges from religious quarters this is also the status quo codified in law in many countries. In Israel abortion is legally more restricted. In 1977 the Israeli Knesset put into law what had been the prevailing practice, permitting abortion in cases of serious hazard to the mother; conception from adultery, child pregnancy, and rape; suspicion of severe birth defects and congenital disease; and of pressing socioeconomic factors which would prevent the parents from providing the essentials of a healthy environment. The last item was a subject of great controversy because the religious party Agudat Yisrael opposed it vociferously. In 1979, as part of the coalition agreement between the Likud party and Agudat Yisrael, the last category was repealed from the law.

In response to the challenge of the environment, most Orthodox rabbis have adopted the more stringent view of abortion. It has become a common practice to cry out against abortion as murder and as a form of genocide. Often the memory of the Holocaust is brought into the discussion, with those supporting and practicing abortion cast as Hitler's accomplices. As against this view, the critics of Orthodoxy and Halakhah have accused Jewish law and tradition of total disregard for the essential human rights of women and subjugation of women to the role of child producers. In the heat of the debate each side often disregards the range of opinions which are in fact represented in the Halakhah through its historical development.

Despite the complexity of the issue, one can make some generalizations about abortion in Jewish law. The Halakhah does not recognize a right of a woman to abort a child because it is unwanted, in order to limit the size of her family, or in order to save herself the pain and suffering which are naturally inherent in giving birth and raising children. But it does recognize as a fundamental principle the right of a woman to protect her life by abortion. It is part of the right, and duty, of self-preservation (*pikuah nefesh*). The strict interpreters of the principle include within it only the protection of life in cases where the fetus threatens the mother with death. The more lenient halakhists include in the principle of self-protection defense against other hazards: pain, mental anguish, and disgrace. But for halakhists of both approaches, abortion is always an extraordinary measure in extreme circumstances.

✶ 10 ✶

RAPE

OUR CONCEPTION of rape has undergone a major change in recent years. Whereas in the past rape was generally regarded as a crime of passion and uncontrollable sexual urges, it is viewed today primarily as an act of violence. It is an act of violence between a man and a woman who are cast in traditional social and familial roles as strong and weak, dominating and subservient, aggressor and victim. This new understanding of rape is based, on the one hand, on psychological studies of men who have committed rape, and on the other hand, on the new awareness of male and female roles and images in our society which feminism has brought into focus.[1]

In the Halakhah we find a complex view of rape. Rape is generally seen as a forced act fueled by sexual urges (even between husband and wife) or alternatively as a man's way of forcibly acquiring a wife by sexually possessing her. But we also find recognition of the aggressive-sadistic element in rape. The Bible includes a number of accounts of rape where the primary motivation is violence, not sexual gratification. The most striking are the descriptions of the gang rape of the Levite's concubine in the town of Givah (Judges 19), and the attempted homosexual rape of Lot's guests (the three angels) in Sodom (Genesis 19). If we compare the two accounts we find many literary similarities, suggesting that the two accounts were fashioned to resemble one another to accentuate their impact as stories of ultimate human barbarism. In the story of Lot the townspeople demand that the three men who came to visit Lot be handed over to them so that they can sexually molest them. Lot attempts to save his guests by offering his two virgin daughters to the crowd instead. But why he prefers to sacri-

239

fice his daughters and have them raped to save his guests is not explained. Presumably this is because of the supreme obligation of a host to his guests, and probably also because rape of a woman was considered less abhorrent than homosexual rape.

In biblical legislation rape is considered from two angles: the assault and the financial damage inflicted upon the woman and her father, respectively, and the involvement of sexual transgression. If the woman who has been raped is an available virgin, in biblical law the crime is primarily against the woman's father, who incurs a financial loss. The crime is a civil matter, settled by appropriate financial compensation. If the woman who was raped was a betrothed virgin, or a married woman for that matter, the rape takes on much greater implications because it involves a sexual transgression and the man is punished accordingly:

[22]If a man is found lying with another man's wife, both of them—the man and the woman with whom he lay—shall die. Thus you will sweep away evil from your midst.
[23]In the case of a virgin who is pledged to a man—if a man comes upon her in town and lies with her, [24]you shall take the two of them out to the gate of that town and stone them to death: the girl because she did not cry for help in the town, and the man because he violated his neighbor's wife. Thus you will sweep away evil from your midst.
[25]But if the man comes upon the engaged girl in the open country, and the man seizes her and lies with her by force, only the man who lay with her shall die, [26]but you shall do nothing to the girl. The girl is not guilty of a capital offense, for this case is like that of a man attacking another and murdering him. [27]He came upon her in the open; though the engaged girl cried for help, there was no one to save her.
[28]If a man comes upon a virgin who is not engaged and he seizes her and lies with her, and they are discovered, [29]the man who lay with her shall pay the girl's father fifty [shekels of] silver, and she shall be his wife. Because he has violated her, he can never have the right to divorce her. [Deut. 22 : 22–29]

Four different cases of illegal sexual relations are considered here:

1. A man and a married woman (another man's wife) have sex by mutual consent.

2. A man and a betrothed virgin have sex in the city, seemingly by mutual consent since she does not protest (cry out).

3. A man takes a betrothed virgin against her will (in the countryside).

4. A man takes an unbetrothed virgin against her will.

The first two cases do not involve rape; sexual relations are not forced upon the woman. The first case is simply the paradigmatic, most common, and least complicated sexual transgression: sexual relations with another man's wife. This is a case of adultery.

The second and third cases involve a betrothed virgin. A betrothed virgin is in a particularly vulnerable position: while she is legally committed to a certain man through betrothal, she is still a virgin living with her own family as if she were single and available. She is not yet under the protection of her husband. The fact that the biblical text focuses on the betrothed virgin is not accidental, nor is it a mere oversight that the Bible does not address the case of a married woman who has been raped. The reason behind this has to do with what rape meant to the author of this legislation. Rape was not seen as a crime of sexual assault against a random woman because she is a female, but rather as a calculated attempt by a man to acquire a woman as his wife against her and her parents' wishes. Thus rape is analogous to illegal seizure. No man in his right mind would try to seize a married woman since he would know that she is forbidden to him. With a betrothed virgin there may be a temptation to force her into marriage since her status is in limbo. Such an attempt is conceivable especially if we imagine a situation where one woman is sought by several suitors and one of the rejected suitors tries to get his way despite the wishes of the woman or her father.[2]

The exceptional vulnerability of a betrothed woman leads the biblical text to devote the most attention to her situation if she is raped. In the first case involving a betrothed virgin the sexual encounter occurs in a town or city, when "a man comes upon her" and "lies with her." In that case we are not dealing with rape: it is assumed by the Bible that the woman consented "because she did not cry for help." Had she been unwilling the betrothed virgin would have called out and would have been at least noticed (the fact of rape thus recognized), if not rescued. In biblical law the

simple fact that the woman was in the city was sufficient to conclude that she was a consenting partner. Postbiblical law, as we
shall see, amended this to include more complex considerations
of the issues of consent and compulsion.

The last case—the virgin who is unbetrothed and thus available
for marriage—is rape, pure and simple, whereas the case of the
betrothed virgin in the field is a compounded one of rape and
sexual transgression. If we compare the punishment meted out in
each case an important distinction emerges. The man who meets a
betrothed virgin in the country where her crying out cannot be
heard, seizes her, and rapes her, is stoned to death. His offense is
twofold: like a murderer, he has attacked his victim and he violated the prohibition of adultery. Yet, the essence of the offense is
having sexual relations with another man's wife. How do we
know that the major offense is having sex with another man's wife
rather than the assault entailed in "violating" her? Because the
punishment for raping a virgin who does not belong to another
man is so much less severe. A man who rapes an available virgin
is punished in two ways: he pays her father fifty shekels, and he
must marry the woman, and is forbidden ever to divorce her, a
right that a properly married man holds. He pays the fifty shekels
to her father as compensation for the loss the father has suffered:
the loss of the "bride money" he could expect for his daughter. It
may also serve to compensate him for the degradation brought
upon the family whose daughter is not married in the proper
customary way. The prohibition on divorcing the woman aims to
protect her. Though she was innocent, her reputation is most
likely to have suffered severe damage. Even later in life she might
suffer from a tainted reputation and be unable to find another
husband were she to be divorced. The man must bear the consequences of his act for all his life and may never cast her away.

But what if the virgin does not wish to marry the man who has
raped her? The biblical legislation does not entertain this possibility. It seems that there are two reasons for this. First, it is assumed
that the woman would wish to marry the man because she has
been "compromised" so that her chances of finding another hus-

band are very slim. Second, rape is not perceived here as a sadistic or perverse act, but rather as a socially improper way of taking a wife.

When we examine postbiblical sources the matter becomes more complicated. On the one hand the rabbis as a rule try to prevent improper sexual relations, whether by consent, seduction, or compulsion by barring the man from marrying the woman. On the other hand they seem to recognize the plight of the woman "violated" by rape or "compromised" by seduction and leave room for resolving the situation by marriage if the woman and her father want it.

In Maimonides' succinct formulation of the law we find an attempt to account for all possibilities and emphasize the protection of the injured party, the woman and her father:

> If a woman is seduced and does not want to marry the seducer or her father does not want to give her [in marriage], or the man does not want to take her: in that case the man pays the fine and goes along—he is not forced to take her. And if they [woman and her father] do want [the marriage] he does not pay a fine, but rather writes her a *ketubah* as for other virgins. But if a woman is raped and does not want to marry the man, or her father does not want her to marry the rapist: in such a case they have the right [to refuse] and he pays the fine and goes along. If she and her father want [the marriage] and he does not—he is compelled to marry her and pay the fine. [Maimonides, *Mishneh Torah*, Nashim, Hilkhot Na'arah Betulah 1 : 3]

In the case of rape, in contrast to seduction, the man must pay the fine in any circumstance. The woman and her father have the right to refuse the marriage but the man does not.

Whether or not the woman wishes to marry the man who has raped her, he must pay damages to her father. In that respect he is like the seducer who has taken away the woman's virginity without her father's consent and without paying the bride money. Both seduction and rape, then, are offenses against the father's property rights and his honor. What distinguishes rape is the act of violence. Therefore the rapist is required to pay an additional fine for the pain he inflicted:

Mishnah: The seducer pays three forms [of compensation] and the violator four. The seducer pays compensation for indignity and blemish and
the [statutory] fine, while the violator pays an additional [form of com-
pensation] in that he pays for the pain.

What [is the difference] between [the penalties of] a seducer and those
of a violator? The violator pays compensation for the pain but the seducer
does not pay compensation for the pain. The violator pays forthwith but
the seducer [pays only] if he dismisses her. The violator must drink out of
his pot but the seducer may dismiss [the girl] if he wishes. What is meant
by "must drink out of his pot"?—Even if she is lame, even if she is blind
and even if she is afflicted with boils [he may not dismiss her].

Gemara: [For the] "Pain" of what?—The father of Samuel replied: For the
pain [he has inflicted] when he thrust her upon the ground.

Rabbi Zera demurred: Now then, if he had thrust her upon silk stuffs
would he for a similar reason be exempt? And should you say that the law
is so indeed was it not [it may be retorted] taught: "Rabbi Simeon ben
Judah stated in the name of Rabbi Simeon: A violator does not pay compensation for the pain [he has inflicted] because the woman would ultimately have suffered the same pain from her husband, but they said to
him: One who is forced to intercourse cannot be compared to one who
acts willingly"? [Ketubot 39a–b]

The discussion in the Gemara of the nature of the pain for which the
violator must compensate is illuminating. The first suggestion of
Samuel's father is that the pain was inflicted when the woman was
thrust on the ground. This is countered by Rabbi Zera's objection
that by this reasoning if the woman was thrown on a bed of silk
there would be no pain. In other words, Samuel's father locates the
"pain" in physical abuse accompanying the rape. Rabbi Zera's
question points out the fact that rape can happen without accompanying bodily hurt. Samuel's father's interpretation is faulty because it locates the "pain" in the attending circumstances rather
than in the sexual act itself. And indeed Rabbi Zera's objection
would have sufficed were it not for another tradition cited here.
According to this tradition Rabbi Simeon held that the rapist
should not have to pay compensation for the pain he inflicted since
the pain is the pain of penetration and that pain would have occurred in any case at the point when the woman first had intercourse. But the rabbis reject Rabbi Simeon with a simple argument:
"One who is forced to intercourse cannot be compared to one who

acts willingly." In other words, the pain is indeed the pain of penetration in intercourse, yet it is not a result of the mere physical
penetration but rather a psychological result of the compulsion.

While the fine paid by the man to compensate the father for the
financial loss is set at fifty silver shekels, the fines for indignity,
blemish, and pain are determined by the father himself. As the
Shulhan Arukh explains, the latter fines reflect the degree of personal injury suffered by the woman and her family, which varies
according to their personal circumstances:

And in the case of a raped virgin who suffers pain [he pays for] pain,
indignity, and blemish. And these are not identical for all people, rather
it all depends on the degree of indignity, according to the one who causes
the shame and the one who is shamed. For the case of one who shames an
important girl from an important family is not like the case of one who
shames a lowly and poor one. And it is not the same for a father who is
shamed by an important man as for one shamed by a lowly and despised
man. Therefore, the court considers his status and her status and such
things as how much her father and her family would have given for this
not to have been done to them by that man; and that is how much he shall
pay.
And pain: they judge according to his smallness [size? age? importance?] and hers, and according to her health and how much she actually
suffered. And that is how much he will pay in addition to the fifty [shek-
els] of the fine. [Shulhan Arukh, Even Ha-Ezer 177 : 4–5]

Personal dignity for the Shulhan Arukh is a function of wealth,
social status, power, and reputation. This is not surprising: in a
hierarchical, rather than democratic society, personal integrity is
not equal for all, but rather reflects one's class, lineage, and
wealth. Traditional Jewish society was primarily hierarchical.
The principle of equal worth of all people only applies to extreme
matters of life and death. This was apparently already the common opinion in the Talmud despite the minority view of Rabbi
Akiva, who held that in matters of personal dignity all are equal
(Baba Kama 90b).

We return to the definition of rape, that is, the question: What
constitutes compulsion? As we saw, the biblical text uses the
word "seize" to describe the two cases of rape: the case of the

betrothed virgin in the field and the case of the virgin who is not betrothed. The case of the betrothed virgin interests the biblical author more because the crime involves sexual transgression and is of much greater magnitude than the assault and financial damage inflicted in the case of the unbetrothed virgin. Therefore in the case of the betrothed virgin we have a more elaborate description of the circumstances of the rape. The text distinguishes between the city and the countryside. In the city the woman could have called out for help, and therefore she is not considered to have been raped. In the countryside the reverse holds: the woman cried out for help but there was no one to rescue her and she is deemed to have been raped.

The distinction between rape and consensual sex is based on a geographic criterion. This answers an implicit problem in the definition of rape by the act of "seizing," namely: How do we know that the man "seized" her? It is in the nature of sexual acts and transgressions that they are not observed by witnesses. The logic of the biblical legislation is that if assaulted and raped, a woman would resist by calling for help. Her calling or not calling for help can therefore be used as the yardstick in determining whether or not the woman had been raped. In the city, if she is not heard one may conclude that she did not object to the sexual act. In the country there is no one around to hear her whether or not she cries out so we assume in all cases in the countryside the woman has been raped.

This rather crude biblical definition of rape bothered some of the medieval commentators. The problem with it was that the definition of rape seemed to rest on an external criterion, i.e., the location of the event. What of a woman who had sexual relations with a man in the country and did not resist by crying out? What of a woman who cried out in the city but was not heard?

About the betrothed maiden: When witnesses see from afar a man seize a maiden and lie with her in the town and they raise their voice and warn them, [then] according to our rabbis they shall both be stoned, since the woman too is considered to be transgressing intentionally because she did not cry out at all. For normally, any woman being raped [*anusah*] cries out in the town for help to be saved.

And if they see her in the field when he holds her and lays with her she is considered raped [*anusah*] and not liable. And the reason for "and she cried out" (Deut. 22 : 27) is [to indicate that] it is *possible* that she cried out. . . . for even if they did not hear her cry out she is not liable because she had no rescuers there. And the general rule is that if she has rescuers there, whether in the town or in the countryside, she is liable, and if she has no rescuers, whether in the countryside or in the town, she is not liable. [Nachmanides on Deut. 22 : 23]

Nachmanides essentially changes the criterion for rape. It is not the location which matters but the question of whether there was possibility for rescue. His "general rule" is: if the woman knew or could see that there were rescuers for whose help she could cry out, regardless of the location, if she cried out it is rape and if she did not she is liable for consenting to illicit sex. On the other hand, if "she had no rescuers there" she is innocent. This may seem just an elaboration of what the biblical text states, but it is not. The critical distinction between the biblical text and Nachmanides' interpretation is between objective fact and subjective judgment. According to Nachmanides the woman's subjective judgment of whether or not there were rescuers available determines the matter. Of course the presence of rescuers could be determined by testimony of others also, but the nature of the event is such that it occurs in privacy, so that even if others attest that rescuers were available, the woman can always claim that she was unaware of their presence and therefore did not call for help.

Nachmanides' interpretation leads to the two extreme cases he presents at the beginning of the passage. In the second case, of a betrothed virgin in the field, even if two witnesses see the man hold her and lie with her but *do not* observe her call out, she is not liable. Because it is in the field she is expected to *assume* that there are no rescuers, even if that is not the case, so that her failure to cry out may not be interpreted as proof that she consented. In the first case, of a woman in the town, because there too it is possible that she believed there were no rescuers, we need explicit proof that she knew she had rescuers. The explicit proof is the observation and intervention of the witnesses. The witnesses must observe the man and the woman and warn them that they are about to transgress. If the couple proceeds to have intercourse nevertheless, then and only then is it absolutely clear that the woman is liable for consenting to illicit relations.

The requirement of testimony of two direct witnesses and a warning preceding the act is not peculiar to the laws concerning rape or sexual transgression. In the case of rape the issue of available rescuers makes the presence of witnesses particularly crucial. However, for all transgressions punishable by a court, postbiblical Halakhah requires two witnesses and explicit warning about the nature of the transgression right before it is committed in order to convict a transgressor.

Nachmanides' interpretation makes the definition of rape more flexible and more amenable to subjective judgment. Significantly, the judgment rests with the woman who is the victim. Nachmanides expands the range of situations where a woman may plead innocence to sexual transgression on the grounds of rape. According to his interpretation, a woman can claim that there would have been no one to rescue her in order to justify not having called out for help. Jacob ben Asher considers another justification for not calling out for help, but rejects it:

"Because she did not cry out" (Deut. 22 : 24): And if she were afraid of him [being afraid to cry out] she could have said that she is crying out because of the pain of virginity. [Ba'al Ha-Turim (Jacob ben Asher), Commentary on Deut. 22 : 24]

Jacob ben Asher rejects the possibility that a woman could justify not calling out because of her fear of some retaliation by the attacker. If that were the case, he argues, she could cry out and justify it to the man by the pain of the rupture of the hymen, "her virginity."

Given the basic view of rape as forced sexual relations, with or without Nachmanides' modification concerning crying out for help, another question arises: What must be the duration of the compulsion in order for it to constitute rape? The problem is formulated in both the Babylonian Talmud and the Jerusalem Talmud. What about sexual relations which began under compulsion

and ended with consent? The Jerusalem Talmud illustrates the
problem with an anecdote:

A woman once came to Rabbi Yohanan and said to him: "I have been
raped." He said to her: "And didn't you enjoy it by the end?" She said to
him: And if a man dipped his finger in honey and stuck it in your mouth
on Yom Kippur [a fast day], is it not bad for you yet enjoyable by the
end?" He accepted her. [Jerusalem Talmud, *Sotah* 4 : 4]

When a woman comes to Rabbi Yohanan and tells him she had
been raped, he challenges the validity of her claim by suggesting
that though at the start she was forced into illicit sexual relations,
by the end she was a willing partner and enjoyed the sexual act.
The woman's response leaves him with no retort and he accepts
her reasoning: the pleasure at the end is irrelevant. What began
under duress is rape no matter what the woman's attitude and
feelings were by the end. There is a similarity here with the attitude expressed in the discussion of the fine paid for the pain
caused in rape (Ketubot 39a–b): the crucial factor is the initiation
of sexual intercourse under duress. The fact that the physical pain
of the rupture of the hymen would have occurred in consensual
relations with the husband is irrelevant: the pain is a result of the
compulsion. Similarly the pleasure or consent by the end is irrelevant in defining rape: the compulsion at the start is the only determining factor.

The Babylonian Talmud goes even further in applying the principle that what began under compulsion is rape, even if it ended
with consent and possibly pleasure. Even if the woman is offered
rescue in the middle of the sexual encounter and turns it down,
she is still considered to have been raped:

. . . for Raba laid down: Any woman the outrage [rape] against whom
began under compulsion, though it is terminated with her consent, even
if she said "leave him alone" for if he had not made the attack she would
have paid him to do it, is permitted [to her husband]. What is the reason?
He plunged her into an uncontrollable passion. [Ketubot 51b]

Raba defines any woman who was initially forced into sexual
relations as a victim of rape, even the extraordinary case of a

woman who refuses to be rescued and wishes for the sexual act which began as rape to be consummated. She too is considered a victim of rape and therefore allowed to return to her husband and resume her marriage even though she had been party to an illicit sexual relation. Normally a married or betrothed woman who has sexual relations with another man is thereafter forbidden to both her husband and the adulterer, but if she was a victim of rape she is permitted to her husband. This issue is mostly discussed in the Halakhah in relation to the problem of women who are taken captive or imprisoned by gentiles, for they are assumed to have been taken advantage of sexually by their captors.[3]

Raba's definition of rape in the case before him warrants a closer look. According to him, even a woman who refuses to be rescued is considered a victim of rape if the sexual act began under compulsion. Why does he rule this way when it seems that the woman is a consenting partner, at least in the latter part of the sexual act? Because, he states, "He plunged her into an uncontrollable passion." This is an interesting illustration of Raba's view of female sexuality. Once a sexual act has begun, a woman is ruled by powers beyond her rational and moral control: her sexual urge overcomes her moral and religious abhorrence of adultery. Raba considers this a fact of nature which absolves the woman of responsibility for the sexual transgression she has committed.

Maimonides' summary of the law concerning rape reveals a similar view to that of Raba in Ketubot 51b: a woman compelled to intercourse is exempt from the guilt of sexual transgression even if the sexual act ended in consent. The agent of duress is at first the man who rapes her, and later "human impulse and nature":

The victim of duress is entirely exempt, both from flogging and from offering a sacrifice; needless to say, she is also exempt from the death penalty, as it is said "and to the maiden you shall do nothing" (Deut. 22 : 26). This holds true only when the victim is the woman, since duress cannot apply to the man, for no erection is possible without his own intention.

A woman who is subjected to the duress at the beginning of intercourse, but finally acquiesces to it, is also entirely exempt; once a man has begun sexual intercourse with her under duress, she cannot but acquiesce, seeing that human impulse and nature compel her to ultimate assent. [Maimonides, *Mishneh Torah*, Issurei Bi'ah (Forbidden Intercourse) 1 : 9]

In a discussion of rape in Sanhedrin we find a different justification for the impunity of a woman who committed adultery under duress. It is not the ongoing compulsion, at first by the man and then by her own sexual impulses, that makes a woman exempt from any transgression when she is raped, but rather her passivity in the sexual act. In a discussion of the three transgressions which one may not commit in public even under threat of death (idolatry, murder, and sexual transgressions), a problem arises: "Did not Esther transgress publicly?" (Sanhedrin 74a). According to some interpretations which understand the word "uncle," *dod*, to mean "husband" (see Song of Songs, where the lover is referred to as *dod*), Mordecai, Esther's "uncle," was her husband. If that were the case, Esther committed adultery in public when she became Ahasuerus's wife and sexual partner in place of the rebellious Vashti (Esther 2, and the commentaries in Mishnah Megillah ch. 13).

How could Esther commit a sexual transgression for which one is commanded to choose martyrdom if threatened: "Commit the transgression or suffer death"? Sanhedrin 74a addresses this very problem, stating that Esther was totally passive in the sexual act: "Esther was merely [like] natural soil [*karka olam*]." Esther was not required to die rather than commit a sexual transgression because she was a passive victim: she did nothing, only received the act. Just like the soil upon which men tread and act is not responsible for their crimes, so a woman who allows herself to be violated sexually, either like Esther or in the case of rape, is not morally or legally responsible for the sexual transgression committed.

The emphasis on the issue of passivity is important for understanding another, and very real, aspect of sex: the sexual relationship between husband and wife. The case of Esther and passive sexual relations under threat of death are a very extreme manifestation of the basic condition of women, their passivity in the sexual act. This passivity also characterizes the sexual relations of

husband and wife, where the husband is perceived to be the initiator and active agent and the wife the passive recipient. This
imbalance of power leads the Halakhah to protect the woman's
sexual needs through the laws of *onah*, and by forbidding a husband to rape his wife.

The notion that rape can occur within marriage has only recently become accepted in contemporary Western society and
law, but it appears very clearly in the Talmud. In fact in a recent
(1982) court case in Israel the Supreme Court convicted a man for
raping his wife and based its decision on the Halakhah as opposed
to the principles of English common law which does not recognize rape between husband and wife.

Rami ben Hama citing Rav Assi further ruled: A man is forbidden to
compel his wife to the *mitzvah* [of *onah*], since it is said in Scripture:
"And he that hastens with his feet sins." (Prov. 19 : 2)
   Rabbi Joshua ben Levi similarly stated: Whosoever compels his wife to
the *mitzvah* will have unworthy children. Said Rabbi Ika ben Hinena:
What is the Scriptural proof? "Also without consent the soul is not good"
(Prov. 19 : 2). So it was also taught: "Also without consent the soul is not
good" refers to a man who compels his wife to the *mitzvah*; "And he that
hastens with his feet sins" refers to a man who has intercourse twice in
succession. But, surely, this cannot be right! For did not Raba state: "He
who desires his children to be males should cohabit twice in succession"? This is no difficulty, since the latter is with [the woman's] consent;
whereas the former, without her consent. [Eruvin 100b]

Eruvin begins with the ruling that a man may not abuse the *mitzvah* of having sexual relations for the sake of *onah* and procreation to force his wife to have sex against her will. The fact that
sex is a positive commandment is not to be used as justification
for imposing it on the woman. The passage in Proverbs "he that
hastens with his feet" is understood as a sexual metaphor about
the man who hastens and presses his wife to the marital act. The
second part of the same verse in Proverbs ("Also without consent
the soul is not good") is also interpreted as a reference to the
sexual act. If sex is initiated without the woman's consent the soul
that will be conceived as a result will be unworthy.

An alternative tradition in the name of Rabbi Ika ben Hinena interprets the sexual references of the verse in Proverbs differently. The second part of the verse ("Also without consent the soul is not good") indeed refers to the prohibition on having intercourse without the woman's consent. The first part refers to a different matter, to having intercourse twice in succession. According to Rabbi Ika, that too is a sinful act. As against this view the Gemara brings the opinion of Raba who recommends having intercourse twice as a way of producing male children. The contradiction is resolved by referring again to the question of the woman's consent. If having intercourse twice is done with the woman's consent it will have the positive effect of producing a male because the woman will be more aroused and thus she will "give forth seed" first (Rashi on Eruvin). If the woman gives forth seed first, her seed will dominate and this will result in the embryo's being formed as a male. The negative view of repeated intercourse applies when the second act is done without the woman's consent. Such an act is sinful even if sex was initially begun with the woman's consent.

Maimonides in his rules concerning marital relations also forbids a husband to coerce his wife to sexual relations. He states: "He may not rape her by having intercourse against her will, but rather, [let him do it] with her consent and in mutual arousal and joy" (*Mishneh Torah*, Hilkhot Ishut 15 : 17). In his instructional book for the pious, *Ba'alei Ha-Nefesh*, Abraham ben David warns a man time and again against compelling his wife to the sexual act. Among nine categories of improper sexual relation between husband and wife which will produce children afflicted by handicaps and various ills, Rabad lists *first* rape between husband and wife:

"These are the children of nine categories [of women]: children of ASNT MS GAH" [acronym for rape, hatred, *niddah*, substitution, rebellious wife, drunkenness, intended divorce, confusion, brazenness]. Interpretation: The children of a raped woman [*anusah*]: You do not need to interpret this that he raped some [other] woman and had a child by her, but simply that he raped his wife in intercourse! And thus we learn in Tractate Kallah: Why does a man have children who are crippled? Because he demands and she does not reciprocate, that is, she does not turn around and desire him too, and nevertheless he satisfies his need for her. Rabbi

Joshua says: Because she says to him during intercourse: "I am being raped [compelled]" and it [sexual intercourse] occurs between them with him wanting it and her not wanting it. And thus they said in Tractate Eruvin: Anyone who compels his wife to a matter of *mitzvah* is called wicked as it says "Without consent the soul is not good."

We find that rape is forbidden in the case of his wife as well. Rather, if he is in need of the act [sex] let him persuade her first and then he may cohabit. [Abraham ben David (Rabad), *Ba'alei Ha-Nefesh*, Sha'ar Ha-Kedushah]

Rabad warns against a husband's raping his wife and details the dynamics of such a situation: the wife "does not reciprocate" to the husband's sexual advances, she "does not turn around and desire him too," and finally she says "I am being raped." The husband does not heed the woman's increasingly explicit objection to intercourse and "nevertheless, he satisfies his need for her." This, concludes Abraham ben David, is rape of a wife and it is forbidden in the Halakhah.

It appears that the Halakhah envisions rape somewhat differently from the way we might today. Rather than understanding rape as a crime of violence in which sex is the means of perpetrating aggression, the biblical and halakhic sources envision rape as a crime of passion. Rape might also be a way of compelling a woman into marriage when she is available (single and unbetrothed) but she or her father do not consent to the match. This is why it is conceivable that the rape would be followed by marriage. As Maimonides states in his discussion of the Halakhah concerning seduction and rape, if the woman and her father want a marriage to take place after the rape, the rapist is compelled to marry her even against his own wishes.

The basic trend in the evolution of the Halakhah concerning rape seems to be an extension of the boundaries which define rape. Whereas the biblical text defines rape in clear-cut and objective terms of location, later Halakhah makes the definition more flexible. It introduces the subjective judgment of the victim regarding the possibility of rescue and the initiation of the sexual act under duress as the critical factors in defining rape. Finally, if a married woman is coerced to sexual relations by her husband, that too is considered rape.

This general trend of expanding the definition of rape represents a conscious effort to protect women from the charge that they were willing participants in a prohibited sexual act, that they "brought it on themselves," or that their hidden wish is to be coerced into intercourse. The talmudic text goes to an extreme, it seems, when it states that even if the woman refuses to be rescued from the rapist she is still considered to be compelled in the sexual act, not by the rapist's brute force but by her own "uncontrollable passion." This argument may be understood in two ways. It probably reflects a mythical, exaggerated view of female sexuality: a woman's passion is boundless, and once released it is uncontrollable.[4] Second, the argument that a woman is compelled to assent to sexual relations by her natural impulse, though unlikely as a psychological reality, serves to compensate a woman for her sexual passivity by clearing her of any liability for a sexual act which was initiated under duress. This position purposefully removes any responsibility from the woman once sex is initiated by force. The contemporary notion of the dynamic of rape would substitute intimidation for "uncontrollable passion" as the psychological factor which compels a woman to acquiesce to rape. Nevertheless the basic point is similar: a woman does not need to be kicking and screaming from start to end in order for us to rule that she has been raped. Sex begun under duress and intimidation is, by definition, rape.[5]

As in the case of other aspects of the Halakhah which protect women and guard their rights, we must recognize a kind of balancing act between the underlying assumption that men are the active agents, in this case in sexual relations, and an attempt to shore up and increase the rights and means of protection available to women. In the case of rape we see a general trend toward expanding as much as possible the definition of rape: rape is any sexual act which begins under compulsion, even if between husband and wife.

EPILOGUE

THE QUESTION of women's role and status in Jewish society is one of the most vital issues in the Jewish world today, particularly in North America. The debate has been developing for over a decade. In the early 1970s the first publications appeared in which the status of women in the Halakhah and in Jewish religious and communal life was challenged. In 1971, in one of the first serious treatments of the subject, Rachel Adler aptly expressed the sense of displacement of Jewish women in the title of her article "The Jew Who Wasn't There."[1] In the ensuing decade, a considerable body of literature has emerged, including works examining and criticizing the role of women in traditional Jewish society and others glorifying and defending that role, studies of women in the contemporary Jewish community, and proposals for reforms in a variety of areas such as abortion, contraception, divorce, the participation of women in the synagogue, the ordination of women rabbis, and new rituals for women.[2]

The vitality and fervor of the debate on women draws on two sources. The first is the profound impact of the feminist movement and its claims on American society and cultural norms. Feminism has won the day in America, not in the sense that women's status is now actually equal to men's, but in that the essential claim that women are equal to men in spiritual and intellectual potential has become an accepted axiom along with other democratic principles. The debate over feminism has become part of the process of coming to terms with American society which has preoccupied American Jews for the past century. Feminism cannot be ignored by Jews any more than any of the other fundamental tenets of American democracy.

256

The second source which feeds the debate on women is the structure of the American Jewish community. Undoubtedly influenced by its environment, the American Jewish community is essentially pluralistic. It includes a full spectrum of positions from Orthodoxy through Conservative, Reconstructionist, and Reform Judaism to secular Jews and others whose opinions do not fit the formal categories but who are actively committed to a Jewish life. Despite many differing opinions, the majority of Jews in America have enough in common, both in terms of Jewish and American values, to engage in a debate.

The importance of this last factor can be appreciated more fully if we compare the lively debate in the American Jewish community to the minimal discourse over the status of women in Judaism in Israel. The Israeli Jewish community is essentially split between the Orthodox and the secular. Since these two communities tend to live quite separate spiritual lives, there is little public debate over worship, synagogue life, and ritual. The only major issue is *dinei ishut*, the laws regulating personal status through marriage and divorce which apply to all Israeli Jews. Since there is no civil law in these areas, secular Israelis have become involved in debates about the Halakhah.[3] The Halakhah has become a part of secular politics. One example of this debate is the abortion law, which was recently changed to satisfy the demands of Agudat Yisrael, an Orthodox political party. But due to the polarization of opinion in Israel, the position of the secular is primarily focused on removing the Halakhah from the public sphere (what is called "opposition to religious coercion," i.e., separation between church and state) rather than changing the Halakhah from within. The Sephardic community is perhaps less polarized between Orthodox and secular, but at least at this time shows no interest in the "Western" concepts of feminism.

Since in America civil law governs matters of personal status, these issues have less urgency than they do in Israel. To be sure, there have been numerous articles and several books addressing questions such as the laws of divorce, the problem of the *agunah*, and especially abortion and birth control.[4] But the most "political" issues in the American Jewish community are the public,

ceremonial ones. Partly as a result of the acceptance of Judaism as
one of the "three great religions" of America whose manifesta-
tions are primarily through organized public worship, and partly
as a result of the waning of the power of the Halakhah, what goes
on in the synagogue takes precedence in the minds of most Jews
over what goes on in the home. The secondary role of women in
the synagogue has therefore become the major arena for debate. A
central issue in this area is the ordination of women as rabbis,
which caused considerable upheaval in the Reform movement a
decade ago.[5] Following the Reform movement's ordination of
women, pressure developed in the Conservative movement to follow suit. On October 24, 1983, the faculty of the Jewish Theological Seminary voted in favor of the ordination of women, but the
matter is by no means settled. Many of the members of the faculty
abstained and there is a danger of a split in the movement.
Another issue that pertains to women's role in public Jewish life
is the laws which disqualify women from testifying in a Jewish
court (except in very special circumstances, such as the case of an
agunah).[6]

The debate over both the "public" and "private" issues in the
Halakhah pertaining to women includes positions from ultra-
Orthodox to very secular. There are those on both ends of the
spectrum for whom feminism presents no real challenge to the
Halakhah, either because they are so traditional that they reject
any response to challenges from the surrounding environment, or
because they are so distant from Jewish law that they have no
interest in even debating against it. Thus David Bleich, a prominent Orthodox rabbi, argues that the Halakhah is a self-contained
system which follows its own internal logic and is always in conflict with "reality." He rejects the call of feminists that Jewish law
accommodate the demand of women for equality. The Halakhah
has its own ideal role for women and the values of the non-Jewish
world constitute no cause for change.[7] Similarly, at the opposite
end of the spectrum we find a Reform thinker like Eugene Mihaly
who also believes that the Halakhah is fundamentally opposed to
the reality of the modern world.[8] But as opposed to Bleich, this is
Mihaly's basis for rejecting the Halakhah entirely. Judaism is not

what is codified in the Halakhah, but what the religious and historical experience is for Jews in each generation. Since the contemporary experience of Jews is totally different from that of the rabbis who formulated the Halakhah, the Halakhah becomes irrelevant.

But between these ironically similar, if opposite, extremes there are a great many Jews for whom the Halakhah and feminist demands are both relevant and require some kind of response. Even those who essentially reject all the demands for a change in the status of women in the Halakhah take the contemporary critique seriously. Such is the case with Moshe Meiselman, an Orthodox rabbi who has written *Jewish Women in Jewish Law*, one of the most extensive treatments of the subject. Meiselman's intention is to refute and reject feminist claims. While he is willing to increase women's involvement in learning and worship, he does so only within traditional male and female roles and rejects any demands for change in either Halakhah or ritual.[9] Similarly another Orthodox writer states categorically: "From a halakhic, psychological and societal view, the Jewish answer may very well be: 'to feminism, no; to women in their full uniqueness and authenticity, absolutely yes!' "[10] In other words, no to change in the Halakhah and role of women, yes to a glorification of the traditional female role and legal status.

There are, however, Orthodox writers who not only take the challenge of feminism seriously, but also accept the need for certain real reforms. Saul Berman, now dean of Stern College for Women at Yeshiva University, wrote a highly influential article on "The Status of Women in Halakhic Judaism" in 1973.[11] Berman's article calls for a nonpolemical and unapologetic response to feminism. He concludes that the Halakhah evolved certain restrictions and exemptions for women "to achieve a particular social goal, namely, to assure that no legal obligation would interfere with the selection by Jewish women of a role which was centered almost exclusively in the home," yet "while the goal of family stability seems to be the motive force behind many of the elements of the status of women, the law recognizes that women are disadvantaged by that position and attempts to compensate to the extent possible."[12] While Berman affirms the centrality of women's domestic role, he does not advocate remaining within its confines. As long as changes in religious life do not substantially interfere with this domestic role, he accepts far-reaching changes to meet the quest of women for greater religious participation. Berman explicitly calls for restructuring the *Mehitzah* so that women are not relegated to the back of the synagogue, including women in study of Torah, and holding women to the same standards as men in terms of synagogue attendance. In addition to these reforms in public religious life, Berman also advocates a change in the area of *agunot*. If the proposed conditional *ketubah* or conditional *get* prove to be unacceptable to halakhic authorities, he advocates turning to civil courts to enforce prenuptial agreements which would force both husband and wife to give and receive a *get* in case of dissolution of their marriage by civil divorce.

A more theoretical and also more radical attempt to reconcile women's rights and the Halakhah from an Orthodox point of view is that of Eliezer Berkowitz.[13] Berkowitz proposes a return to Maimonides' view of the Halakhah in the *Guide for the Perplexed*. For Maimonides, the *mitzvot* are educational tools geared to the understanding of the common person and designed to increase belief in monotheism. They are products of specific historical circumstances and are therefore instruments for a higher goal. Berkowitz follows this logic. He holds that there is a central ethos to Judaism which is beyond the specific *mitzvot*. This ethos is equivalent to the moral conscience of Judaism and includes the recognition that all human beings are of equal worth. The fact that certain *mitzvot*, such as those relating to the Hebrew slave, seem to contradict this ethos suggests that these *mitzvot* were the product of limited historical circumstances and they fell into disuse when times changed. The same principle applies to the Halakhah pertaining to women. Elements of the Halakhah contradict the moral conscience of Judaism and can therefore be changed. An example of this process is the law which requires a woman to wash her husband's feet as one of her primary "wifely" duties. This law has fallen into disuse among the Orthodox because they feel intuitively that it contradicts the essential ethos of the Halakhah. For Berkowitz, the solution to the problem of women is not to reject the Halakhah, but rather to explore the possibilities within the Halakhah for approaching its ideals more closely. Berkowitz advocates starting with the inclusion of women in study of the Torah.

Berkowitz's argument is not far from that of a number of Conservative thinkers who also call for halakhic reforms in the status of women. For Conservative Judaism, change in the Halakhah represents less of a problem than for the Orthodox since one of the cornerstones of Conservative ideology is that the Halakhah evolves historically. A recent argument for such a position was made by Robert Gordis, who has also argued passionately for equality for women.[14] Gordis asserts that the challenge of real life is not alien to the Halakhah but is a legitimate part of its internal dynamic. Throughout history changes in the "popular will" have led to changes in the Halakhah. But it is not that the demands of reality force the Halakhah to bend against its will, but rather that response to reality is in fact one of the central characteristics of Jewish law.

More cautious figures in the Conservative movement have also tried to balance the challenge of the "popular will" against the internal dynamic of the Halakhah. Thus David M. Feldman, the author of *Marital Relations, Birth Control and Abortion in Jewish Law*, and "Women's Role and Jewish Law,"[15] focuses on finding past permissive rulings and lenient stands in the Halakhah in order to accommodate modern sensibilities. He often suggests that the minority opinions which are preserved in the Talmud and afterward are the legitimate keys for change in the law. As opposed to the Orthodox, many Conservative thinkers hold that the original intention behind the preservation of minority opinions was the recognition that Judaism consists not of one eternally true interpretation but of many interpretations which are correct for different times and places.

Three women writers have made particularly important contributions to the attempt to win acceptance of feminism within the halakhic framework: Blu Greenberg, Cynthia Ozick, and Rachel Adler. Greenberg, who recently published a book on women and Judaism, adheres to the Halakhah, but also believes that feminism is both just and necessary for the spiritual life of Orthodox women. While she presents no easy solutions, she grapples seriously with the tension between the demands of the Halakhah and those of feminism. Although she is not certain that they can be totally reconciled, she argues that both are essential for Jewish life.[16]

Cynthia Ozick presented her views on the issue of women in Jewish life in a piece entitled "Notes Towards Finding the Right Question."[17] Ozick's first point is that the problem of the status of Jewish women ("the Right Question") is not a theological problem but a social one. The Jewish understanding of God is first and foremost a monotheistic vision cleansed of all anthropomorphic thought. Thus the problems of the "masculinity" of God in traditional Judaism and the attempts to redress it by creating a new "female" theological language are misguided. The essence of the problem of women in Judaism is their sociologically inferior status. Ozick has no patience for what she considers the apologetic attempt to mask the inferiority of women by glorification of their role as different from yet complementary to men's role in society and law.

The inferior role of women in Judaism is plainly a question of injustice. The injustice is of such magnitude that it seriously threatens our reliance on the most fundamental ethical vision of Jewish law (what Ozick means by "Torah"), namely, posing moral principles to militate against a world which is by nature given to exploitation, subjugation, and injustice. Furthermore there has been a void in traditional Jewish consciousness when it came to women: the injustice done to women by relegating them to inferior status was never recognized, and the loss of women's potential contribution to Jewish intellectual and religious life never felt.

The injustice and loss must be undone and repaired. Ozick directs her call for "repair and renewal" to "the most traditional elements of the community" because "it is they who make the claim of being most in the mainstream of authentic Jewish expression; of being most representative of historic Jewish commitment; and, finally, it is they who dedicate themselves to being models for Jews who are less stringent in striving to live conscientiously within the frame of Torah."[18] Ozick argues that the repair of the injustice must come as a totally new idea: the Torah never recognized that the inferior status of women was unjust. The recognition of the injustice poses a new situation which Ozick compares to the new era begun by the establishment of the school at Yavneh. The destruction of the Temple necessitated creating a new focal point for Jewish cultic life: the Torah lacked this alternative and it had to be invented. "When the Temple was destroyed . . . we came to Yavneh and invented the Synagogue in order to save Torah."[19] A similar new invention is necessary to create a precept which is missing in the Torah, a precept which says: "Thou shalt not lessen the humanity of women."[20]

To create a commandment against casting women in an inferior status "what we must do is find . . . a Yavneh that will create the conditions for the precept."[21] Yet Ozick does not clearly spell out where this modern-day "Yavneh" is to be found. She does, as we have said, call on the traditional rabbinate to assume the primary responsibility for repairing the injury done to women. Yet she must be well aware of the conservatism of this leadership and the lack of a figure like Yohanan ben Zakkai, someone with the authority, ingenuity, and daring to do something totally new and contrary to the general trend, within the Orthodox community. She does not, however, propose an alternative to the traditional rabbinate, nor suggest another milieu from whence a Yohanan ben Zakkai might arise.

Rachel Adler, in her call for a change in the status of women in Judaism, does just that. She proposes an alternative source of law for Jewish women in the event that traditional rabbinical leaders turn a deaf ear to the demands of women for justice and equality. Like Ozick, she states that the essential problem of Jewish women is the problem of inferior status: "we are viewed in Jewish law and practice as peripheral Jews."[22] The peripheral status of women in Jewish law results in laws which exclude women from the central activities of Jewish life as well as laws which make them dependent on men and vulnerable to exploitation and denigration.

Adler argues that certain laws can be changed rather easily since such changes would not involve transgressions against actual prohibitions. Among these she cites allowing women to study Torah, allowing *aliyot* for women, and permitting women to assume the obligation of performing time-bound positive *mitzvot* from which they are exempt. The more difficult problems, such as the counting of women in a *minyan* and the *mehitzah*, must also be addressed and modified. Adler advocates that women should constitute themselves as a powerful pressure group and relentlessly press rabbis to study these problems in a fresh light and issue rulings that women can accept. If such pressure bears no fruit, she calls for the drastic step of breaking away from the recognized halakhic authorities and making independent rulings. "If they continue to turn a deaf ear to us, the most learned and halakhically committed among us must make halakhic decisions for the rest."[23] Thus Adler calls for women to form their own halakhic constituency and establish their own legal leadership. Ironically, although this is one of the most radical proposals ever made, it is less problematic from a strictly halakhic point of view than it might seem. Recognized halakhists draw their authority from the fact that their followers accept their opinions. Although such authorities are without exception ordained by recognized seminaries and *yeshivot*, their ordinations draw their legitimacy from consensus rather than from laws within the Halakhah. Thus if women achieve learning in the Halakhah and develop a constituency, they may be able to change the Halakhah themselves without waiting for the existing authorities.

The notion of new authorities' leading a revolution in Jewish values is not new in Jewish history. The transition from biblical to talmudic law which took place in the centuries immediately before and after the beginning of the Common Era was headed by the Pharisees or rabbis, a group whose authority only became unchallenged after the destruction of the second Temple. The rabbis succeeded in radically changing the law without discarding the Bible as no longer relevant.[24] The Oral Law, although essentially new, is presented in the Talmud as a natural outgrowth of the Bible.

The rabbinical revolution was based on new concepts about justice and society. The biblical notion of "an eye for an eye; a tooth for a tooth" was no longer acceptable and was reinterpreted to mean monetary compensation. Capital punishment generally disappeared. As we have seen repeatedly throughout this book, the status of women was also fundamentally altered. The ordeal of the *sotah* became obsolete. The laws of marriage which permitted a man to take a wife simply by having sexual relations with her were altered to make marriage into a public ceremony. Divorce was changed from a unilateral act of the husband into a complex procedure which included considerable measures to protect the woman.

This revolution could provide a model for Jews today. In the modern world, however, there are several factors militating against change in the Halakhah. The Orthodox community is divided and fragmented. There is no recognized halakhic leadership of the stature of Rabbenu Gershom Me'or Ha-Golah who could institute bold new rulings. In addition, since the Halakhah has become a voluntary system, those who do not agree with it tend to abandon it rather than agitate for change. In the medieval world where all Jews lived under the umbrella of Halakhah there were considerable forces for change and flexibility, but the impetus for change has greatly diminished in a world where dissidents can escape the Halakhah.

Thus for meaningful change to take place in women's status in Jewish law, new authorities must emerge to transform the Halakhah. Just as the Bible was maintained as the vital root of mishnaic and talmudic legislation despite far-reaching changes, so today the Halakhah must be maintained as the focus for discussion. The Halakhah as it is presently constituted does not accept women as equal to men, despite Orthodox apologies to the contrary. But even as we reject the traditional view of women in favor of equality, we need not reject the halakhic framework. We must revolutionize the view of women within the Halakhah, but that very process will necessarily revolutionize the Halakhah itself. We can draw upon minority opinions in the Halakhah, some of which have been presented in this book, but ultimately the changes must be even more radical because we are bringing a new set of values into the Jewish tradition.

I believe that the call for women to become leaders within the Jewish world must be extended. Certainly the ordination of women rabbis is a step in this direction. But authority in the Jewish tradition comes less from formal titles than from learning. Jewish women of all religious persuasions and commitments must become learned in the Halakhah, even if they do not actually live by it, for it is the framework and vocabulary of Jewish life. The first and most important step in the dialectical revolution of preserving and changing is *talmud torah*: the serious study of the Halakhah. Only those who explore the historical roots of the Halakhah and master its logic may become part of its future growth.

NOTES

Pentateuch passages are quoted from the Jewish Publication Society translation of the Torah and passages from the Babylonian Talmud are quoted from the Soncino translation, unless otherwise noted for either. Occasionally I have made minor changes in the above translations. When a Pentateuch verse is quoted in the Babylonian Talmud I have maintained the Soncino translation which may vary from the JPS translation cited earlier on in the text. Translations of all other texts are mine unless otherwise indicated in the notes.

Chapter 1. Women and the Mitzvot

1. See the summary in David Feldman, "Women's Role and Jewish Law," *Conservative Judaism* 26, no. 4 (Summer 1972): 29–39, and a more conservative view in Moshe Meiselman, *Jewish Woman in Jewish Law* (New York, 1978), Chap. 9.

2. See Saul Berman, "The Status of Women in Halakhic Judaism," reprinted in *The Jewish Woman*, edited by Elizabeth Koltun (New York, 1976), pp. 114–28. For a "pro-feminist" Orthodox view, see Blu Greenberg, *On Women and Judaism: A View from Tradition* (Philadelphia, 1981), Chaps. 1 and 2.

3. See Meiselman, *Jewish Woman in Jewish Law*, Chaps. 8 and 9.

4. Exceptions to the rule regarding *tefillin* and *tzitzit* are discussed in the Talmud, e.g., Rosh Ha-Shanah 33a, which cites cases of women (Mikhal, daughter of King Saul) who according to the Midrash wore *tzitzit* and *tefillin*. For a discussion of the *mitzvah* of blowing the shofar, see Arlene Pianko, "Women and the Shofar," *Tradition* 14, no. 4 (Fall 1974): 53–62. See also Meiselman, *Jewish Woman in Jewish Law*, Chaps. 21 and 22.

5. The subject of *tehinot* and women's historical relation to prayer remains hardly touched by scholarly work. In his overview of Jewish prayer *Jewish Worship* (Philadelphia, 1971), Abraham Milgram devotes one and a half pages (pp. 473–74) to the subject. For biographical details about women who composed *tehinot*, see Solomon Ashkenazi, "Women Authors of *Piyyutim*, *Tehinot*, and Prayers" (Hebrew), *Mahanayim* 109 (1967): 75–82; as well as Ashkenazi's *Woman in the Jewish Perspective* (Hebrew) (Tel Aviv, 1957). Some new "women's prayers" have recently been composed for occasions such as giving birth and Rosh Hodesh. See Arlene Agus, "This Month Is for You: Observing Rosh Hodesh as a

Woman's Holiday," and Daniel Leifer and Myra Leifer, "On the Birth of a Daughter," both in Koltun's The Jewish Woman. A particularly emotion-laden issue has been the question of women reciting Kaddish for their parents: see Sara Reguer, "Kaddish from the 'Wrong' Side of the Mehi-tzah," in Susannah Heschel, On Being a Jewish Feminist (New York, 1983), pp. 177–81.

6. Feldman, "Women's Role and Jewish Law," p. 36. For a view advo-cating counting women in a minyan in the Conservative Movement, see Phillip Sigal, "Women in a Prayer Quorum," Judaism 23 (Spring 1974): 174–82.

7. As cited in Feldman, "Women's Role and Jewish Law"; see there for more detailed discussion of Ran's position.

8. See Rabbenu Tam's view in Tosafot on Rosh Ha-Shanah 33a, and Menahem Ha-Meiri, Bet Ha-Behirah on Megillah 23a. For a derivation of Torah reading from the mitzvah of hak'hel, see Abraham Gumbiner, Ma-gen Avraham (Commentary on the Shulhan Arukh), Orah Hayyim 282 : 3. See also Meiselman's discussion, in Jewish Woman in Jewish Law, Chap. 9.

9. The basis for this view is the position of Jacob Landau (fifteenth century); see the discussion in Feldman, "Women's Role and Jewish Law."

10. See Meiselman, Jewish Woman in Jewish Law, Chap. 20.

11. The practice in regard to aliyot varies from one Conservative con-gregation to another as the Rabbinical Assembly decided to allow each Conservative synagogue to rule according to its own members' wishes. For background discussion, see A. Blumenthal, "An Aliyah for Women," Proceedings of the Rabbinical Assembly of America 19 (1955): 168–81. For more recent articles, see Ora Hamelsdorf and Sandra Adelsberg, Jew-ish Women and Jewish Law: Bibliography (Fresh Meadows, N.Y., 1980).

12. My translation.

13. For this view, see Meiselman, Jewish Woman in Jewish Law, Chap. 20.

14. On the obligation of children toward their parents, see Gerald Blid-stein, Honor Thy Father and Thy Mother: Filial Responsibility in Jewish Law (New York, 1975).

15. See Judith Hauptman, "Women in the Talmud," in Religion and Sexism, edited by Rosemary Ruether (New York, 1974). For an analysis of the most prominent learned woman in the Talmud, Beruriah, the wife of Rabbi Meir, see Ann Goldfeld, "Women as Sources of Torah in the Rab-binic Tradition," Judaism 24, no. 2, reprinted in Koltun, The Jewish Woman.

16. For a comprehensive review of the Halakhah and attitudes toward teaching women, and a strong Orthodox advocacy of institutionalized Jewish education for girls, see Rabbi Techoresh, "Regarding the Educa-

tion of Girls" (Hebrew), *Noam* 12 (1969): 77–81. See also Arthur Silver, "May Women Be Taught Bible, Mishnah and Talmud?" *Tradition* 17 (Summer 1978): 74–85. On the Bais Yaakov schools, see Deborah Weissman, "Bais Yaakov: A Historical Model for Jewish Feminists," in Koltun, *The Jewish Woman*. This article is a brief summary of an unpublished master's dissertation on Bais Yaakov.

17. Leibowitz holds that there is absolutely no reason for women to have any desire to perform *mitzvot* from which they are exempt since the only meaning of a *mitzvah* is the fact that it has been commanded. The *mitzvot*, in his view, have absolutely no intrinsic value. This view is rather similar to Sa'adia Gaon's view of the *mitzvot shim'iyot*.

18. As cited in *Ha-aretz* daily newspaper (abbreviated from an article in the religious journal *Amudim*), May 4, 1983.

19. For the debate on the ordination of women rabbis in the Reform movement, see Central Conference of American Rabbis (CCAR), "Report of the Committee on Ordination of Women," *CCAR Yearbook* 66 (1956): 9–93.

20. The faculty of the Jewish Theological Seminary voted to approve the ordination of women rabbis in October, 1983. The debate over ordination of women in the Conservative movement generated many articles. For a summary, see the following: "Commission for the Study of the Ordination of Women, Final Report," *Conservative Judaism* 32 (Summer 1979): 63–80; Fishel Pearlmutter, "Report on the Decision of the Commission to Study the Ordination of Women," The Rabbinical Assembly, New York, Feb. 2, 1979; *Proceedings of the Rabbinical Assembly*, Statements before the Commission on the Ordination of Women, dated Sept. 7, 1979, and Dec. 3, 1979. See also Gerson Cohen, "On the Ordination of Women," *Conservative Judaism* 32 (Summer 1979): 56–62; and an article by Ruth Wisse which aroused much criticism by "pro-feminists," "Women as Conservative Rabbis," *Commentary* 68 (Oct. 1979): 59–64.

Chapter 2. Marriage

1. Genesis 24.

2. My translation.

3. See Ze'ev Falk, *Jewish Matrimonial Law in the Middle Ages* (Oxford, 1966); and A. H. Freiman, *Seder Kiddushin Ve-Nisu'in* (Jerusalem, 1964). For a more detailed work on Jewish marriage, see Kalman Kahana, *The Theory of Marriage in Jewish Law* (Leiden, 1966).

4. There is a debate in the Halakhah as to which is better: to violate the ban against polygyny or to violate the ban on divorcing a woman against her will when the marriage is untenable and the woman refuses to accept a *get*. See, for example, Benjamin Rabinowitz Teomim, "A Release from

the Ban of Rabbenu Gershom in the Case of a Cripple" (Hebrew), *Noam* 2 (1959): 284–316.

5. See the discussion in Freiman, *Seder Kiddushin Ve-Nisu'in*, passim.

6. My translation.

7. Translation by David Biale.

8. For a discussion of the *Simphon*, see Freiman, *Seder Kiddushin Ve-Nisu'in*, pp. 11–13.

9. Yevamot 94b and 107a. See also the symposium on the issue of conditional *kiddushin* in *Noam* 1 (1958): 52–110.

10. The traditional blessing at the marriage ceremony includes the statement "Blessed be He who forbade us the *arusot* [women betrothed but not yet married] and permitted us the *nesu'ot* [women taken in both betrothal and *nisu'in*]." For an interesting reflection of the gradual fusion of the two ceremonies, see Rashi, Responsa (Elfenbein edition), No. 194.

11. See, e.g., Niddah 31b: "Rabbi Dostai's students said to him: Why does a man court a woman but a woman not court a man? [He answered] It is like a man who loses something: who goes looking for whom? The one who lost the thing goes looking for it!" See also Berakhot 10b.

12. See *Birkei Yosef*, the commentary on the *Shulhan Arukh*, by Hayyim Yosef David Azulai (eighteenth century). "*Hirhur* [sexual thoughts] is not relevant to women" (*Even Ha-Ezer* 1 : 16). For a more detailed discussion, see below, Chapter 5 on sexuality and marital relations, and Louis Epstein, *Sex Laws and Customs in Judaism* (New York, 1967), Chaps. 1 and 4.

13. On the issue of child marriages, see Jacob Katz, "Family, Kinship, and Marriage among Ashkenazim in the Sixteenth to Eighteenth Centuries," *Jewish Journal of Sociology* 1 (1959): 4–22. A more detailed and technical article appeared in Hebrew: Jacob Katz, "Marriage and Marital Life at the End of the Middle Ages," *Zion* 10 (1945): 21–54.

14. See David Biale, *Childhood Marriage and the Family in the Eastern European Jewish Enlightenment*" (American Jewish Committee, 1983).

15. We have not discussed the question of the economic side of marriage here. For an excellent review of the economic rights and constraints which apply to a married woman, see Samuel Morell, "An Equal or a Ward: How Independent Is a Married Woman According to Rabbinic Law?" *Jewish Social Studies* 44, nos. 3–4 (Summer-Fall 1982): 189–210, especially Part 1 (pp. 189–97).

Chapter 3. Divorce

1. Malachi 2 : 14–16 (my translation).

2. See Evald Lovetam, "Divorce and Remarriage in the New Testament," *The Jewish Law Annual* 4 (1981): 47–65.

3. In the final analysis Bet Hillel and Rabbi Akiva hold similar views

as regards the practical possibilities for a man to initiate divorce, since in both cases the grounds for divorce would be what the husband subjectively desires or finds distasteful. Yet their analysis of the text is very different.

4. In the mishnaic text the quote attributed to Bet Shammai actually inverts the word order to read *devar ervah*. This reading is the more natural grammatical order for the meaning that Bet Shammai assign to the phrase.

5. See the discussion in Yair Zakovitch, "The Woman's Right in the Biblical Law of Divorce," *The Jewish Law Annual* 4 (1981): 33–34.

6. An adulteress is forbidden to both her husband and her lover: "*asurah le-ba'alah u-le-vo'alah*" (Sotah 27b).

7. For a succinct summary of the laws of divorce, see Blu Greenberg, "Jewish Divorce Law," *Lilith*, 1, no. 3 (1977): 26–29; and Simon Greenberg, "And He Writes Her a Bill of Divorce," *Conservative Judaism* 24 (1970): 75–141. For the Conservative movement's position on divorce, see Edward Gershfield (ed.), *The Jewish Law of Divorce* (New York, 1968).

8. On the history of the *ketubah*, see Louis Epstein, *The Jewish Marriage Contract* (New York, 1927); and Moses Gaster, *The Ketubah* (reprinted; New York, 1974). On the artistic tradition of illuminated *ketubot*, see David Davidovitch, *The Ketubah: Jewish Marriage Contracts through the Ages* (Hebrew and English) (Tel Aviv, 1968).

9. The *ketubah* often includes additional details of the financial agreement between the couple. These were called *tena'im* (conditions). In some cases, when the bride came from a wealthy family the *tena'im* included a provision allowing her to engage in business on her own behalf. For a detailed discussion of such clauses and the question of a woman's right to engage in business for herself, see Samuel Morell, "An Equal or a Ward: How Independent Is a Married Woman According to Rabbinic Law?" *Jewish Social Studies* 44, nos. 3–4 (Summer-Fall 1982): 190–97.

10. For extensive discussion and more examples, see Zakovitch, "The Woman's Rights."

11. See Mordechai Friedman, "Divorce upon the Wife's Demand as Reflected in Manuscripts from the Cairo Geniza," *The Jewish Law Annual* 4 (1981): 103–26.

12. Ketubot 61b.

13. See Rashi and Tosafot on Ketubot 61b.

14. Ketubot 63b.

15. See the *Shulhan Arukh*, Even Ha-Ezer 77, and commentaries there.

16. See similarly the discussion of the use of contraception in Chapter 8 on procreation and contraception, where one cannot be expected to rely on divine mercy to prevent a dangerous pregnancy (Yevamot 12b).

17. Maimonides, *Mishneh Torah*, Hilkhot Ishut 15 : 17.

18. Ibid., 15 : 18. For further discussion of the rebellious wife, see Morell, "An Equal or a Ward?" Part 3, pp. 198–201.

19. Quoted in Moses Isserles's commentary on the *Tur: Darkhei Moshe*, Even Ha-Ezer 154 : 11. However, another source (Responsa of Binyamin Ze'ev, No. 88) cites the Maharam of Rothenburg as one of the authorities who permit physical punishment to chastize a wife. For further discussion of the range of opinions on wife-beating (primarily as a form of punishment for her cursing the husband's parents), see Morell, "An Equal or a Ward?" Part 2, pp. 197–98, and the extensive footnotes for this section.

20. Binyamin Ze'ev, Responsa No. 88.

21. Moses Maimonides, *Mishneh Torah*, Hilkhot Ishut 21 : 3, 10. The Rabad (Avraham ben David of Posquieres), in his commentary on the *Mishneh Torah*, expresses great surprise at this ruling and rejects it altogether.

22. See *Prime Minister's Office Commission on the Status of Women* (Jerusalem, 1978). The commission was established in 1975 and was headed by Knesset member Ora Namir. It submitted a summary of its findings and its recommendations in February 1978 and a full report in August 1978. There is a recent article on wife-beating among American Jews: Mimi Scarf, "Marriage Made in Heaven? Battered Jewish Wives," in Susannah Heschel, *On Being a Jewish Feminist* (New York, 1983), pp. 51–64. However, a more extensive treatment of the problem in both quantitative and analytical terms remains to be written.

23. This *mishnah* is also cited in Gittin 88b.

24. For a concise discussion of the Paris proposal and other reform proposals for the solution of the *agunah* problem, see Moshe Meiselman, *Jewish Woman in Jewish Law* (New York, 1978), Chap. 17. For a more detailed discussion, see Meir Ha Meiri (Feuerwerger), *Ezrat Nashim* (London, 1955). See also Mark Washofsky, "The Recalcitrant Husband: The Problem of Definition," *The Jewish Law Annual* 4 (1981): 144–66. For further discussion, see below, Chapter 4, "The *Agunah* and the *Yevamah*."

Chapter 4. The Agunah and the Yevamah

1. For an extensive compilation of halakhic material on *agunot*, see Isaac Farkas Kahan, *Sefer Ha-Agunot* (Jerusalem, 1954). For rabbinic and comparative sources on the *agunah* and the *yevamah*, see S. Belkin, "Levirate and Agunate Marriage in Rabbinic and Cognate Literature," *Jewish Quarterly Review*, 40 (1970): 275–329. For a review of the proposals for resolution of the *agunah* problem, see Moshe Meiselman, *Jewish Woman in Jewish Law* (New York, 1978), Chap. 17.

2. In Jewish law an illegitimate child (*mamzer*) is only the product of an expressly forbidden union, not a child born out of wedlock. A *mamzer* may not marry any Jew/Jewess unless the other person is also a *mamzer*.

A man who is a *mamzer* may also marry a woman who converts to Judaism.

3. The details regarding reported death of a husband are discussed in Tractate Yevamot, primarily Chapter 15. For a detailed synopsis, see Gad Navon, "Prevention of Wartime *Agunot*" (Hebrew), *Noam* 19 (1977): 61–109.

4. Both passages from Yevamot 114b are my translation.

5. For example, Meir HaMeiri (Feuerwerger) in his *Ezrat Nashim* devotes special attention to the problem of women who became *agunot* due to the Holocaust, and argues the need for his book on this basis. The particular problem of *agunot* of wars in Israel has been addressed by Gad Navon, chief rabbi of the Israeli Defense Forces, in his article "Prevention of Wartime *Agunot*."

6. For a discussion of conditional divorce, see Eliezer Berkowitz, *Tenai Be-Nisu'in U-ve-Get* (Jerusalem, 1967).

7. For an extensive discussion of annulment of marriage, see A. H. Freiman, *Seder Kiddushin Ve-Nisu'in* (Jerusalem, 1964), Chapt. 1; the symposium in *Noam*, volume 1 (1958); and M. Kasher, "Regarding a Conditional Clause in Marriage" (Hebrew), *Noam* 11 (1968). See also David Novak, "Annulment in Lieu of Divorce in Jewish Law," *The Jewish Law Annual* 4 (1981): 188–206; and J. David Bleich, "Modern Day Agunot: A Proposed Remedy," *The Jewish Law Annual* 4 (1981): 144–66; as well as M. Chigier, "Ruminations over the Agunah Problem," *The Jewish Law Annual* 4 (1981): 207–25.

8. See *Proceedings of the Rabbinical Assembly*, 1954 pp. 64–68. For a discussion and critique of the "Lieberman addendum," see Norman Lamm, "Recent Additions to the Ketubah," *Tradition* 2, no. 1 (Fall 1959): 93–118. For a clear summary of the controversy over proposed solutions to the *agunah* problem and the question of the validity of the Conservative *ketubah* as tested out in actual court cases, see Meiselman, *Jewish Woman in Jewish Law*, Chap. 17.

9. See E. Bohnen et al.'s proposal "Tnai Be-Kiddushin," *Proceedings of the Rabbinical Assembly*, 1968 pp. 229–241.

10. For a review of court cases, see David Ellenson and James Ellenson, "American Courts and the Enforceability of the Ketubah as a Private Contract," *Conservative Judaism* 35, no. 3 (Spring 1982): 35–42; and Bernard Meislin, "Pursuit of the Wife's Right to a 'Get' in United States and Canadian Courts," *The Jewish Law Annual* 4 (1981): 250–71.

11. See Nat Hentoff, "Who Will Rescue the Jewish Women Chained in Limbo?" *The Village Voice*, Sept. 13, 1983, and letters regarding this article in the October 4 issue of *The Village Voice*.

12. See the discussion in E. G. Ellinson, *Nisu'in She-Lo Ke-Dat Moshe Ve-Yisrael* (Tel Aviv, 1975), Chap. 5, esp. pp. 86–92. See also Ya'akov Emden, *Responsa She'elat Ya'avetz* vol. 2 Responsum #15.

13. See Shulamit Aloni, *The Status Quo: From State of Law to State of Halakhah* (Hebrew) (Tel Aviv, 1970).

14. My translation.

15. My translation.

16. For a detailed discussion, see Freiman, *Seder Kiddushin Ve-Nisu'in.*

17. For a detailed discussion of the problems of a *yevamah* who "falls before a *levir,*" see Meir Ha Meiri, *Ezrat Nashim,* Chaps. 5–14; Isaac Jacob Vachtfogel, "Regarding a *Yevamah*" (Hebrew) *Noam* 6 (1963): 112–18; and Abraham Moshe Fingerhut, "Regarding the Woman Who Requires *Yibum*" (Hebrew), *Noam* 6 (1963): 119–23.

Chapter 5. Sexuality and Marital Relations

1. For general works on sexuality in Jewish law and tradition, see Roland Gittelsohn, *Love, Sex and Marriage: A Jewish View* (New York, 1976); Robert Gordis, *Love and Sex: A Modern Jewish Perspective* (New York, 1978); as well as his *Sex and the Family in Jewish Tradition* (New York, 1967). See also Maurice Lamm, *The Jewish Way in Love and Marriage* (San Francisco, 1980). For a wealth of material on sexuality in the view of the Rabbis see Louis Epstein, *Sex Laws and Customs in Judaism* (New York, 1967). A good many of the pronouncements on sexuality in the Talmud and the Midrash (including some of the more daring and surprising ones) have been collected in the Hebrew anthology by Shlomo Shva, *Ahavah Doheket et Ha-Basar* (Tel Aviv, 1979).

2. On masturbation and touching of the genitals by men, see the statement "in the case of a man the hand that reaches below the belly-button should be chopped off" (Niddah 13a). On homosexuality, see Chapter 7, below.

3. The tension between the strength and covertness of female sexuality is expressed by another passage in the Talmud which forbids a court order to supply a woman with wine (as part of a *ketubah* settlement). Wine is dangerous because it loosens the restraint and releases the hidden sexual impulse: "Rabbi Eliezer said: We do not order a woman to be supplied with wine since wine accustoms a person to desire sexual intercourse. For we have learned: one glass is beneficial for a woman, two glasses are a disgrace [*nivul*], three—she demands sex with her mouth, four—she demands even a donkey in the market and has no restraints.

"Raba said: all of that [is the case] if her husband is not with her, but if her husband is with her—it is permitted" (Ketubot 65a).

4. There are innumerable traditional and scholarly commentaries on the two Genesis stories. I recently found a new insight in an article by Meir Shalev ("Bible Now" [Hebrew], *Ha-Aretz* daily newspaper, May 21,

1983) in which he points out the fact that in the second story Adam and Eve are punished with the very same things which are their blessings in the first story, namely, taking dominion over the earth for Adam and procreation for Eve.

5. For the talmudic discussion of the nature of the affliction, *innui*, in sexual relations, see Ketubot 48a and Yoma 77a. For a good discussion of *onah* and, especially, the quality of the marital relationship, see David M. Feldman, *Marital Relations, Birth Control and Abortion in Jewish Law* (New York, 1974), Chaps. 4 and 5.

6. This issue should be understood as part of a larger one, the conflict between marriage and Torah study. This conflict is epitomized by the talmudic discussion of whether a man should study first or marry first, and the phrase "With a millstone around his neck how he can study Torah?" (Kiddushin 29b). There are also a number of stories illustrating this tension, most famous among them are the stories about Akiva and his wife Rachel. Most of these stories have been collected in David Zimmerman's book *Eight Love Stories in the Midrash and the Talmud* (Hebrew) (Tel Aviv, 1981).

7. There is also a rule about initiating sex on the night after the immersion in the *mikveh*: Jerusalem Talmud Tractate Ta'anit 1 : 6 (it does not appear as an explicit *halakhah* in the Babylonian Talmud) and *Tur* and *Shulhan Arukh*, Even Ha-Ezer 76.

8. One of the first authorities to rule this way due to the sexual mores of his time was Yonah Landsofer (Prague, end of the seventeenth century) in his responsa *Me'il Tzedakah*.

9. My translation.

10. My translation.

11. For Maimonides' strict view on sexuality, see *Guide to the Perplexed*, Book 3, Chap. 49; and Fred Rosner, *Sex Ethics in the Writings of Moses Maimonides* (New York, 1974).

12. *Iggeret Ha-Kodesh* has been translated into English by Seymour Cohen under the title *The Holy Letter: A Study in Medieval Jewish Sexual Morality* (New York, 1976).

13. For rabbinical speculation on female seed, see Leviticus Rabbah Chapter 11, and for speculation on the secret to the birth of male children, Eruvin 100b and Niddah 71a. For an excellent presentation on the notion of female seed and ideas about conception, see Feldman, *Marital Relations*, Chap. 7. On the preference for male children, the following colorful text is characteristic of rabbinical attitudes: "The Sages said: The world cannot exist without males and females! Woe to him who has female children! A daughter is like a trap for her father: for fear for her he does not sleep at night. When she is small he fears that she might be seduced; when she is a maiden—that she become promiscuous; when she matures—that she might not marry; when she marries—that she might

not produce children; when she grows old—that she would practice witchcraft" (Sanhedrin 100b).

Chapter 6. Niddah: *The Laws of the Menstruant*

1. See Janice Delaney, *The Curse: A Cultural History of Menstruation* (New York, 1976); and Penelope Shuttle, *The Wise Wound: Eve's Curse and Everywoman* (New York, 1978).

2. See Jacob Neusner, *A History of the Mishnaic Law of Purity* (Leiden, 1974), for a general discussion of the laws of purity and impurity, and his article, "From Scripture to Mishnah: The Origins of the Mishnaic Tractate Niddah," *Journal of Jewish Studies* 29 (1978): 135–48, for a specific discussion of the evolution of the laws of *niddah*.

3. See, for example, Rachel Adler, "*Tum'ah* and *Taharah*: Ends and Beginnings," in *The Jewish Woman*, edited by Elizabeth Koltun (New York, 1976), pp. 63–71.

4. The distinction of types of blood was particularly difficult in premodern times because medical and physiological knowledge of the female genital and reproductive systems was very limited. In modern times rabbis have often relied on medical diagnosis and expertise to resolve problems of women with unusual menstruation patterns. See, for example, Shlomo Zalman Auerbach, "A Proposal for a Solution for Women in the Matters of *Niddah*" (Hebrew), *Noam* 7 (1964): 134–74; and the response to this suggestion in the subsequent issue of *Noam* by Menahem Kasher (7 : 293–349). For more general information about the laws of *niddah*, including speculations about the religious and psychological value of these laws, see Moshe Meiselman, *Jewish Woman in Jewish Law* (New York, 1978), Chap. 19; and Blu Greenberg, *On Women and Judaism: A View from Tradition* (Philadelphia, 1981), Chap. 4, "In Defense of the 'Daughters of Israel': Observations on Niddah and Mikveh." For more specific details, see Moses Tendler, *Pardes Rimonim* (Jerusalem, 1970).

5. The kinds of punishments which a court can impose on an offender, including the different forms of capital punishment, are discussed in detail in Tractate Sanhedrin.

6. A woman of wealth is also required by the rabbis to engage in weaving in order to keep away from idleness, since "idleness leads to sin" (Ketubot 64b).

7. My translation.

8. The commentaries on the *Tur* and *Shulhan Arukh* include a lengthy discussion of this matter as well as other related questions, such as should a woman have special clothing to be worn during her *niddah* period, may these be pretty clothes, and may she demand such clothing from her husband.

9. Kalman Kahana, *Daughter of Israel: Laws of Family Purity* (New York, 1970).

10. Shlomo Pines's translation of *The Guide to the Perplexed* (Chicago, 1963).

11. On the *Baraita De-Niddah*, see C. M. Horowitz, *Tosefta Attikata* 4 and 5 (1980) and *Encyclopedia Judaica*.

12. For some modern attempts to deal with the psychological and spiritual value of the laws of *niddah*, see Meiselman, *Jewish Woman in Jewish Law*, Chap. 19. Meiselman sees it as a way of "injecting the Divine Presence into a sphere where it can all too easily be forgotten" and as a way to enrich the marital relationship by forcing the couple to see each other as spiritual, not only sexual partners. Many Orthodox writers have also argued for the medical soundness and value of the laws of *niddah* (especially claiming that their observance is the cause for the low incidence of cervical cancer among Jewish women), for example, Moses Tendler, *Pardes Rimonim*. For another perspective, presenting the laws of *niddah* in terms of their effect on marital life and Jewish marital ideals, see Norman Lamm, *A Hedge of Roses* (New York, 1968). For a feminist Orthodox analysis of the laws of *niddah*, see Greenberg, *On Women and Judaism*, and Adler, "*Tum'ah* and *Taharah*: Ends and Beginnings." For a psychological analysis of the laws of *niddah*, see David Appelbaum, "Psychosomatic Aspects of the Menstrual Cycle in Jewish Law," *Journal of Psychology and Judaism* 2, no. 1 (Fall 1977): 55–70.

13. See Auerbach, "A Proposal."

Chapter 7. Sexuality Outside of Marriage

1. See, for example, Josephus, *Antiquities* XV, 2, 6, regarding homosexuality, and *Avodah Zarah* 22b regarding bestiality and the excessive lust of "the heathens." Compare these with the statement: "Israelites are not suspect in regard to bestiality" (Kiddushin 82a). For further discussion, see Louis Epstein, *Sex Laws and Customs in Judaism* (New York, 1967), Chap. 5.

2. For a discussion of this notion, see Yair Zakovitch, "The Woman's Rights in the Biblical Law of Divorce," *The Jewish Law Annual* 4 (1981): 32.

3. In addition, an uncle's wife is also prohibited. The prohibition on marrying a brother's wife is reversed if the brother dies childless (i.e., levirate marriage; see Chapter 4, above). The prohibition on marrying a wife's sister was violated by Jacob, who married Leah and then her sister Rachel.

4. In fact marrying a sister's daughter is considered a special act of kindness and merit; see Yevamot 62b.

5. Translation by Shlomo Pines.

6. See a similar argument on the function of these laws as a way of taking in female relatives from outside the immediate family in Stephen E. Bigger, "The Family Laws of Leviticus 18 in Their Setting," *Journal of Biblical Literature* 98 (1979): 187–203.

7. See David Biale's discussion of the impact of early marriage on the adolescence of men in eastern Europe in *Childhood Marriage and the Family in the Eastern European Community* (American Jewish Committee, 1983).

8. For details see Louis Epstein, *Sex Laws*, pp. 119–123.

9. For example, Judges 19, 1 Samuel 25, 2 Samuel 11. For a detailed discussion of this thesis, see Zakovitch, "The Woman's Rights," esp. pp. 32–41.

10. I am indebted for the analysis of the *sotah* passage to Prof. Jacob Milgrom, Near Eastern Studies Department, University of California at Berkeley.

11. The subsequent discussion in Sotah outlines the specific rules pertaining to the conduct of the ordeal and the husband's behavior.

12. For further discussion, see Epstein, *Sex Laws*, Chap. 9.

13. See ibid., esp. p. 212.

14. The Halakhah tries to protect the children of an adulteress by a general ruling that the children are considered to be the children of the *husband* (not the lover), even if the woman testifies otherwise (Sotah 27a). This rule is questioned only in the case of a woman who has committed adultery repeatedly (*Shulhan Arukh*, Even Ha-Ezer 4 : 15, 29).

15. See Louis Epstein, *Sex Laws*, Chap. 7; and E. G. Ellinson, *Nisu'in She-Lo Ke-Dat Moshe Ve-Yisrael* (Tel Aviv, 1975), Part 1.

16. See Ellinson, *Nisu'in*, Part 2, Chap. 7.

17. The crucial distinction between actual intercourse and other sexual acts is also evident in the discussion of the mother's fondling her son in Sanhedrin 69b and from several discussions in the Talmud of the exact degree of penile penetration which constitutes intercourse (*bi'ah*), for example, in Yevamot 55a–b and Sotah 4a.

18. Two males may also sleep together since homosexuality is normally not suspected among Jews; however, they should not sleep facing each other (Kiddushin 82a).

19. On homosexuality in the Halakhah, see Norman Lamm, "Judaism and the Modern Attitude to Homosexuality," *Encyclopedia Judaica 1974 Yearbook* (Jerusalem, 1974), pp. 194–205.

Chapter 8. Procreation and Contraception

1. The most comprehensive treatment of the issues of procreation, contraception, and abortion in the Halakhah is David M. Feldman, *Mari-*

tal Relations, Birth Control and Abortion in Jewish Law (New York, 1974). Feldman has been criticized by E. G. Ellinson for overemphasizing the "permissive" positions in the Halakhah; see his review in *Dinei Yisrael* (Hebrew with English abstracts) 7 (1977): 97–118. I believe that Ellinson is essentially correct in arguing that Feldman emphasizes the more lenient rulings in the Halakhah. Nevertheless his book remains an outstanding work on the subject, and much of my discussion in this chapter and Chapter 9 on abortion is based on his work.

2. Technically the commandment of procreation is derived in the Talmud from a different passage in Genesis (Gen. 9 : 1) where it is addressed to Noah and his sons, as well as from Genesis 35 : 11 where it is addressed to Jacob. Genesis 1 : 28 is interpreted as a *blessing* rather than a commandment.

3. See Shmuel Shilo, "Impotence as a Ground for Divorce," *The Jewish Law Annual* 4 (1981): 127–43.

4. See Yevamot 64a. However, this was generally not enforced if the couple wished to stay married. See Shir Ha-Shirim Rabbah 1 : 34 and the discussion in Feldman, *Marital Relations*, pp. 40–45.

5. See the stories cited in Ketubot 62a–b.

6. I have modified the Soncino translation of this passage to reflect the ambiguity of the text.

7. The pronouncement of the Sages is actually open to another interpretation, that it is actually only in reference to the last issue under discussion: the definition of a minor. This would then mean that the statement "the one as well as the other carries on her intercourse in the usual manner" only refers to the minor at risk, that is, between eleven and twelve years of age, and not to the first two women mentioned. However, this possible interpretation is not considered in the Gemara or in subsequent halakhic discussion. But it might shed light on the possible original intent of the mishnah.

8. See the discussion in Feldman, *Marital Relations*, pp. 212–13.

9. The issue of *hashhatat zera* is complex and we cannot enter into it here. Its greatest practical significance is in terms of the halakhic preference for certain contraceptive methods (i.e., those that do not interfere with normal procreative ejaculation). For a detailed discussion, see Feldman, *Marital Relations*, Chaps. 6, 8, 12, and 13.

10. Translation by David Feldman.

11. For a detailed discussion of self-sterilization for a woman, see Moses Herschler, "On the Law Regarding Surgery and the Prohibition of Castration in a Woman" (Hebrew), *Noam* 20 (1978): 153–62.

12. See Menahem Elon, "*Hapalah Melakhutit*" (Hebrew), *Ha-Encyclopedia Ha-Ivrit*, Suppl. vol. 2 (Tel Aviv, 1983).

13. Translated in Feldman, *Marital Relations*, p. 201.

14. Translated in ibid., p. 192.

15. Translated in ibid., pp. 225–26 (I have made a few modifications in the translation for greater clarity).
16. Translated in ibid., p. 211.

Chapter 9. Abortion

1. The most extensive treatment of abortion in the Halakhah is David M. Feldman, *Marital Relations, Birth Control and Abortion in Jewish Law* (New York, 1974), Part 5. There have been many other articles written on the subject. Some articles in English are: David Bleich, *Contemporary Halakhic Problems* (New York, 1977), chapter XV: 325–371, and Fred Rosner, "The Jewish Attitude toward Abortion," *Tradition* 10 (Winter 1968): 48–71; Victor Aptowitzer, "The Status of the Embryo in Jewish Criminal Law," *Jewish Quarterly Review* 15 (1924): 84–118; G. B. Halibard, "Abortion in Jewish Law: A Recent Judgment," *The Jewish Law Annual* 3 (1980): 139–53; Robert Gordis, "Abortion: Major Right or Basic Wrong?" *Midstream* 24: 3 (March 1978): 44–49. See also several articles in a symposium conducted in Sh'ma, Dec. 9 and 23, 1977, Blu Greenberg, *On Women and Judaism: A View from Tradition* (Philadelphia, 1981), Chap. 6, "The Issue of Abortion." In Hebrew see D. M. Maeir, "Abortion and Halakhah: New Issues," *Dinei Yisrael* 7 (1976): 137–150; Moshe Yonah Ha-Levi Zweig, "On Abortion," *Noam* 7 (1964): 35–56; Issar Yehudah Unterman, "On the Question of Danger to Life and a Fetus," *Noam* 6 (1963): 1–11; and Menahem Rakover, "Bibliography on Abortion in Hebrew Law," *Beri'ut Ha-Tzibbur* 17, no. 4 (1975): 305ff.
2. On abortion in Christianity, see John T. Noonan, Jr. (ed.), *The Morality of Abortion: Legal and Historical Perspectives* (Cambridge, Mass., 1970), pp. 1–59.
3. This of course is also a problem with adults, as in the celebrated case of Karen Ann Quinlan. However, in the case of a newborn in the Halakhah the considerations are somewhat different because of the ruling that a neonate is not considered *bar kayma* (viable) until it reaches its thirtieth day.
4. For further discussion of the nature of mental anguish as a hazard for the mother which warrants abortion, see Moshe Spero, "Psychiatric Hazard in the Halakhic Disposition toward Abortion: The Role of the Caseworker," *Journal of Jewish Communal Services* 53:2 (Winter 1976): 155–164.
5. Translation by Feldman, *Marital Relations*, p. 276.
6. For a detailed discussion of this complex issue, see Feldman, *Marital Relations*, Chap. 15.
7. Issar Unterman, *"Be-Inyan Pikuah Nefesh shel Ubar,"* *Noam* 6 (1964): 1.

8. For further discussion of the analogy of the ship's cargo as "pursuer," see Feldman, *Marital Relations*, Chap. 15.

9. Menahem Elon, "*Hapalah Melakhutit*," *Ha-Encyclopedia ha-Ivrit*, Suppl. vol. 2 (Tel Aviv, 1983).

10. Moshe Yonah Ha-Levi Zweig, "On Abortion" (Hebrew), *Noam* 7 (1964): 36–56.

11. Yehiel J. Weinberg, "Abortion in a Sickly Woman" (Hebrew), *Noam* 9 (1966): 193–215.

Chapter 10: Rape

1. See Susan Brownmiller, *Against Our Will: Men, Women, and Rape* (New York, 1975).

2. In recent years there have been a few cases of rape in Israel among immigrant Georgian Jews where it became apparent that rape was being used as a way of forcing a marriage against parental wishes. In some cases such rape was a way of forcing marriage against the civil laws which prohibit marriage before the age of seventeen for women and eighteen for men.

3. For a detailed discussion of the laws pertaining to the captive woman, see Gerald Blidstein, "The Status of Women Captives and Converts in Medieval Halakhah" (Hebrew), *Hebrew Law Annual* 3–4 (1976–1977): 35–116. See also Meir HaMeiri, *Ezrat Nashim*, Chap. 4, who analyzes the Halakhah in regard to women held captive in concentration camps and rules leniently that they are all permitted to their husbands, Israelites and *kohanim* alike.

4. See, for example, Ketubot 65b and Avodah Zarah 17a.

5. For further discussion of rape in the Halakhah, see Ben Zion Scherschevsky, *Dinei Mishpahah* (Jerusalem, 1967), pp. 49–51 and 316; and Louis M. Epstein, *Sex Laws and Customs in Judaism* (New York, 1967), Chap. 8.

Epilogue

1. Rachel Adler, "The Jew Who Wasn't There," first published in *Davka* (Summer 1971): 7–11, reprinted in *On Being a Jewish Feminist*, edited by Susannah Heschel (New York, 1983), pp. 12–18. For a similar viewpoint from a historical perspective, see Paula Hyman, "The Other Half: Women in the Jewish Tradition," *Conservative Judaism* 26: 4 (Summer, 1972): 14–21 and her "The Jewish Family: Looking for a Usable Past," reprinted in Heschel, pp. 19–28.

2. For a bibliography (including English publications only), see Aviva Cantor, *Bibliography on the Jewish Woman* (Fresh Meadows, N.Y., 1979), esp. Sect. 3; and the more extensive Ora Hamelsdorf and Sandra Adels-

berg, *Women and Jewish Law: Bibliography* (Fresh Meadows, N.Y., 1980). For more recent material, see articles in journals such as *Conservative Judaism, Judaism, Lilith, Moment, Present Tense, Response, Sh'ma,* and *Tradition.*

3. See Shulamit Aloni, *The Status Quo: From a State of Law to a State of Halakhah* (Hebrew) (Tel Aviv, 1970).

4. For the recent literature on these issues, see the references cited in the notes to Chaps. 3, 4, 8, and 9, above.

5. See Central Conference of American Rabbis (CCAR), "Report of the Committee on Ordination of Women," *CCAR Yearbook* 66 (1956): 9–93; and Sally Priesand (the first woman rabbi ordained by the Reform movement), *Judaism and the New Woman* (New York, 1975). There has been a plethora of articles on the issue of ordination of women in the Conservative movement. See Hamelsdorf and Adelsberg, *Jewish Women and Jewish Law* (Fresh Meadows, 1980), passim. Some of the most significant publications are in the notes to Chap. 1, "Women and the *Mitzvot*," n. 20.

6. On women as witnesses, see Moshe Meiselman, *Jewish Woman in Jewish Law* (New York, 1978), Chap. 13.

7. David Bleich, "Halakhah as an Absolute," *Judaism* 29 (1980): 30–37.

8. Eugene Mihaly, "Halakhah Is Absolute and Passé," *Judaism* 29 (1980): 68–75. An extreme feminist view is that of Rosalyn Lacks, *Women and Judaism: Myth, History, and Struggle* (New York, 1980).

9. See Meiselman, *Jewish Woman in Jewish Law*, Introduction.

10. Reuven P. Bulka, "Women's Role: Some Ultimate Concerns," *Tradition* 17, no. 4 (Spring 1979): 38.

11. Saul Berman, "The Status of Women in Halakhic Judaism," *Tradition* 14, no. 2 (Fall 1973): 5–28. Reprinted (abridged) in Koltun, *The Jewish Woman*, pp. 114–28.

12. Ibid., in Koltun, pp. 122, 123.

13. Eliezer Berkowitz, *Crisis and Faith* (New York, 1976), pp. 97–121.

14. Robert Gordis, "A Dynamic Halakhah: Principles and Procedures in Jewish Law," *Judaism* 28 (Summer 1979).

15. David M. Feldman, *Marital Relations, Birth Control and Abortion in Jewish Law* (New York, 1974); and his "Women's Role and Jewish Law," *Conservative Judaism* 26 (Summer 1972): 29–39.

16. Blu Greenberg, *On Women and Judaism: A View from Tradition* (Philadelphia, 1981). See also her "Feminism: Is It Good for the Jews?" *Hadassah Magazine* 57: 8 (April 1976): 10–11, 30–34; and her "Women's Liberation and Jewish Law," *Lilith* 1, no. 1 (Fall 1976): 16–19, 42–43.

17. Cynthia Ozick, "Notes Towards Finding the Right Question," reprinted in Heschel (ed.), *On Being a Jewish Feminist*, pp. 120–51.

18. Ibid., p. 142.

19. Ibid., p. 150.

20. Ibid.
21. Ibid.
22. Adler, "The Jew Who Wasn't There," in Heschel, pp. 13–14.
23. Ibid., p. 17.
24. Jacob Neusner has argued in many places that the Mishnah is really ahistorical and does not relate closely to the Bible. It is the Gemara which makes the connection to the biblical sources with its typical investigation of what the biblical source is for each mishnaic ruling. See his "Halakhah and History," *Judaism* 29 (1980): 52–56.

HALAKHIC SOURCES

NOTE: This list of halakhic sources includes only the major texts cited in this book.

Bible
Medieval biblical commentaries:
  Rashi (Rabbi Solomon ben Isaac, 11th century)
  Abraham Ibn Ezra (12th century)
  Ramban (Rabbi Moses ben Nachman, Nachmanides, 13th century)

Mishnah (ca. 200 C.E.)
  Commentary on the Mishnah, Moses ben Maimon (Maimonides, 12th century)

Talmud (consists of the Mishnah and the Gemara-commentary on the Mishnah)
  Jerusalem (or Palestinian) Talmud (ca. 400 C.E.)
  Babylonian Talmud (ca. 500 C.E.)
  Medieval talmudic commentaries:
    Rashi
    Tosafot (a school of French and German commentators, 12th–13th centuries)
    Sefer Ha-Yashar, Rabbenu Tam (Rashi's grandson, a member of the Tosafot school, 12th century)
    Yam Shel Shlomo, Solomon Luria (16th century)

Codes and Commentaries
  Mishneh Torah, Moses ben Maimon (Maimonides)
  Sefer Mordecai, Mordecai ben Hillel (13th century)
  Sefer Mitzvot Katan, Isaac of Corbeil (13th century)
  Sefer Abudarham, David Abudarham (14th century)

Tur *(Arba'ah Turim)*, Jacob ben Asher (14th century)
 Bet Yosef, Joseph Karo (16th century)
 Darkhei Moshe, Moses Isserles (16th century)
Shulhan Arukh, Joseph Karo
 Glosses of Rema, Moses Isserles
 Magen Avraham, Abraham Gumbiner (17th century)

Responsa (rabbinical rulings on specific cases)
 Ezrat Nashim, Meir HaMeiri (20th century)
 Hatam Sofer, Moses Sofer (19th century)
 Havat Yair, Yair Bachrach (17th century)
 Hemdat Shlomo, Solomon Lifschutz (19th century)
 Igrot Moshe, Moshe Feinstein (20th century)
 Maharam Rothenburg, Meir of Rothenburg (13th century)
 Mishpetei Uziel, Ben Zion Uziel (20th century)
 Noda Bi-Yehudah, Yehezkel Landau (18th century)
 She'elat Ya'avetz, Jacob Emden (18th century)
 Tshuvot, Hai Gaon (10th century)
 Tshuvot Rashi, Solomon ben Isaac (Rashi, 11th century)
 Tzitz Eliezer, Eliezer Judah Waldenberg (20th century)

Non-legal Literature
 Ba'alei Ha-Nefesh, Abraham ben David (Rabad, 12th century)
 Iggeret Ha-Kodesh, ascribed to Nachmanides (see above)
 Sefer Hasidim, Judah He-Hasid (12th century)

GLOSSARY

agunah (pl. *agunot*) A woman who is "bound" in marriage to a husband with whom she no longer lives. Generally, the husband has either disappeared, died without direct witnesses to his death, or refuses to grant his wife a divorce even though they are separated. An *agunah* is unable to remarry.

aliyah, aliyah la-Torah (pl. *aliyot*) Being "called up to the Torah." A symbolic reading of the Torah by members of the congregation; (the person who has an *aliyah* usually reads only the blessings while a cantor/reader chants the actual Torah portion).

Amora (pl. *Amoraim*) Rabbi(s) of the Talmudic period who are cited in the *Gemara**.

bet din A Jewish court ruling according to the *Halakhah**.

Bet Hillel An early first century school of *Tannaim** who followed the teachings of Hillel: traditionally thought of as more "liberal" than the competing tradition of *Bet Shammai**.

Bet Shammai A school of *Tannaim** following the teachings of Shammai.

ervah A sexual transgression: a violation of one of the prohibited sexual relations.

Gemara The Talmudic commentary on the *Mishnah**.

get A Jewish writ of divorce.

Halakhah The corpus of traditional Jewish law; a specific ruling within Jewish law.

halitzah The ceremony in which a *levir** renounces his obligation to marry his *yevamah** and releases her to marry anyone of her choosing.

hashhatat zera "Destruction [or spilling] of seed": ejaculation of semen outside the vagina.

herem A ban of excommunication from the Jewish community.

ketubah The Jewish marriage contract given by the groom to the bride specifying his obligations during the marriage and in the event of its dissolution.

kiddushin Betrothal: the actual legal act effecting marriage.

levir The brother of a married man who dies without children, upon whom the obligation of *levirate marriage** falls.

levirate marriage The marriage of a widow whose husband died childless to one of her deceased husband's brothers.

mamzer A bastard: the child of an adulterous union.

midrash The genre of rabbinic commentary that expands and explicates the biblical text. In this book, as in many other works, the term is used to refer to the non-legal commentaries (*midrash aggaddah*).

mikveh A ritual bath used for purification.

minyan A group of ten people (traditionally adult males) constituting a quorum for public prayer.

Mishnah The oral tradition codified in 200 C.E. under the direction of Rabbi Judah Ha-Nasi.

niddah A menstruating woman.

nisu'in The ceremony marking the beginning of married life signified by the *huppah* (canopy) and specified blessings.

onah The sexual rights of a married woman; the marital obligations of a husband.

responsa Collections of legal opinions written by rabbis in response to questions about actual cases.

shiddukhin An engagement; generally a prerequisite for *kiddushin**.

takanah (pl. **takanot**) Rabbinic legislation in the post-Talmudic period that can alter or amend the law.

Talmud A compilation of the *Mishnah** and *Gemara** codified in a Babylonian version circa 500 C.E. and a Palestinian version (the Jerusalem Talmud) in the preceding century. (Unless otherwise stated, all references to the Talmud in this book are to the Babylonian Talmud.)

Tanna (pl. **Tannaim**) Rabbi(s) contributing to the oral tradition codified in the *Mishnah**.

yevamah A woman whose husband dies without children who is subject to the *levirate marriage**.

yibum A *levirate marriage**.

zenut Sexual promiscuity or prostitution.

zonah A prostitute; a woman who engages in *zenut**.

INDEX

Abortion: accidental, 219–20; in Christianity, 220–21; elective, 219, 225–28, 234–38; and law of Gentiles, 227–29; as murder, 229–30, 232, 235, 238; problem of *rodef*, 229–34; therapeutic, 221–22, 228, 230–31, 238

Abraham ben David (Rabad), 6, 132–34, 136, 253–54

Abudarham, David ben Joseph, 13–14

Adler, Rachel, 256, 261, 263–64

Adultery, adulterous marriage, 33, 105, 155, 175, 183–89; and abortion, 226

Agunah, 102–13, 260; definition of, 102; as result of early marriage, 68

Akiva, Rabbi, 163, 245; on adultery, 189; on divorce, 74; marriage of, 39; on prostitution, 191

Aliya la-Torah, 25, 28–29, 41, 264

Annulment of marriage, 57–58; in case of *agunah*, 109–10, 112

Asher ben Yehiel (Rosh), 92–93, 103

Ashi, Rav, 57

Assuming obligations, 12, 41–43, 264. *See also* Mitzvah

Ba'al keri (nocturnal emission), 65

Bachrach, Yair, 226–27

Bais Yaakov schools, 38

Baraita De-Niddah, 169–72

Barren woman: sex with, 216–17

Bastard (*mamzer*), 101, 103, 105, 190, 227

Ben Azzai, 33–36

Benyamin Ze'ev, 93–94

Berkowitz, Eliezer, 260–61

Berman, Saul, 259–60

Beruriah, 35

Bestiality, 155

Bet din (rabbinic court): power to compel husband to divorce wife, 97, 99, 100. *See also* Court

Bet Hillel, 47, 73–78, 129

Bet Midrash, 39

Betrothal (*kiddushin*), 46–49, 53; in Bible, 45–47; improper, 53–61. *See also* Marriage, *kiddushin*

Bet Shammai, 47, 73–78, 87, 129

Bi'ah. *See* Sexual intercourse

Bleich, David, 258

Blessing, 12, 17–19

Blood, 152–53; purity of, 71; of virginity, 68

Bulka, Reuven, 259

Child, children, 16–18, 26–27, 30–31, 36, 64, 201–2, 214–15, 217–18

Childbearing: and curse of Eve, 123–24

Childbirth, 151–52, 218, 223–24

Christianity: and polygyny, 50; prohibition on divorce, 71

Circumcision (*brit milah*), 10, 29–30, 63

Cohabitation (*pilagshut*), 111. *See also* Concubine

Commandment. *See* Mitzvah

Companionship: as reason to marry, 6?

Conception, 147, 173–74, 204–5, 220

Concubine (*pilegesh*), 83

Conditional divorce, 108–9

Conditional marriage, 59, 110

Conjugal duties. *See* Onah

Conservative movement, 25, 110, 257–58, 261

Contraception, 202–18

Court, non-Jewish or civil, 97–100, 110–11

"Cup of roots" (*kos ikarin*). *See* Sterilization

David ben Zimra, 103–4
Deborah, 11
Divorce, 5–6, 52, 127, 260; biblical
    laws of, 70–72; civil, 110–11; com-
    pelling husband to give, 84–100;
    reasons for, 73–79. See also Get
Domestic role of women, 13, 17, 38,
    159–60, 259–60

Edah (congregation), 21–22
Eliezer, Rabbi, 33–36, 37, 62–63, 193–
    94
Elon, Menachem, 235
Elopement (nisu'ei seter), 56–59
Embryo, 224. See also Fetus
Emden, Jacob, 225–28, 233
Engagement. See Shiddukhin
Enlightenment. See Haskalah
Erotic. See Sexual
Ervah, 26–27, 36, 177. See also Sexual
    transgressions, Incest
Ervat davar (matter of indecency): as
    cause for divorce, 70, 73–78
Esther: and laws of rape, 251
Eve, curse of, 122–23, 125

Feibish, Samuel, 107
Feinstein, Moshe, 133
Feldman, David, 22–23, 27, 261
Female seed, female semination, 141–
    43
Female sexuality. See Sexuality
Feminism, feminists, 28, 256, 259,
    261–62
Fetus, 131, 136, 219–22, 224–37

Galanti, Moses, 119
Genitals, 65, 138, 193; discharge, 149–
    51. See also Zavah
Geniza, Cairo, 84
Gershom, Rabbenu, 6, 50–51, 81–83,
    100, 265
Get (writ of divorce), 6, 70, 72, 79, 81,
    90, 260; and civil divorce, 111; co-
    erced, 97. See also Divorce
Gikatilla, Abraham, 140
Giluy arayot. See Incest, Sexual trans-
    gressions
Gordis, Robert, 261

Greenberg, Blu, 261–62
Gumbiner, Abraham, 19–20

Hai Gaon, 214–15
hak'hel, 16, 25
Ha-Levi, David, 168
Ha-Levi, Isaac, 42
halitzah, 102, 114–19
hallah, 40
Hannah, 19
hashhatat zera (improper emission of
    seed), 64–65, 137, 210, 216–17
Haskalah, maskilim (Enlightenment,
    enlighteners), 67, 119
Hisda, Rabbi, 144–45
Hiyya, Rabbi, 39
Holocaust, 108, 235–36
Homosexuality, 155, 175. See also Les-
    bianism
Huna, Rav, 193–94
huppah, 56

Ibn Ezra, Abraham, 123–24, 156
Iggeret Ha-Kodesh, 140–44
Impurity, 71, 154, 157–58
Incest, 154–55, 175, 179–83; in Bible,
    181. See also Sexual transgressions
Intercourse. See Sexual intercourse
Islam, and polygyny, 51
Israel, State of: laws of abortion, 237;
    problem of agunot, 112; laws of di-
    vorce, 99–100; problem of levirate
    marriage, 117, 120; prohibition on
    polygyny, 51; status of Judaism in,
    257; wife-beating in, 96
Isserles, Moses, 18, 37, 41; on divorce,
    82; on niddah, 168–69; on women
    studying Torah, 40; on wife-beating,
    95–96

Jacob ben Asher, 62–63, 92, 248
Joshua ben Levi, 23
Judah Ha-Nasi, 107, 138, 189
Judah, Rav, 4, 29, 97–98

Kabbalah, kabbalistic, 140–41
Kaddish, 21, 24
Kahana, Kalman, 163–64
Karo, Joseph, 37, 139; on niddah, 164–

65; on *onah*, 133–34; on wife-
beating, 94; on women studying
Torah, 43. *See also Shulhan Arukh*
Ketubah (marriage contract), 6, 58, 127,
196, 199, 210, 260; and conservative
movement, 110–11; as divorce insur-
ance, 80–83; loss by wife, 90
Kiddushin (betrothal): as stage in mar-
riage, 59. *See also* Betrothal,
Marriage
Kinyan (acquisition in marriage), 47–
48
Kohen, kohanim. See Priest
Kvod ha-tzibbur, 26–28

Landau, Yehezkel, 67, 172, 231
Leibowitz, Yeshayahu, 38
Lesbianism, 192–97
Levirate marriage (*yibum*), 113–19
Levite, 24, 27
Licentiousness (*pritzut*), 26
Lulav, 15
Luria, Solomon, 168, 215–18

Maharam. *See* Meir of Rotenburg
Maimonides, Moses (Rambam): on abortion, 229–33; on divorce, 91–92; on
marriage, 55–56, 64; on incest, 180–
81; on lesbianism, 195–96, on Levirate marriage, 116–17; on *mitzvot*,
42, 260; on *niddah*, 165; on prayer,
19–20; on rape, 243, 250–51, 253; on
sexual practices, 145–46; on wife-
beating, 94–95
Mamzer. See Bastard
Marriage: age of, 65–68; in Bible, 44–
45; civil, 112; consent of woman, 59–
60; ways of effecting, 45–53. *See also*
Betrothal
Masturbation, 122
Maturation, female, 11, 205–7
Megillah, reading of, 21, 23–24, 26, 42
Mehitzah, 26, 260, 264
Meir, Rabbi, 84–85, 203, 207–17
Meir of Rotenburg (Maharam), 27–28,
50, 93
Meiselman, Moses, 22, 259
Menstruation, menstruant. *See Niddah*
Mesharsheya, Rabbi, 97–98

Mesolelot. See Lesbianism
Mihaly, Eugene, 258
Mikhal, 41
Mikveh, 156, 164, 172. *See also* Purity,
Tevilah
Minor. *See* Child, children
Minyan, 21–24, 220
Miscarriage, 220
Mishneh Torah. See Maimonides
Mitzvah, mitzvot, 10–43; assuming ob-
ligation, 41–43; exemption of wom-
en, 11–17; prayer, 17–24; Torah read-
ing, 24–29; Torah, study of, 29–41
Modesty (*tzni'ut*), 38
Mokh, 203, 207–17
Mordecai ben Hillel, 96
Moredet. See Rebellious wife

Nachmanides, Moses (Ramban), 140;
on divorce, 70–71; on *niddah*, 170–
71; on prayer, 21; on rape, 246–48;
on sexuality, 123–24, 128
Nefesh, 221–22, 230–35
Niddah, (menstruation, menstruant), 7,
10, 38, 40, 121–22, 147–73
Nissim, Rabbenu (Ran), 23–24
Nisu'in: as stage in marriage, 59
Nursing, 204, 214–15

Onah (sexual rights of woman), 6, 40,
121–22, 173; definition of, 125–27;
and divorce, 86; frequency of, 129–
34; and polygyny, 49; quality of, 126,
129, 135. *See also* Sex
Ordination of rabbis, 7–8, 264
Orthodox movement, 25, 38, 39, 257
Oshri, Ephrayim, 235–36
Ozick, Cynthia, 262–63

Parents: consent in marriage, 59–61
Paternity, 11
Patriarchs, and polygyny, 50
Pidyon ha-ben, 10, 15, 30
Polygyny, 49–51. *See also* Gershom
Prayer, 17–24, 28, 41, 168; men's, 20;
women's, 40. *See also* Tehinot
Pregnancy, pregnant woman, 203–5,
223–26; danger in, 211–18; sexual
relations during, 131, 217

Priest, priesthood, 11, 13, 24, 27–28, 71, 109, 193–94
Priestess, 11
Procreation, 62–63, 136, 148, 173, 198–203
Prohibited relations, 175–79. See also Incest, Sexual transgressions
Promiscuity (zenut), 190–92
Prostitute, prostitution. See Promiscuity
Purity, purification, 147–49. See also Mikveh, Tevilah

Raba, 49, 131–32, 159–60, 193–94, 249–50
Rachel, 44, 170
Rachel (wife of Rabbi Akiva), 39
Rambam. See Maimonides
Ramban. See Nachmanides
Rape: in Bible, 239–43; in postbiblical texts, 243–55; in marriage, 252–54
Rashi (Rabbi Shlomo Yitzhaki): on abortion, 222, 224, 229–31; on agunot, 108; on contraception, 208–13, 216–17; on curse of Eve, 123, 132; on divorce, 78, 90; on Levirate marriage, 116–17; on niddah, 161–62, 165, 168–69; on onah, 135; on prayer, 19, 21; on sexual foreplay, 144–45
Rav, 39, 53–55, 86–87
Rebellious husband, 88
Rebellious wife (moredet), 88–89, 165
Reconstructionist movement, 39, 257–58
Reform movement, 25, 39, 257
Reischer, Jacob, 60–61
Rubella, 236
Ruth, and problem of Levirate marriage, 114

Sabbath, 12, 25, 36, 40
Samuel, 53–55, 86–88, 159–60, 224–25
Schneersohn, Menachem Mendel, 213–14
Seduction, 243–44
Sefer Hasidim, 35–36
Sefer keritut, 184. See also Get
Sefer Mitzvot Katan, 135–36

Sex: extramarital, 65, 183, 190–92; refusal by wife, 88–89
Sexual arousal, 123
Sexual distraction: by woman's voice, 26, 28
Sexual foreplay, 144–45
Sexual impulse (yetzer ha-ra), 26, 64
Sexual intercourse, 123, 128–29, 197; abnormal practices in, 137–38; abstinence from, 87, 151; in Kabbalah, 140–43; to effect marriage, 45, 53, 55, 58; during niddah, 167
Sexual intimacy, 159–65
Sexual pleasure, 64, 173–74; man's, 135; woman's, 135, 139
Sexual promiscuity (be'ilat zenut), 58. See also Promiscuity
Sexual rights. See Onah
Sexual temptation, 36, 121
Sexual transgressions, 73–78, 105, 155–56, 175–79; and rape, 240, 242, 248–51. See also Adultery, Incest
Sexuality, 122; female, 123–25, 131–35, 137; imbalance between sexes, 6–7; male, 137
Shema, 17, 18, 168
Shiddukhin (engagement): as stage in marriage, 54, 56
Shlomo Zalman of Posen, 212–14
Shneor Zalman of Lublin, 233
shofar, 15, 42
shtar (deed effecting marriage), 52
Shulhan Arukh, 30, 31, 38; on niddah, 168; on prayer, 18–19; on rape, 245; on sexual pleasure and onah, 130, 133, 139; on study of Torah, 36–37, 43. See also Karo
Simha ben Shmuel of Vitri, 94
Simphon (marriage agreement), 59
Slave, 17–18, 26, 125–26, 260
Sofer, Moses (Hatam Sofer), 211–12
Soloveitchik, Hayyim, 232
Sotah (ordeal of the bitter waters), 33, 184–88, 265
Steinsaltz, Adin, 144
Sterilization, 202, 211–12, 217–18
Sukkah, 15
Synagogue, 7, 40, 148, 167–69, 258, 260

Tam, Rabbenu Jacob: on *agunot*, 108–9; on assuming obligations, 42; on contraception, 208–10, 212, 214, 216–17; on divorce, 90–91; on Levirate marriage, 117

Tamar: incestuous relations with Amnon, 181; and problem of Levirate marriage, 113

Tay Sachs disease, 236–37

Tefillin (phylacteries), 15, 17, 29, 41, 43

Tehinot, 20. *See also* Prayer: women's

Tevilah (ritual purification), 165. *See also Mikveh*, Purity

Thalidomide, 236

Torah: reading, 17, 21, 24–29, 168; study of, 25, 29–41, 43, 129–30, 260, 264, 266

Tosafot: on abortion, 225; on age of marriage, 66–67; on assuming obligations, 43; on contraception, 208; on divorce, 90–91; on prayer, 19

Tur (*Arba'ah Turim*), 61–63, 66, 92–93, 133. *See also* Jacob ben Asher

Tzedakah, 38

Tzitzit, 15

Unterman, Isar, 232–35

Uziel, Ben Zion, 28, 222–23, 234

Waldenberg, Eliezer, 237

Warhaftig, Z., 112

Weil, Michael, 99

Weinberg, Yehiel Jacob, 236

Wife-beating, 93–96

Witness: women accepted as, 104–5

Yetzer ha-ra. See Sexual impulse

Yevamah. See Levirate marriage

Yishmael, Rabbi, 228–29

Yohanan, Rabbi, 15–16, 249

Yohanan ben Dahbai, 137–38

Yohanan ben Zakkai, 188, 263

Yom Kippur, 15, 168

Zav, Zavah, 149–53, 157

Zonah (prostitute). *See* Promiscuity

Zweig, Moshe Yonah Ha-Levi, 236